Llewellyn's 2024

Sabbats
ALMANAC

Samhain 2023
to
Mabon 2024

Llewellyn's 2024 Sabbats Almanac
Samhain 2023 to Mabon 2024

© 2023 Llewellyn Worldwide Ltd.
Llewellyn is a registered trademark of Llewellyn Worldwide Ltd.

Cover art © Carolyn Vibbert
Editing by Hanna Grimson
Interior Art © Carolyn Vibbert, except on pages 13 and 205, which are by the
    Llewellyn Art Department

You can order annuals and books from *New Worlds*, Llewellyn's catalog. To
request a free copy, call 1-877-NEW WRLD toll-free or order online by visiting
our website at http://subscriptions.llewellyn.com.

ISBN: 978-0-7387-6900-4

Llewellyn Worldwide Ltd.
2143 Wooddale Drive
Woodbury, MN 55125-2989
www.llewellyn.com

Printed in China

2023

JANUARY						
S	M	T	W	T	F	S
1	2	3	4	5	6	7
8	9	10	11	12	13	14
15	16	17	18	19	20	21
22	23	24	25	26	27	28
29	30	31				

FEBRUARY						
S	M	T	W	T	F	S
			1	2	3	4
5	6	7	8	9	10	11
12	13	14	15	16	17	18
19	20	21	22	23	24	25
26	27	28				

MARCH						
S	M	T	W	T	F	S
			1	2	3	4
5	6	7	8	9	10	11
12	13	14	15	16	17	18
19	20	21	22	23	24	25
26	27	28	29	30	31	

APRIL						
S	M	T	W	T	F	S
						1
2	3	4	5	6	7	8
9	10	11	12	13	14	15
16	17	18	19	20	21	22
23	24	25	26	27	28	29
30						

MAY						
S	M	T	W	T	F	S
	1	2	3	4	5	6
7	8	9	10	11	12	13
14	15	16	17	18	19	20
21	22	23	24	25	26	27
28	29	30	31			

JUNE						
S	M	T	W	T	F	S
				1	2	3
4	5	6	7	8	9	10
11	12	13	14	15	16	17
18	19	20	21	22	23	24
25	26	27	28	29	30	

JULY						
S	M	T	W	T	F	S
						1
2	3	4	5	6	7	8
9	10	11	12	13	14	15
16	17	18	19	20	21	22
23	24	25	26	27	28	29
30	31					

AUGUST						
S	M	T	W	T	F	S
		1	2	3	4	5
6	7	8	9	10	11	12
13	14	15	16	17	18	19
20	21	22	23	24	25	26
27	28	29	30	31		

SEPTEMBER						
S	M	T	W	T	F	S
					1	2
3	4	5	6	7	8	9
10	11	12	13	14	15	16
17	18	19	20	21	22	23
24	25	26	27	28	29	30

OCTOBER						
S	M	T	W	T	F	S
1	2	3	4	5	6	7
8	9	10	11	12	13	14
15	16	17	18	19	20	21
22	23	24	25	26	27	28
29	30	31				

NOVEMBER						
S	M	T	W	T	F	S
			1	2	3	4
5	6	7	8	9	10	11
12	13	14	15	16	17	18
19	20	21	22	23	24	25
26	27	28	29	30		

DECEMBER						
S	M	T	W	T	F	S
					1	2
3	4	5	6	7	8	9
10	11	12	13	14	15	16
17	18	19	20	21	22	23
24	25	26	27	28	29	30
31						

2024

JANUARY						
S	M	T	W	T	F	S
	1	2	3	4	5	6
7	8	9	10	11	12	13
14	15	16	17	18	19	20
21	22	23	24	25	26	27
28	29	30	31			

FEBRUARY						
S	M	T	W	T	F	S
				1	2	3
4	5	6	7	8	9	10
11	12	13	14	15	16	17
18	19	20	21	22	23	24
25	26	27	28	29		

MARCH						
S	M	T	W	T	F	S
					1	2
3	4	5	6	7	8	9
10	11	12	13	14	15	16
17	18	19	20	21	22	23
24	25	26	27	28	29	30
31						

APRIL						
S	M	T	W	T	F	S
	1	2	3	4	5	6
7	8	9	10	11	12	13
14	15	16	17	18	19	20
21	22	23	24	25	26	27
28	29	30				

MAY						
S	M	T	W	T	F	S
			1	2	3	4
5	6	7	8	9	10	11
12	13	14	15	16	17	18
19	20	21	22	23	24	25
26	27	28	29	30	31	

JUNE						
S	M	T	W	T	F	S
						1
2	3	4	5	6	7	8
9	10	11	12	13	14	15
16	17	18	19	20	21	22
23	24	25	26	27	28	29
30						

JULY						
S	M	T	W	T	F	S
	1	2	3	4	5	6
7	8	9	10	11	12	13
14	15	16	17	18	19	20
21	22	23	24	25	26	27
28	29	30	31			

AUGUST						
S	M	T	W	T	F	S
				1	2	3
4	5	6	7	8	9	10
11	12	13	14	15	16	17
18	19	20	21	22	23	24
25	26	27	28	29	30	31

SEPTEMBER						
S	M	T	W	T	F	S
1	2	3	4	5	6	7
8	9	10	11	12	13	14
15	16	17	18	19	20	21
22	23	24	25	26	27	28
29	30					

OCTOBER						
S	M	T	W	T	F	S
		1	2	3	4	5
6	7	8	9	10	11	12
13	14	15	16	17	18	19
20	21	22	23	24	25	26
27	28	29	30	31		

NOVEMBER						
S	M	T	W	T	F	S
					1	2
3	4	5	6	7	8	9
10	11	12	13	14	15	16
17	18	19	20	21	22	23
24	25	26	27	28	29	30

DECEMBER						
S	M	T	W	T	F	S
1	2	3	4	5	6	7
8	9	10	11	12	13	14
15	16	17	18	19	20	21
22	23	24	25	26	27	28
29	30	31				

Contents

Contents

Lammas

Mabon

Introduction

NEARLY EVERYONE HAS A favorite sabbat. There are numerous ways to observe any tradition. The 2024 edition of the *Sabbats Almanac* provides a wealth of lore, celebrations, creative projects, and recipes to enhance your holiday.

For this edition, a mix of writers—Melissa Tipton, Enfys J. Book, Irene Glasse, Mickie Mueller, Deborah Castellano, and more—share their ideas and wisdom. These include a variety of paths as well as the authors' personal approaches to each sabbat. Each chapter closes with an extended ritual, which may be adapted for both solitary practitioners and covens.

In addition to these insights and rituals, specialists in astrology, history, cooking, crafts, and spells impart their expertise throughout.

Bernadette Evans gives an overview of planetary influences most relevant for each sabbat season and provides details about the New and Full Moons, retrograde motion, planetary positions, and more. (Times and dates follow Eastern Standard Time and Eastern Daylight Time.)

Natalie Zaman explores history, myths, and practices from around the world and how they connect to and sometimes influence each sabbat. Featuring a "royal court" of seasonal characters, this section is the place for celebration.

Mickie Mueller conjures up a feast for each festival that features seasonal appetizers, entrées, desserts, and beverages.

Lupa offers instructions on DIY crafts that will help you tap into each sabbat's energy and fill your home with magic and fun.

Dallas Jennifer Cobb provides nature magic tips and spells to celebrate and utilize the unique forces in each season.

About the Authors

Kate Freuler lives in Ontario, Canada, and is the author of *Of Blood and Bones: Working with Shadow Magick & the Dark Moon*. She is a maker, artist, and generally creative introvert who is constantly starting new projects and occasionally finishing them. Visit her at www.katefreuler.com.

Suzanne Ress has been practicing Wicca for about twelve years as the leader of a small coven, but she has been aware of having a special connection to nature and animal spirits since she was a young child. She has been writing creatively most of her life—short stories, novels, and nonfiction articles for a variety of publications—and finds it to be an important outlet for her considerable creative powers. Other outlets she regularly makes use of are metalsmithing, mosaic works, painting, and all kinds of dance. She is also a professional aromatic herb grower and beekeeper. Although she is an American of Welsh ancestry by birth, she has lived in northern Italy for nearly twenty years. Suzanne has written three novels, available on Amazon: *The Trial of Goody Gilbert*, about witchcraft in colonial Connecticut; *The Beeman*, about beekeeping and spiritual/cultural change in post–Civil War America; and *The Dream Book*, about gods, goddesses, time travel, and the Gundestrup cauldron in northern Italy.

Charlie Rainbow Wolf is an old hippie who's been studying the weird ways of the world for over fifty years. She's happiest when she's got her hands in mud, either making pottery in the "artbox" or tending to things in the yarden (yard + garden = yarden). Astrology, tarot, and herbs are her greatest interests, but she's dabbled in most metaphysical topics in the last five decades because life always has something new to offer. She enjoys cooking WFPB recipes and knitting traditional cables and patterns, and she makes a wicked batch of fudge. Charlie lives in central Illinois with her very patient husband and her beloved Great Danes.

Deborah Castellano (New Jersey, US) is the author of *Glamour Magic: The Witchcraft Revolution to Get What You Want* (Llewellyn, 2017) and *Magic for Troubled Times: Rituals, Recipes and Real Talk for Witches* (Llewellyn, 2022). She is an independent maker of ritual perfume and other fineries. In 2006, she founded the first steampunk convention, SalonCon. She enjoys old typewriters and record players, St. Germain, and reality television. Visit her at https://www.deborahcastellano.com.

Enfys J. Book (they/them) is a high priestx (3rd degree) of the Assembly of the Sacred Wheel tradition in the mid-Atlantic. They are the author of *Queer Qabala: Nonbinary, Genderfluid, Omnisexual Mysticism & Magick* (Llewellyn, June 2022). They have taught many classes on tarot, Hermetic Qabala, and queering one's magical practice, including "The Genderqueer Tree of Life," "Qabala's Queer Connections," and "Queering Your Magickal Practice." As a nonbinary, bisexual Pagan, Enfys employs a queer lens to break down limiting binaries in magickal theory and practice, and to advocate for bi, trans, nonbinary/genderqueer, queer, and asexual visibility and inclusion. They are also the creator of Major Arqueerna, a website devoted to queer magickal practice with a focus on Qabala, and they host a biweekly livestream interview show called "4 Quick Q's: Book Talk with Enfys," wherein they interview Pagan authors using questions determined by a roll of the dice.

Lupa is an author, artist, and naturalist in the Pacific Northwest. She is the author of several books on nature-based Paganism, as well as the creator of the Tarot of Bones and Pocket Osteomancy divination sets. More information about Lupa and her works may be found at http://www.thegreenwolf.com.

Irene Glasse is a mystic witch based in Western Maryland. She is a longtime teacher of witchcraft, meditation, and magic in the mid-Atlantic. She has performed, taught workshops, and led rituals at many festivals and conferences over the years, including but not limited to the Sacred Space Conference, EarthSpirit's Twilight Co-vening and Rites of Spring, Fertile Ground Gathering, Free Spirit Gathering, the Shenandoah Midsummer Festival, and more. Irene is the main organizer of the Frederick Covenant of Unitarian Universalist Pagans (Frederick CUUPS), offering events, rituals, classes, and workshops to a large, vibrant community. She is the coauthor of *Blackfeather Mystery School: The Magpie Training* and blogs weekly at GlasseWitchCottage.com.

Natalie Zaman is the author of the award-winning books *Color and Conjure* (with Wendy Martin) and *Magical Destinations of the Northeast* and is a regular contributor to various Llewellyn annual publications. Visit Natalie online at http://nataliezaman.blogspot .com.

Bernadette Evans has worn many hats—or toques (she's from Canada)—over the years, from daughter and sister to mother and now grandmother, as well as being a clinical counselor, astrologer, hypnotherapist, and writer. Her daily and monthly forecasts were a mainstay on *Conscious Community Magazine*'s website for four years. When she is not working with clients or writing, you can find her with her nose in a book, going to the movies, singing around the house, or taking a class to gain more knowledge. Her new love is playing with her grandson. She hopes to travel more and soak up some sun. You can contact her at bernadetteevansastrology.com or email her at bbevans001@gmail.com. You can also follow her on Facebook and Instagram.

Mickie Mueller is a witch, author, illustrator, tarot creator, and YouTube content creator. She is the author/illustrator of multiple books, articles, and tarot decks for Llewellyn Worldwide, including *Mystical Cats Tarot*, *Magical Dogs Tarot*, *The Witch's Mirror*, and

Llewellyn's Little Book of Halloween. Her magical art is distributed internationally and has been seen as set dressing on SYFY's *The Magicians* and Bravo's *Girlfriends' Guide to Divorce.* She runs several Etsy shops with her husband and fellow author, Daniel Mueller, in their studio workshop. Her YouTube videos are shot in her studio where she creates art, writes on the subject of witchcraft and folklore, and manifests her own style of eclectic everyday magic. She's been a witch for over twenty years, and she loves to teach practical and innovative ways to work magic using items and ingredients in your home. Visit her at https://www.mickiemueller.com.

Dallas Jennifer Cobb lives in a magickal village on Lake Ontario. A Pagan, mother, feminist, outdoorswoman, and animal lover, she enjoys a sustainable lifestyle with a balance of time and money. Widely published, she writes about what she knows: brain injury, magick, herbs, astrology, healing, recovery, and vibrant sustainability. When she isn't adventuring with her golden retriever, she likes to correspond with like-minded beings. Reach her at dallasjennifer.cobb @outlook.com.

Raechel Henderson is a dual class seamstress / shieldmaiden. She is the author of *Sew Witchy: Tools, Techniques & Projects for Sewing Magick* as well as *The Scent of Lemon & Rosemary: Working Domestic Magick with Hestia,* both from Llewellyn Worldwide. You can find her on Instagram, Facebook, or at her blog (idiorhythmic.com) where she writes about magick, creativity, living by one's own life patterns, her family and books.

Melissa Tipton is a Jungian Witch, Structural Integrator, and founder of the Real Magic School, where she teaches online courses in Jungian Magic, a potent blend of ancient magical techniques and modern psychological insights. She's the author of *Living Reiki: Heal Yourself and Transform Your Life* and *Llewellyn's Complete Book of Reiki.* Learn more and take a free class at www .realmagic.school.

Samhain

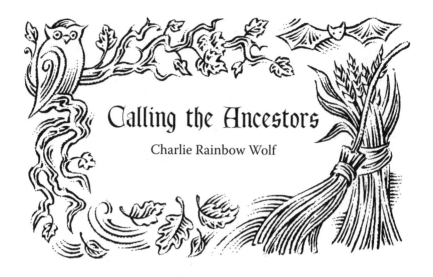

Calling the Ancestors

Charlie Rainbow Wolf

SAMHAIN IS THE TIME of year when ghosts, goblins, eight-legged beasties, and things that go bump in the night are said to be closer to our world than at any other time of the year. It's the time when trick-or-treaters don their Halloween costumes and go out in search of goodies. All Hallows' Eve is celebrated on October 31, followed by All Saints' Day on November 1, then All Soul's Day on November 2. The first and second of November are also when Mexico celebrates its "Day of the Dead" (Día de los Muertos). It is said that this is the only time that the spirits of their dead can return to earth. I love the way the two cultures blend at this time of year when it comes to remembering those who have passed.

The Last Fire Festival

My elders taught me that Samhain was a fire festival and the last of the harvest festivals. It was at this time the year was said to close, ready for the grip of winter. It's easy to see why it was viewed as a time of death; the fields were empty, their stubble glowing into the night as it was burned off, ready to rest the land. The skeletons of naked trees stood bold against a sun that set ever earlier each evening. All fruit had been gathered and bushes were bare, although after a good harvest pantries were plentiful. My late aunties often told how they would butcher a pig around this time of year, keeping the meat for themselves but making pork pies and sausage rolls and black puddings to share among their neighbors so that everyone had food going into the cold months.

Samhain is opposite Beltane on the calendar, and Beltane is also a fire festival. One of the customs that was practiced during both seasons when I lived on the farm all those years ago was to light two fires and walk the herds of cattle between them. I believe I remember the local old folk referring to this as "the time of the blessing." It was said the fires would protect the herds from ailments during the upcoming season.

The fires of Samhain are different from the fires of Beltane. I was taught the Beltane fire welcomed the heat of the coming summer Sun, while the Samhain fire was to chase away the cold and dark. Many times in the past we have written down what we wanted to purge from our lives, then fed the papers to the Samhain fire so it could eat and destroy that energy, taking it into the darkness and helping us to surrender to the changes we desired to make.

In other Samhain fires we have all taken some of the cold clinkers home with us. Doing this meant we had something from the last fire of the old year to use when we lit the first fire of the new year. In this way, the same fire passed from year to year, continuing the cycle and keeping the energy of those who no longer walked this earth alive with the memories of the fires that they had attended.

Sometimes at Samhain we have simply honored the fire. So many times we feed the fire in order to destroy or to transform something we're working on, but sometimes it's nice (and good magic) just to be one with the fire, to thank it for its presence and to celebrate it rather than feed it because we need something from it. We have done this with Samhain fires in the past and had howling success with sparklers and different salts that color the flames. You'd be surprised at how differently the fire responds to the different energies!

Divination

This is another important part of Samhain festivals. When I was a kid at school, we all thought it was great fun to hold a séance—well, as much of a séance as any group of giggling twelve-year-old girls was capable of holding! Divination is a part of many contemporary Samhain practices, and this seems to be something that has endured through the centuries.

My daddy was adamant we should have apples over Halloween, and my late Nanny Ruby said to peel the apple in one long strip, then toss it over my shoulder to find the initial of the man I was going to marry! When I was older and engaged to be married, my Aunt Martha told me to take off my engagement ring and tie it to one of the hairs plucked from my head and hang it over the palm of my hand. It was said it would tell me how many children I was going to have—back and forth for boys and around in circles for girls.

Other divination practices from the past involved scrying. This is when a bowl of water, dark mirror, crystal ball, or other such object is gazed into until images of the future start to appear. I have a quartz crystal that I use for such purposes. It is semi-translucent, cloudier on some days than on others depending on my mood and the weather! It also changes hue slightly too. Nearly anything—even the Samhain fire itself—can be used for scrying when the right mindset is cultivated.

Modern-day divination often revolves around oracles and tarot cards, and there are several decks that are Halloween or Samhain based. One of my favorites is *The Halloween Oracle* by Stacey Demarco and Jimmy Manton. Most of the Halloween oracles are readily available and easy to use. I like this one because the artwork is glorious, and the accompanying book is simple yet thorough.

Another favorite is Marcus Katz and Tali Goodwin's *The Ghost Train*. They have written many books on using the tarot, and in *The Ghost Train* they explore what they call "gated spreads" designed to unlock the past so the here and now can be better understood to create the desired future (Katz and Goodwin, 2013). Any deck of tarot cards can be used—although I do suggest one in keeping with the Rider-Waite artwork might be most appropriate; something like the *Llewellyn's Classic Tarot* by Barbara Moore and Eugene Smith works very well. This isn't specifically a Halloween book; I've used *The Ghost Train* many times and in different seasons, but it always seems the most profound when I do it over Samhain.

Honoring the Dead

My father died over three decades ago during the last week of October. Ever since then, Samhain has had a special place in my heart, for it is always when I remember Daddy the most. As the years have passed and I have lost more loved ones, it just seems fitting that I remember them at this time, at the festival that marks the end of the harvest and the dying of one year so the next might commence.

A few years ago, a friend told me she was writing down the names of those to be remembered at Samhain, and I thought that was such a good idea that I have adopted it myself. I write down the names of those close to me who have passed in the previous year, and then I continue to add the names of those who no longer walk this earth but whose love still lives in my heart. The older I get, the longer the list becomes. I speak these names out loud over the Samhain proceedings, breathing my vitality into them, keeping their memories alive.

Recording the names of loved ones who have passed is just one way the dead can be honored. I don't necessarily resonate with the phrase "respecting the dead" though. I prefer to think of it as "remembering the living." These people were once animated, once full of life; they had stories to share, people they loved, and things that were important to them. For me, it is more fitting to celebrate their lives than to mourn their deaths, even though I miss some of them with emotions so strong that they fill my heart to overflowing and the feelings leak out of my eyes, leaving a salty path along my cheeks.

Remembering the Living

Throughout this article, I've mentioned many people who made a great impact on me and who no longer walk this earth. I see Samhain predominantly as a time for celebrating the lives of the ancestors, both those I knew personally and those who are long gone. Some have called me a necromancer, and I'll wear that title, even though I do believe that it is gravely misunderstood.

Usually, a necromancer is defined as someone who conjures or speaks to the spirits of the dead for magical purposes. I suppose a lot of this depends on how the word *conjure* is interpreted, for not all definitions pertain to magic. Thoughts can be conjured, for example, by bringing someone or something to mind. I "conjure" my father's energy when I make pickles because I am doing them the way he taught me. I "conjure" my dear friend when I make fudge, for she is the one who taught me how to tell when it was stirred enough and ready to set up. I "conjure" my medicine elder when I share the lessons that he taught all those years ago.

If you talk to your deceased loved ones at holidays or festivals, if you plant things in your garden in their name, if you remember them fondly when you are making their favorite recipes or working at a craft they taught you, if you have their photo or ashes on a mantle or shelf and you say good morning to them as you pass, then you, too, have practiced necromancy. It's not that terrifying.

There's always a "however," though, and this is it: Just because someone is dead doesn't mean they are automatically enlightened. There are some malevolent beings out there, just as there are some not-so-nice people who walk the planet. Don't go headfirst into this without some basic preparation. Practice grounding and centering and shielding so that you know you are protected and you know what feels right and what does not. Be as discerning with the spirits as you are with the company you keep in your everyday life.

When doing ancestral work or seeking an audience with those who have passed, I find grounding, centering, and shielding essential. This practice is one of the most basic forms of protection and

I do it every morning, never mind before every ceremony or ritual. Grounding is just that: the energy is anchored so that you are grounded and not flying willy-nilly. Centering is done by anchoring your energy or your incorporeal body with your physical being. Shielding is putting up an energy barrier; I usually envision myself wrapped in rose quartz or a mirror, depending on the situation. A quick internet search will reveal many different articles on how to do this; if you're unfamiliar with it, I urge you to choose the method that resonates the strongest with you and then start putting it into practice. The day is less likely to unravel when you do!

With Samhain being the festival of the dead, it's only fitting that the dead are a major part of the proceedings. They can be honored in either a group ritual or by those who work as solitary practitioners. I'm a big believer in intent being one of the main ingredients of any mystical or spiritual work. The more you put into it, the more you will get out of it.

Reference

Katz, Marcus, and Tali Goodwin. *The Ghost Train*. Keswick, UK: Forge Press, 2013.

Cosmic Sway

Bernadette Evans

EVERYTHING IN LIFE IS a cycle, whether it's astrology cycles or sabbats. The Wheel of the Year, as it is commonly known, consists of eight sabbats in total that witches and Pagans come together to celebrate. Some of the sabbats are more well-known than others, Samhain being one of them, as it falls on the more famous holiday, Hallowe'en.

This year, during Samhain the Moon will be in Gemini, which is an air sign. Air signs love to connect, and Gemini enjoys communicating and gathering information to share with others. Mercury, who rules Gemini, is in the sign of Scorpio, as is the Sun and Mars. These three planets together are not lightweights. You may be ready to do a deep dive into a new area, one you're passionate about. Its fascinating and mysterious subject matter has a way of drawing you in.

Any gathering you attend on Samhain could have the earmarks of being quite thrilling, passionate, and intense. The rituals you practice will bind you closer to your friends and to the universe. Enjoy your celebrations!

Scorpio Season

The Sun will enter the sign of Scorpio on October 23 at 12:21 p.m. There are four elements associated with the zodiac signs: fire, earth, air, and water. Scorpio is in the watery realm. Water is connected with sensitivity, intuition, creativity, and feelings. When the Sun makes its yearly pass through this sign of the zodiac, emotions run deep. Conversations could have a more serious tone. You want to understand the nuances of life. It could get intense dissecting every feeling, but you might learn something about yourself and others. This is how transformation happens: diving deep into scary territory. Besides emotions, this energy is associated with sexual energy. Of course, intercourse is on the table … or anywhere! Sexual energy is more than just sex; it's about creation—whether you're using it to create life or using it to create a piece of art. Have fun!

Full Moon

There's a Full Moon and a partial lunar eclipse on October 28 at 4:24 p.m. at 5 degrees of Taurus. This Moon is called the Full Hunter's Moon or the Blood Moon. Whenever there's an eclipse, the energy is amplified. A Taurus Full Moon wants life to move at a slow and steady pace. It's a time to take practical steps; use this lunar energy to build a foundation. There are times you may want to laze around and not do much, but really, how much laying around can you do? Getting a handle on your finances and your partnerships is vital to your peace of mind. It helps you feel secure and gives you breathing room.

Mercury and Mars are conjoin in Scorpio and opposing Jupiter in Taurus, which is retrograde. Your conversations and actions are more serious; maybe obsessive thoughts keep playing in your mind. If you've been hurt, you may think it's time to cut someone out of your life; only you can make that call. With all the Scorpionic energy, you don't want to cross someone or be trifled with. You'll be presented with a choice of either going to a deeper, more profound level or ruminating on thoughts and actions. One direction can lead to growth while the other could keep you stuck.

Samhain

On October 31, it's time to celebrate the first of the sabbats. Samhain is a celebration of the end of harvest. It's the halfway point between the fall equinox and the winter solstice, a time to give thanks for the bounty of the earth. While it is about endings and going inward, it's also about beginnings. It's the Celtic New Year, when the cosmic wheel turns again. The waning Moon is in the sign of Gemini, which is ruled by Mercury, the winged messenger of the Romans. Since the sign of Gemini is known for communication, this seems perfect for those wanting to speak with their relatives on the other side. Communication will be easier and messages will be heard from both sides.

There are three inconjuncts today that could present some challenges. Compromising and adjusting to circumstances are the name of the game. The Venus-Uranus trine could bode well for an unusual encounter, maybe a love interest. Pay attention to the signs the universe brings you.

All Soul's Day

All Souls' Day is on November 1. The Moon is void-of-course from 8:36 a.m. until 5:30 p.m., when it enters the sign of Cancer. This is a great time to cook up a feast or just be with family members, or those whom you consider family. Any act of nurturing, whether it's for others or yourself, lines up with this Moon energy.

Saturn Direct

On November 4, Saturn will station direct at 3:03 a.m. Saturn is the great timekeeper. What have you been planning? Saturn has been retrograde since June 17. Have you been revising your plans? You will be rewarded if you've done the work. Now is the time to start thinking about your next course of action.

Dark Moon

On November 13 at 4:27 a.m., there is a New Moon at 20 degrees of Scorpio. This is the time of year when you think about regeneration. What needs to go to make room for something new? A New Moon is about planting the seeds of new ideas. Take time to go within and discover what you desire. Mars is conjoin the Sun and Moon and opposing Uranus. Expect the unexpected whenever Uranus is in the mix. With the Sun, Moon, and Mars all in Scorpio, you could be diving deep, exploring new sides of yourself. You may even want to see a psychologist who can help you uncover areas that keep you stuck. Old patterns need to be discarded to make way for new pathways. New opportunities could suddenly present themselves. Say yes to the synchronicities of the universe.

With all this Scorpionic energy, we have to talk about sex. It's energy and it's fun! Enjoy playing and connecting with another or yourself. Finances, and specifically other people's money, are at the forefront. Do you have debts that are due, or does someone owe you money? Get it sorted out.

Sagittarius Season

The Sun enters the sign of Sagittarius at 9:03 a.m. on November 22. This is a fiery sign, one that likes to play and have fun, whether it's with a gathering of friends or traveling to far-off places. You may be ready to pack a bag and begin anew! Being impulsive and ready for adventure has its gifts and challenges. There could be a pull to immerse yourself by learning something new. Sagittarius is the seeker of truth—it's just that everyone's truth looks different. Find what resonates for you and let others have their beliefs.

In the morning, the Moon in Pisces will trine Mars in Scorpio, making it easier to tune in to your intuition and follow your hunches. By afternoon, the Moon enters the sign of Aries, so it will trine the Sun. All that fire encourages you to get moving!

Thanksgiving

November 23 is Thanksgiving Day in the United States. You may choose to spend time with the people who mean the most to you. It's a time to give thanks for everyone and everything that has woven the tapestry of your life.

The Moon is in the sign of Aries and opposes Venus in Libra. There are always a few ways for every aspect and situation to unfold. A fiery Moon can get overheated. You could say something you'll regret tomorrow. Likewise, try not to get offended if someone says something they shouldn't; let it roll off you. Use this energy to reach out to someone you haven't spoken with in a while. After all, Venus in Libra is about connecting with other people.

Full Moon

On November 27, there's a Full Moon at 4:16 a.m. at 4 degrees of Gemini. This Full Moon is sometimes called the Full Beaver Moon, since the beavers were seen getting ready for the colder months to come. The Celts called it the Mourning Moon or the Darkest Depths Moon.

During this Full Moon, the emphasis is on information, travel, and siblings. The Full Moon is about releasing. Is there a sibling that you haven't spoken to and need to mend fences with? Are you trying to take in too much information? Can you really digest all of it? As difficult as it may be, slow down and learn one thing really well instead of skimming the surface of twenty things. Is there a short trip you'd like to go on?

Mars is conjoin the Sun and opposite the Moon, so there is an assertive energy—a desire to learn, travel, and take in all the excitement the world has to offer. Again, be careful of trying to consume everything in your wake. You'll wear yourself out. Add in Mercury squaring Neptune and your head could be spinning. Confused about which direction to move, what to study, what to do next? Go within and listen to what your higher self already knows.

Neptune Direct

On December 6, Neptune turns direct at 8:20 a.m. The planet of illusion has been retrograde since June 30. Now the blinders are back on, and you may see what you want to see. When Neptune's direct, you can easily slip back into your dreams and fantasies. This can be helpful if you need to call on your imagination for your work or a hobby. Neptune is also compassionate. Take time to tune in to your heart.

Dark Moon

On December 12, there is a New Moon at 6:32 p.m. at 20 degrees of Sagittarius. Whenever Sagittarius is highlighted, you want to explore and taste all that life has to offer. Sometimes that means traveling. Have you always had a desire to visit a certain country or city? Now may be the perfect time to go! Maybe you're in the mood to take a class or study something new.

This New Moon energy can make you hungry to know more about others and how they live. This knowledge about others not only widens your perspective, it helps you grow. One other thing: Sagittarius energy wants to feel free; it doesn't want to be fenced in. The Sun and Moon are quincunx Uranus, which means you could be changing your plans at the last minute. These things happen; just bob and weave and go with the flow.

Mercury Retrograde

Mercury stations retrograde on December 13 at 2:09 a.m. at 8 degrees of Capricorn. It will retrograde back to 22 degrees of Sagittarius and will be retrograde through the New Year, up until January 1, 2024. Take time to review and revise your plans. Be sure to back up any photos or documents so you don't lose anything that's important to you. This is a wonderful time to slow down and get clear on the direction you want to take. Once you have that figured out, then you can start planning how it will look. You can launch your new passion project once Mercury is direct.

Until it turns direct, don't start anything new, if possible. Remember not to sign any contracts right now. If these are unavoidable, go over them carefully; get another set of (trusted) eyes to look over the contract as well. Mercury retrograde in Capricorn could point to a setback at work or in your career. Maybe your reputation takes a hit.

Then Mercury keeps going and enters Sagittarius territory. When it's retrograde here, there could be delays if you're travelling somewhere. Maybe your studies aren't progressing as smoothly as you'd like. As Mercury is about communication, watch what you say. Be careful of putting your foot in your mouth and saying something that's difficult to smooth over after the fact.

References

Buckle, Anna, Aparna Kher, and Vigdis Hocken. "Traditional Full Moon Names." Time and Date. Accessed December 8, 2022. https://www.timeanddate.com/astronomy/moon/full-moon -names.html.

"Full Moon Names for 2023." *The Old Farmer's Almanac.* Yankee Publishing, Inc. January 5, 2023. https://www.almanac.com /full-moon-names.

Tales and Traditions

Natalie Zaman

I'M PART OF A generation that's betwixt and between. Gen X is that small segment of the population with feet in both the past and the future. It gives us a unique perspective. Part of that perspective is that when Halloween rolled around (about forty or so years ago), one of the most anticipated events of the year was the annual airing of *It's the Great Pumpkin, Charlie Brown* (at least here in the United States). It came on at a precisely scheduled time that, if you missed it, well, you missed it, and had to wait 365 days for your next chance.

It was the same throughout the year. Specific faces appeared in their given seasons, sometimes around or on a particular holiday. For example, *The Wizard of Oz* aired on or around Easter, and monster movies cropped up in the summer (for those days when it was just too hot to go outside). *King Kong* barreled into living rooms for Thanksgiving—a pre-dinner treat probably timed to keep the kids busy while all hell was breaking loose in the kitchen. These characters and their stories defined the seasons for me, and they still do—although I have a different perspective on the seasons and the holidays of my childhood.

A Cast of Sabbats Characters

The year's turning points have many associations. As the years go by and more and more people delve into elder ways, they tell the stories of the Wheel of the Year in their own voices and apply their unique experiences to them. These retellings make ancient ways relatable. What follows here and for each subsequent sabbat are the associations I've made in my life thus far, characters that I've encountered that have brought seasons, sabbats, and holidays to life for me. I've arranged them into an archetypal royal court: "rulers of the sabbats," if you will. There are direct connections to old traditions, subtle links that give me pause, and hints that we are all connected in the spiral dance of time.

Why are these characters so special? Each is endearing or memorable, but they also seem to embody a particular time of the year because of the things they do and say and how they look. They also feel comfortable and familiar. In many ways, their stories are my own; I've made similar journeys:

Jack Skellington's **search for inspiration.**
The White Witch's **doomed efforts to prevent change.**
Mary Poppins's **impossible perfection.**
Dorothy Gale's **journey to maturity.**
Darth Vader's **raging inner battle.**
Godzilla's **destructive awakening from slumber.**
Willy Wonka's **creation of a utopia.**
Brienne of Tarth's **quest for identity and acceptance.**

Human, monster, or a combination of both, their tales tug at heartstrings and deep DNA strands. And even though they are relatively new, their spirit hearkens to older times. We've been here before, seen this before. There's an old saying that there is nothing really new, and there are only so many stories. The hero's, antihero's, or even villain's journey follows a loosely set pattern:

1. We meet them.
2. We discover their strengths and weaknesses.

3. They go out to seek their fortune.
4. Sometimes, many times, they lose almost everything, and then...
5. They discover their power and use it to affect...
6. The ending.

It may not be "happily ever after," but it's only temporary. An ending is only the jumping-off point for a new beginning. Does this not happen each time the Wheel of the Year comes full circle? Each year the sabbats are the same, but the tales are different because the world and the people in it are different; herein lies variety.

Jack Skellington: The Pumpkin King

Samhain is the season of endings and slumber. Life is eternal, and at this time of the year, the world is very much alive, though sometimes it's hard to tell. *The Nightmare Before Christmas* came out just before I turned twenty-three, and as my love of all things goth turned out *not* to be a phase, I was a little more than excited. I grew up on holiday reruns of Claymation and stop-motion specials (e.g., *Rudolph the Red-Nosed Reindeer*, *The Year Without a Santa Claus*, *Santa Claus Is Comin' to Town*, etc.). Everything about *Nightmare*—the storytelling, the aesthetics, the cinematography—was, and still is, magic.

Jack Skellington is an obvious choice to represent Samhain simply because he is the Pumpkin King of Halloween Town. But there are other compelling reasons:

- At Samhain, the veils between the worlds are thin, demonstrated when Jack, who has clearly been the Pumpkin King for goodness knows how long, stumbles into the clearing that leads him to Christmas Town. He discovers the latest step in his destiny in Samhain's waning hours, crossing the veil to commune with another world.
- At Samhain, not all is as it seems. Halloween Town is populated with frightening monsters—with no malice. In fact,

most are lovable, even Boogie with his bugs. Jack attempts to bring this topsy-turviness to Christmas (Yule), but that season has its own unique order that is not so easily overturned.

- At Samhain, we honor those who exist behind the veil and try to communicate with them. There is a great deal of this going on in *Nightmare*, from Sally trying to communicate with Jack in an attempt to help him understand his own feelings, Jack trying to penetrate the mysteries of Christmas, to the whole of Halloween Town trying to understand Christmas. Samhain and *Nightmare* are about grasping the mystery.

Samhain *prêt-à-porter par Nightmare ...*

One of the easiest (and most fun) ways to celebrate a sabbat and honor its archetypal characters is to "get into character." This is an age-old tradition for Samhain: putting on a costume. But in this case, I don't mean the traditional Halloween costume or cosplay (although you can certainly do that too!). Fashion has long been a means of self-expression. Clothing and accessories can be tools. (Think Princess Diana and her cleavage-hiding clutch bags, First Ladies wearing specific designers to show multilevel support, or wearing a power suit to an interview or a meeting.)

These are practical sartorial choices that can be incorporated into everyday outfits: *prêt-à-porter*, ready to wear. Sometimes they're so subtle that only the wearer knows their meanings. Messages are delivered in pieces of jewelry; attitude is expressed in color and pattern. So how can you put on Samhain as defined by dear Jack Skellington?

- **Pinstripes:** Don a pair of vertically striped pants, a jacket, or a combo of both to channel Jack's power. Stripes in general are a favorite Tim Burton aesthetic—but Jack's pinstripe suit carries a hefty history. In the nineteenth century, London banks started issuing uniform pin-striped trousers to their workers (each bank had its own unique color). Add a matching jacket in the twentieth century and *bam!*—the pin-striped power suit was born. Nowadays, the rule is the wider the stripe, the more informal the suit. Jack's pinstripe suit is quite formal, even funereal. How will you show your stripes?

- **Orange:** Jack *is* the Pumpkin King—not to mention that the color is incorporated into many of the stripes seen around Halloween Town. This addition imparts a candy-like sweetness to the surrounding darkness. Orange is the color of the sacral chakra, the body's center of creativity. Jack draws on significant reserves of imagination to make each Halloween special. Orange accessories like scarves and socks and tights will bring a dash of creativity to your Samhain celebrations.

- **Bats:** Jack has only one accessory: a live bat bow(ish) tie. Bats are symbols of death and rebirth and can be found in pieces of Victorian mourning jewelry and even carved on tombstones and chapels in eighteenth- and nineteenth-century cemeteries. Honor Samhain and these winged guardians of the night Jack's way with a bat pin or brooch, big and bold or subtle and secret.

Books and Films to Read, View, and Inspire
Selick, Henry, dir. *The Nightmare Before Christmas*. 1993; Burbank, CA: Touchstone Pictures.

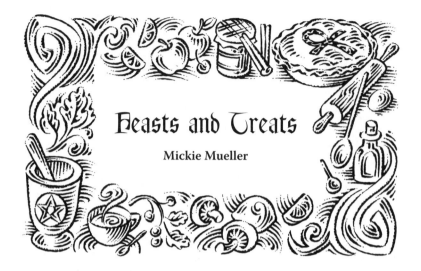

Feasts and Treats

Mickie Mueller

Samhain means different things to different people, and to many of us, it's a day that combines fun with reverence. I love many of the traditional foods associated with Samhain: apples, corn, spices, and sweets all have a place on my Samhain table. Since it's a time when we think about death and our ancestors, it's a great time to use old family recipes to soothe our spirits and welcome traveling souls of our dearly departed. I also love a meal that's quick and easy and can be eaten when you feel like it just in case any goblins ring your doorbell and demand treats. I love to share meal plans that include make-ahead dishes and easy "day of" dishes so that the cook gets to have fun too!

Chicken Paprika Skillet Stew

I first discovered chicken paprikash while reading Bram Stoker's *Dracula*. The way he described it sounded delicious, and I went on a quest for recipes and made the most authentic ones I could find. I later discovered that I had ancestors from Hungary, so maybe that's why these flavors sing to my soul. This is a slimmed-down version of the classic dish, but it's just as delicious and comforting, and a family favorite at my house. I've even made vegetarian versions of this using store-bought vegan chicken substitute and veggie broth.

Prep time: 10 minutes
Cooking time: 12–15 minutes
Servings: 4

2–3 tablespoons olive oil for cooking
4 chicken breasts, cut into bite-size pieces
Salt
Pepper
3 bell peppers, cut into 1-inch pieces
1 onion, cut in half then sliced
3 heaping tablespoons of smoked Hungarian paprika
1 teaspoon flour (regular or gluten free works)
1 cup chicken broth or bone broth
Optional: ¼ cup sour cream

Heat 1 tablespoon of olive oil in a skillet over medium heat. Toss the chicken in salt and pepper, and brown in the skillet. Add bell peppers and onion and continue to sauté until soft. Push all ingredients to the side of the skillet and add another tablespoon of olive oil, all the paprika, and the flour. Mix until it forms a paste and cook for a minute or two. Stir it into all the other ingredients in the skillet, add broth, and mix. Cover and simmer for 5 minutes or until the sauce thickens. If you're going with the sour cream option, stir it in at the end. Serve over rice or broad noodles.

Samhain Flatbread

I love to have bread with my Chicken Paprika Skillet Stew to soak up all that good sauce. This flatbread is really yummy; it's made without yeast and is easy enough for even a baker with very little experience. I also have gluten-free and dairy-free versions. These little flatbreads are good on their own or for sandwiches, but the toppings bring them up to star status!

Prep time: 10 minutes
Cooking time: 20 minutes
Servings: 8 flatbreads

Flatbread

1½ cups self-rising flour or gluten-free self-rising flour (or 1½ cups all-purpose wheat or all-purpose gluten-free flour blend, plus 3 teaspoons baking powder and ½ teaspoon salt)

1 cup Greek yogurt or dairy-free Greek yogurt

Topping

1 tablespoon olive oil

¼ cup sun-dried tomatoes

2 cloves minced garlic

Pinch of salt

Fresh ground Parmesan cheese or dairy-free shreds

Combine flatbread dry ingredients and Greek yogurt in a large bowl until it comes together into a soft ball of dough. You can make little adjustments to the ratios of flour to yogurt if needed; it should be a soft, workable dough. Do not overwork this dough or it will become tough. Turn it out onto a floured board and divide into 8 pieces. One at a time, roll each of the 8 pieces of dough between two sheets of waxed paper using a rolling pin until they're about ¼ inch thick. Preheat a dry skillet over medium heat. Gently peel off the waxed paper and cook in the skillet 2–2½ minutes on the first side, turn, and cook about 2 minutes more on the other. Repeat for each flatbread.

Blitz olive oil, tomatoes, garlic, and salt in the blender or food processor until it's a slightly chunky but spreadable consistency. Spread the tomato mixture onto one side of each flatbread and sprinkle with Parmesan cheese (or dairy-free cheese). Toast under a broiler until the cheese is bubbly, 1–2 minutes.

Popcorn Three Ways

Popcorn has been traditional this time of the year since October 31 celebrations first came to America. Since variety is the spice of life, I have three recipes for big bowls of popcorn, enough to share. One version is sweet, one savory, and one is both salty and sweet. You can even make all three. They're perfect if you're doing scary movie night—an easy dessert or snack that even uses a little chocolate. You can prepare these ahead of time!

Prep time: 10 minutes, each flavor
Cooking time: 10 minutes, each flavor
Servings: 6, 2 per flavor

Samhain Sprinkles Popcorn

8 cups popped popcorn
½ cup white chocolate melts
2–3 tablespoons of orange and black sprinkles, aka jimmies, the little ones that don't break your teeth

First, melt the chocolate. I use the microwave; it takes less than two minutes. Stop it and stir every 15–30 seconds and stir until completely melted. Drizzle over popcorn and toss; add the sprinkles and toss again before the chocolate is set. Turn out onto a baking pan until set, then break it apart and put it back in the bowl.

Chocolate and Sea Salt Popcorn

8 cups popped popcorn
½ cup dark chocolate melts
Sea salt to taste

Melt the chocolate melts. I use the microwave; it takes less than two minutes. Stop it and stir every 15–30 seconds and stir until completely melted. Pour over popcorn and toss; sprinkle with sea salt to taste and toss again before the chocolate sets. Turn out onto a baking pan until set, then break it apart and put it back in the bowl.

Garlic and Herb Popcorn

8 cups popped popcorn
1 tablespoon melted butter or plant butter
1 tablespoon olive oil
1 teaspoon garlic powder (adjust to taste; we like a lot of garlic)

1 teaspoon very fine salt (you can powder it in mortar and pestle)
1 teaspoon Italian seasoning
1 tablespoon grated Parmesan or vegan shreds

Put the butter, olive oil, and seasonings in a microwaveable dish and microwave less than a minute until the butter is melted. Pour it onto the popcorn and toss to coat. Then add the Parmesan while it's still warm and toss again.

Hot Mulled Apple Cider

This is a classic drink that's spicy and delicious, great anytime for cool weather but is quite festive for Samhain. *Mulling* is when you warm a beverage and sweeten it with fruit and spices; you can mull wine as well using the same spices and fruit, and it's delicious. In many areas of the world, *cider* refers to a fermented beverage, but in the United States (where I live) and much of Canada, apple cider is fresh, unpasteurized juice made from pressed apples. Apple cider's more processed cousin is regular apple juice. You can use apple juice if you don't have sweet apple cider in your area. If you can find apple cider, I think you'll love it, as it's very fresh and more flavorful than the processed and pasteurized apple juice.

Prep time: 5 minutes
Cooking time: 1 hour
Servings: 8

1 gallon local fresh unpasteurized apple cider, substitute apple juice if needed
3 cinnamon sticks, or 1 teaspoon ground cinnamon
6 allspice berries, or ½ teaspoon of ground allspice
1 whole nutmeg, or 1½ teaspoons nutmeg
3 slices of ginger root, or 1 teaspoon ground ginger
10 whole cloves, or ⅛ teaspoon ground cloves
3 whole star anise, or ½ teaspoon ground star anise
1 orange, sliced
⅓ cup fresh cranberries

The thing to remember about this recipe (and all recipes) is that if there's a spice that you don't like or don't have, just leave it out. There are many variations of mulled cider out there, so use what you like.

Pour the cider into a large cooking pot on low temperature or into a slow cooker on high. If you're using whole spices like cinnamon sticks, allspice berries, etc., you can release more flavor from them if you toast them first. Put them in a dry frying pan over medium heat and roll them around a bit until they begin to release a strong aroma. Then you can put them in your cider. If you're using any ground spices, I recommend that you put them into a coffee filter and then tie the coffee filter closed tightly with some kitchen twine. This will allow all the flavor to infuse into the cider without gritty spices in your cup. Add the sliced orange and fresh cranberries and cook 1 hour on the stove or 4 hours in the slow cooker. Ladle into small mugs.

Crafty Crafts

Lupa

FALL IS A FABULOUS time for fungi! Cool temperatures and the return of rain prompt many fungus species to produce their fruiting bodies, known more commonly as mushrooms. These temporary reproductive structures are how fungi spread their spores to create the next generation of their species. Some of them, like chanterelles and oyster mushrooms, are safe for most people to eat. Others, such as fly agaric and sulfur tufts, are poisonous enough to make you sick, and a few such as destroying angel and death cap can be deadly if eaten.

Mushrooms come in a wide variety of colors and shapes. However, most only last a few days to a couple of weeks and lose their color when dried. Plus, they don't always pop up in the same place each year, meaning that the flush of colorful saffron milk caps you found last year may be barren this time around. This can make finding, eating, and decorating with mushrooms quite challenging.

Merry Mushroom Mosaic

Thankfully, we can create our own mushrooms out of clay! Not only will they not decay into mush after a few weeks, but they'll retain their color too. Plus, you don't have to be an expert mushroom hunter to add them to your decor; all you need are a few art supplies and reference photos to get started. You also don't have to be the most amazing artist in the world—this craft is about having fun creating something inspired by nature, regardless of how much artistic skill you have. Using FIMO clay, air-dry clay, or epoxy putty, sculpt a variety of mushrooms (whole, caps, etc.) and paint them as you like. Then use them to fill a wooden frame or tray for hanging or other display.

Materials
Choice of clay

Optional: bendable wire, eyepin, sculptor's tools, acrylic paint, acrylic spray sealant

Cost: $10–$75 depending on how many optional materials you choose

Time spent: 1–2 hours not including curing/baking time

You're certainly welcome to create these out of traditional kilnfired clay. There are lots of fun glazes for colors and other effects, and they can be painted after firing as well. And you have unlimited work time; until you fire the clay, it will remain malleable. But not everyone has access to a kiln. Thankfully, there are several options that will cure on their own or can be cured in a regular oven in your kitchen.

Polymer clays like Sculpey and FIMO allow you to make a rainbow of mushrooms with just a few small packets of polymer clay in various colors, and you can even blend your own custom colors. No paints needed! Polymer clay can be cured in a standard oven or even a toaster oven (directions may vary depending on size of oven and the piece you are curing).

Air-drying clay is another good option. It's lightweight and inexpensive and will dry on its own, usually within twenty-four to seventy-two hours depending on the size of the piece and the ambient humidity and temperature. My favorite sculpting medium is two-part epoxy putty. It cures within twenty-four hours through a chemical process regardless of ambient temperature and humidity.

It also lends itself well to carving and sanding after it has cured, allowing you to fine-tune your sculpture. Do be aware that it can irritate some people's skin, so I recommend putting a barrier cream like Gloves in a Bottle on your hands before using it, wearing rubber gloves while mixing the two parts together, and then washing your hands thoroughly once you're done working with it.

Once you've selected your medium of choice, it's time to start sculpting. If you don't have any mushrooms in your area to photograph, you can look online for reference photos of different sorts of mushrooms, especially those that grow in the fall. I especially like http://commons.wikimedia.org, as there are some public domain photos as well as those released under various Creative Commons licenses. These photos can inspire your creativity and help you make your mushrooms more lifelike if you so choose. However, there's nothing wrong with more fanciful, imaginative designs, either!

Decide whether you want your mushrooms to be freestanding or as part of a decorative piece like a picture frame or wreath. If they're going to be on their own, you may need a sturdy but bendable wire to create an armature, at least for the stipe (stem), especially for bigger mushrooms. For the cap, a ring of wire works well as an armature, even if it isn't attached to the stipe. If you're going to turn one of your mushrooms into a pendant, get an eyepin with a wire long enough to put a ninety-degree angle into, then sculpt the cap around that. That way your eyepin won't slide out unexpectedly, and it adds a little more structure to the cap.

If you're incorporating your mushrooms into an art piece, you can create them independently and then attach them after curing or sculpt them directly onto the structure. Another fun idea is to just sculpt the caps so you have lots of flat, round pieces that have more surface area for gluing or otherwise attaching to things. Remember that polymer clay has to be oven-cured, so you probably won't be able to add them to something else until after they've been cured.

For sculpting, you can get packets of sculptor's tools at most craft stores. However, all sorts of household items make great

sculpting tools too, like pencils (both ends!), toothpicks, the ends of paintbrushes, etc. And, of course, your fingers can create a wide array of textures and effects with a little creativity.

Some people find it easiest to sculpt the entire mushroom all at once. Others sculpt the cap and the stipe separately, then put them together after curing. The same goes for clusters of mushrooms; some people may find it easier to sculpt each one individually, then construct an assemblage of all of them after curing. It may help to make a base that you can then "plug" the individual cured mushrooms into.

If you're going to try to sculpt something really delicate, like mushroom gills, sculpt the heavier, less-detailed parts first, cure them, then go back in and sculpt or carve in the fine details. This is because when you're handling uncured clay, it's all too easy to accidentally squish the finest bits! Polymer clay can be put in the oven multiple times as long as the temperature isn't too high, and you can add to air-drying clay or epoxy putty even after it has cured.

All of these clays lend themselves well to painting. I'm especially fond of acrylic paints because they're inexpensive, they come in a lot of colors that are easy to mix together, and they clean up easily. Whether you stay true to the natural colors or let yourself explore fanciful hues, make sure you seal the paint afterward to help protect it for years to come.

The Natural Magic of Connection

Dallas Jennifer Cobb

AS PAGANS, OUR STRONG association with nature has been central to our faith, rituals, spells, and magical practices for millennia. Sabbats have their roots in seasonal archetypes and timely agricultural practices and are associated with natural elements.

But of late, social media has turned Pagan practices into thinly veiled consumerism, requiring the purchase of candles, oils, herbs, and incense. For many, our Craft has drifted away from nature.

Moving beyond this paradigm, let this year be the cycle in which we bring nature back, placing it at the center of our rituals, altars, spells, and lives. For each sabbat this year, enjoy a nature magic theme, ritual, and spell.

These magical practices are written to be accessible to anyone, anywhere. Whether you live in a city or remote wilderness, you can undertake these practices. There are no special tools, supplies, goods, or substances needed that cannot be commonly found.

These essays are written from a Northern Hemisphere perspective. However, if you live in the Southern Hemisphere, I trust you can choose the seasonally appropriate section to read and practice by matching the celebrations of light and dark to your local environment.

Samhain marks the end of the harvest season, and in Celtic Pagan practice it was celebrated as the end of the old year and the beginning of the new year. As we mark the death of the growing season on October 31, let us choose to allow our old, outgrown ways to die also. And as we welcome the new year at sundown on November 1, let us consciously welcome new habits and new ways of being into our lives.

Samhain is the day of connection between the end and the new beginning, so that we don't just "throw away" our old stuff, but learn from it and allow our connection to it to teach us as we move forward. Think of it as the agricultural act of composting. Let go of consumerism and the pressure to purchase Pagan paraphernalia, and this year choose to bring nature back to the center of our lives, celebrations, and sabbats.

Though commonly misattributed to Chief Seattle, the following statement by screenwriter Ted Perry captures the sentiment: "The earth does not belong to man; man belongs to the earth... All things are connected... Man did not weave the web of life; he is merely a strand in it. Whatever he does to the web, he does to himself" (Perry 1987, 528).

One Family Ritual

After sunset, create a small altar dedicated to what is coming to an end. On it place that nameless crystal you bought on Kijiji, the so-called spell that came in a plastic bag, and that mauve "mystically charged incense" you paid too much for. Go through your home and gather anything that needs to be let go of.

Choose a spot near some crossroads or cross paths on your property, like where your walkway meets the sidewalk, or where your drive meets the road, and erect your offering altar there. (Don't worry, kids love to see stuff like this on Hallowe'en night.) Adorn the altar with a small sign that reads "Free." Place it in an easily visible location.

Take your shoes off, placing your bare feet on the earth. Connected physically to the earth, let your spirit and intentions align with the organic intentions of earth, nature, and this planet.

Light a small candle in a wind-safe jar and call upon Hecate to be with you. (Safety is always important. Be aware of the power of fire and use it responsibly.) Incant:

Blessed Hecate, who oversees magic, witches, and creatures of the night,
Goddess of good and evil, keep me in your sight.

Offer up the goods of consumerism. Lay them out side by side, like small dead bodies. Let these be your offerings at the crossroads, and be aware of what you are letting go of.

May these offerings find their perfect new homes,
May they be blessed as they roam.
May they find goodness and appreciation,
And forever be free of consumer association.
As these tools to new homes fly,
Free me from the obligation to buy.

Open your hands wide, palms upturned. Feel your feet on the ground.

Fill my feet and hands with nature's power,
Transformational elements, trees, and flowers,
As spirit flows through me and to my spells,
May my works help keep Mother Nature well.

Breathe in your intention, put on your shoes, and blow out the candle, taking it with you as you turn and walk away without looking back.

Overnight, meditate on composting the colonial idea that "man [*sic*] has dominion over the earth," nourishing instead an earth-based spirituality that holds sacred the notion that the earth creates and sustains us. On November 1, as the new year begins, return to the offering site and clean up what remains. Barefoot once more, invoke Hecate:

> *Guide me this year in a new direction,*
> *Learning and deepening my nature connection.*

Stand with feet wide apart and allow the energy of the earth and nature to possess you. There at the crossroads, envision wild roots growing from your feet into the dark soil of possibility, green shoots of inspiration snaking skyward from your hair, the waters of your sacred creativity flowing freely to nourish passion and pleasure, and the wildfire within your heart rekindling. Envision your family, friends, neighbors, and community joining you in a powerful circle, one family.

Turn so that your back faces the site where you offered up your consumer goods. Put on your shoes. Facing a new direction, walk away.

Connected to the Great Mother Spell

These foundational emotional experiences are considered to be the basics of good parenting: connection, safety, attunement, security, attachment, love, belonging, and healing. As the Wheel of the Year turns, let us connect to nature, to the earth, to our planet in a way that nurtures and sustains us, acknowledging earth as our Great Mother.

We know about the positive effect nature has upon the human nervous system. Let's orient toward the healing available, feeling the support and resources that come from being connected to a creative and sustaining "parent": nature. Whether or not you experienced good parenting or the foundational emotional experiences that good parenting bestows in your early life, know that these are available to you now as you return to the Great Mother.

Today, cast the spell that sets your intention. Say:

> *May the Great Mother heal and teach me,*
> *Connecting me to nature and my earth family.*

I devote this year to reconnection,
Consciously returning to nature's love and protection.

It is time now to walk forward into the new year.

Reference

Perry, Ted. "Version 3—Written by Ted Perry." Quoted in Rudolf Kaiser. "Chief Seattle's Speech(es): American Origins and European Reception." In *Recovering the Word: Essays on Native American Literature*, edited by Brian Swann and Arnold Krupat. Berkeley and Los Angeles, CA: University of California Press, 1987.

Samhain Ritual

Charlie Rainbow Wolf

THIS IS A VERY simple ritual, but it is one that is very powerful. I designed it several years ago when attending a wedding. They started with the customary father-daughter dance, and I had to excuse myself. It hit me like a ton of bricks that I had never danced with my father. I don't even know if he *could* dance, and there is no one left alive for me to ask. However, I can reach out to him in spirit, through rituals such as the one below, and make peace with my memories in that manner.

Dancing with the Dead

You won't need any special tools or a lot of preparation for this, but there are some steps involved—no pun intended! You will need some quiet time to yourself, perhaps an hour or more, and if doing this in a group, you will need to decide on the music to be played beforehand. You will also need a bit of space; nothing brings a magical working back to reality faster than a dramatic mishap!

Take some time choosing the music. Your favorite sounds may not be those of the person or timeline you wish to remember. You're not just doing this for yourself, but rather, you are doing this for both of you. Try to find somewhere to meet in the middle. My dad was an ardent bluegrass fan, but he did like some old western music. I was more into pop and soft rock and songs that told stories. We met in the middle with some of the stuff Willie Nelson did.

Next, you will want to think about things you enjoyed together. Again, this has to be somewhere you can meet in the middle. My daddy loved his black coffee; I've never been able to drink coffee. I'm a tea drinker through and through. We both liked iced tea, though, also the English "mild" beer. Choose a beverage (nonalcoholic is preferred) or a food that the two of you shared or one that pertains to the culture you wish to embrace, and spend time talking with the ancestral spirits as you prepare it.

Smells are important in this ritual too. I remember from my college psychology class that the sense of smell is the strongest of the five senses and the one that links most profoundly to emotions and memory. I know this to be true; I only need to catch a whiff of Old Spice aftershave and I am back in my childhood home, my daddy getting ready to take my mum out for the evening.

I frequently work with dried herbs in the form of incense and dream pillows. I have a special blend that I use when I want to be particularly close to my daddy. It smells of tobacco and hops, of cedar and sage and lilacs. If you associate a particular smell with a pleasant memory, then recreate that if you can. Perhaps it is the smell of freshly baked bread, newly mown grass, freshly harvested apples, or a campfire. Incense and candles are two easy ways to bring a scented memory into the ritual—but keep in mind those who may have allergies and adjust things accordingly.

Finally, prepare yourself. In my traditions, this is having a bath or a shower, putting on clean clothing, and having nothing to eat or drink (except for water) until after the ceremony. I take this tradition one step further, using a ritual soap or shower steamer and putting on clothing that reminds me of my daddy—I've been known to wear his boots before! I also like to have candlelight or moonlight rather than electric lighting, and I pick candles in my daddy's favorite colors.

The spirit you choose to dance with does not need to be someone you knew personally. Perhaps you wish to honor an ancestor from long ago or even to immerse yourself in the energy of a particular spirit from history. This is perfectly okay. I have spent many wonderful Samhain's dancing around stone circles in my mind with ancestors from ancient Britain, just as I have danced around fires with my Cherokee medicine elders. I firmly believe it is all connected, and to create a link with the energy of our ancestors we merely have to reach out to them.

If you desire to dance with someone unknown to you, take a bit of time to research who they were and how they lived, and prepare your setting accordingly. You might want to include things from that culture or timeline in the way of music, decorations, or clothing. Add the food and drink or the colors and the smells via candles and herbs. The more effort you put into setting the stage, the more enriching the dance will be for you.

At your chosen time, when you have prepared everything, including yourself, spend some time in thought with your loved one. Think about what they would think of things today. How would you welcome them and make them feel at home? What would you talk about? Have that conversation with them in your mind, in your heart, in your soul. When you feel their presence, when you know they are near, then invite them to dance.

You don't have to be Fred Astaire or Ginger Rogers to do this. (Yes, I'm a black and white film fan, and I'm probably showing my age!) The idea is just that you move. Give up your energy to the vibrations of the music and let it take you where you want to go. Hold your ancestor close. Keep conversing with them, envisioning them as alive and vibrant, as close as your next breath. Feel them in your heartbeat.

All good things have to come to an end, though, and the time will come when it is right for you to enter fully back into the here and now, releasing them to return back to their realm. At this time, turn off the music, brighten the lights a bit if possible, and have something to eat or drink: the food and beverage that you prepared to share with them. This will start to ground your energy and allow them to start their own journey home.

The Afterglow

The dance with your loved one has ended, but your time with them has not. Every time you speak of them, every time you think of them, every time you are reminded of them, that is when they are close to you. Thomas Campbell (1777–1844) said, "To live in hearts we leave behind, / Is not to die" (1828, 198). As long as you carry those you love in your heart, neither time nor distance nor even death itself can separate you.

Dancing with the departed opens a door for them to come closer to you. It's all to do with the vibrations of the music. Sound is a frequency. Your own vitality—your aura, if you want to see it that way, the energy that makes you alive and vibrant—is also a frequency.

When you set all of this in motion with the dance, the echo lingers on. It is written in the past, and it will be there anytime you want to call upon it. You may even find the more you work with this vibration, the easier it becomes to sense your loved ones close and to be with them. I know my daddy is with me every time I open my throat to sing. He loved singing himself, and sometimes I sing the songs I remember him crooning over the sink as he did the dishes.

It's easy to take the ancestors and other loved ones forward into your daily life by doing things they would have approved of or doing things in their name that help to bring light and positive energy into the dark corners of the world. It doesn't need to be elaborate or expensive; even small, random acts of kindness will release good vibes. Plant something in their name (I'm big on doing trees for Daddy, as he loved them so very much) in a park or even in your own garden, maybe do a spontaneous cleanup in one of their favorite locations, or volunteer a bit of your time to one of their favorite organizations.

I do want to point out that it is quite possible you have less-than-fond memories of some people, or perhaps you have ancestors who were not known for their kindness. History is painted with those who were less than compassionate, and many of those people procreated! While you don't have to dance with them as in the ritual above, it's possible to do things to help bring their energy back into balance. For example, if you know one of your ancestors was a misogynist, you could do something to help a women's shelter. If you have an ancestor who was known for self-medicating, you could do something to help those on the road to recovery.

I've said it previously, but it bears repeating that intention is important. If you feel someone's presence, act on it. If they were not kind, then do something kind in their memory. If they were loving and giving in life, keep that energy alive by doing something loving and giving in their name. Act now as you wish others to think of you in the future. Even if you have no children of your own, one day you, too, will be an ancestor, and others will most certainly remember you; thus, the cycle continues.

Conclusion

Honoring the ancestors and those who no longer draw breath does not need to be complicated. The veil is thinner at Samhain than at any other time of year, but the connection is not limited to this festival. Your connection with your loved ones is something that is alive; it is something that is malleable and evolving because you are alive and malleable and evolving. As you go deeper into working with the ancestors, you will find innumerable ways of connecting with them and keeping their memory alive.

We all die. The goal isn't to live forever,
the goal is to create something that will.
—Chuck Palahniuk

Further Information

1. I touched a bit on necromancy and ways to remember the living in this article. Lonnie Scott has an excellent podcast that deals with all kinds of wonderful weirdness (it's in the name), and this is a fascinating episode where he talks to Mortellus about necromancy and other practices relating to the dead: Lonnie Scott and Mortellus. "Episode 74—Mortellus Talking Necromancy." *Weird Web Radio*. Podcast. 1:15:56. April 13, 2022. https://weirdwebradio.com /episode-74-mortellus-talking-necromancy/.

2. *Ancestral Medicine* by Daniel Foor is one of the best books written on different ways to connect with—and if needed, make peace with—your ancestors.

3. Jason Miller's book *Consorting with Spirits* is a wonderful next step when it comes to working with otherworldly entities.

4. I mentioned Mortellus above, and *The Bones Fall in a Spiral*, with a foreword by Morgan Daimler, is a deeper look into deathwork.

Reference

Campbell, Thomas. "Hallowed Ground." In *The Poetical Works of Thomas Campbell in Two Volumes*. Vol. 2. London: Henry Colburn, 1828.

Palahniuk, Chuck. *Diary: A Novel*. New York: Doubleday, 2003.

Notes

Notes

Notes

Yule

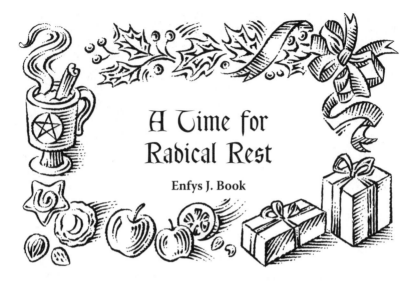

A Time for Radical Rest

Enfys J. Book

EVERY YEAR, I PROJECT-MANAGE my Yule. I'm not bragging. I learned early on that I *have* to do this for the sake of my own mental and physical health.

I have a list of giftees, and I track where they are in the process: gifts not purchased yet, gifts purchased but not wrapped, gifts wrapped but not shipped or given, and gifts complete. I have a little card for each person that I move between these states on a board so I can see at a glance how close I am to finishing the annual gift-making-buying-giving extravaganza. I will often purchase or make gifts early in the year and stow them away until December, when those of us in the Northern Hemisphere celebrate Yule.

If this sounds over the top, trust me, I know. I am organized to a *fault*. I made extensive use of a wall calendar when I was a kid to track my obligations, count days until my birthday, and note homework due dates. My dad bought me a very fancy, professional planner when I was fifteen, and I carried it everywhere and used it religiously. And now everything I need to know or remember lives in my smartphone. (Why yes, I *do* have a lot of Virgo in my chart, why do you ask?)

I learned early in my life that I have to do this because—confession—I am a complete scatterbrain. I have to externalize everything into a list or I'll crumble into a pile of anxiety about what I could possibly be forgetting, because my brain is *very good* at forgetting, and I hate disappointing people. I take my promises, social obligations, and gift giving very seriously, so I thoroughly plan out all of those things. Which means that my already-very-busy life—one that involves regularly rehearsing and performing with my comedy band, leading a coven, writing professionally, and running a blog, with a full-time day job on top of all of that—gets even busier leading up to Yule.

And I'm not alone in that. Everyone I know is stretched thin, overbusy, and exhausted no matter the time of year. But Yuletide seems to push people absolutely beyond their limits. It's a season of heightened expectations, so there are a lot of responsibilities we place on ourselves and others to get everything *just right* for Yule. We must celebrate all the things. We must attend all the things. We must buy all the things. We must bake all the things. We must make cherished memories. And we must be happy, darn it. If we fail to do any of these things, we have failed the holiday season, our families will be upset, and we will feel terrible. I don't see many magickal people putting the same high expectations on Beltane, Imbolc, or any of the other sabbats. The majority-Christian, capitalist culture that surrounds me and many other Pagans and polytheists puts a huge amount of importance on the things we do—or fail to do—specifically during the Yuletide season.

Ironically, this mindset runs counter to the actual vibe of Yule. Yule, which we celebrate as the shortest and darkest day of the year, is a time of peace, a time of reflection, a time of rest, a time of gratitude and hope, a time to exhale and release before we inhale and take on everything the new year brings. Filling the season with the proverbial *hustle and bustle* makes that rest harder to achieve or, worse, makes *rest* feel like yet another project to manage. While there's a lot of joy in giving and receiving gifts, baking, and socializing, by living a go-go-go life in the Yule season, we start our new year already burned out and exhausted.

Why is it so hard for us to rest during what *should be* the quietest and most restful season of the year, when the land is dark, quiet, and cold?

What Kinds of Rest Do You Need?

I think part of the problem is that we usually define *rest* as "sleep" or "inactivity." Those things *can* be restful, particularly for the physical body, but there are lots of other ways to recharge different aspects of yourself (Dalton-Smith 2017, 15). Rest is not just lying or sitting still. Rest, at its core, is about finding balance in your life so that you are energized for the things that require energy.

Consider the Temperance card in the major arcana of the tarot. In the classic image of the card, you see a figure peacefully pouring water between two cups. They pour the water back and forth, each cup replenishing the other, symbolizing not only the dynamic of work and rest, but also the alchemical process of balance bringing about something new, something better: a life greater than the sum of its parts.

A life so balanced, it is greater than the sum of its parts. Sounds like a dream, right? Is such a thing possible? I think it is, but more importantly, I think the practice of striving for a balanced life can make our lives better if we approach it thoughtfully and intentionally.

Consider: What parts of your life feel off-balance right now? What is draining you? What do you need rest to recover from? What would replenish you?

Rest can be simply doing something different than what you normally do. For example, if you have a full-time job that is very repetitive and doesn't require a lot of deep, creative thought, spending time on a creative hobby, like writing, painting miniatures, or woodworking, can actually be restful. Conversely, if your job requires a lot of brainpower, or if you spend a lot of time on social media or reading the news, you can find rest in doing something physical, repetitive, and meditative, like weeding a garden, crocheting, or stuffing envelopes for a nonprofit. Spend a lot of time sitting? Going for a walk or doing gentle, mindful stretching can be restful for your body by moving out of the stressful sitting position.

Some types of rest can be trickier to achieve depending on how your life and living environment are structured. For example, if a lot of your day involves having to put on a pleasant, customer-service face or voice, you may find rest in creating a place of emotional safety: one where you can let down your guard and just *be*, or cry, or rage without worrying how others will see you or worrying about others' immediate needs of you (Dalton-Smith 2017, 58). Sometimes this kind of rest can only be found alone; sometimes you may have someone in your life—a close friend, partner, health care provider, or therapist, perhaps—who can hold nonjudgmental emotional space for you while you drop your shields and feel your feelings. For example, a close friend and I have a daily practice of doing a "real check-in," where we record videos for each other saying how we're *actually* doing. Both of us are used to leading groups and being a public presence, so this practice is really helpful for reconnecting with and giving voice to our own feelings and needs hidden beneath our public personas.

For those who have been caretakers for a long time, you may be so used to taking care of others that you forget that you need caretaking too. For example, my partner is an acupuncturist. His days are spent caring for others, and it's particularly important to me that he has moments where he himself receives care. Early in our relationship, when he visited me, I would make him a cup of tea and bring it to him. That small moment of being cared for struck him profoundly, and he realized how much he needed and appreciated gestures like that in his life. I still make and bring him tea because I know it's a small thing I can do to give him a moment of rest from caretaking.

Many magickal people are proud to be highly sensitive and empathic, but we may not consider the sheer quantity of mundane inputs we receive during the day that may impact us. Do you get overwhelmed in noisy environments, places full of bright fluorescent lights, or while surrounded by lots of people? Do you get aggravated by feeling the tag on your shirt brushing against your neck or smelling something unpleasant? If so, sensory rest may be worth exploring. To regain energy lost from being surrounded by overwhelming stimuli, try lying in a dark, quiet room for a while. Put away or turn off your electronic devices, wear noise-canceling headphones playing soft music, curl up under a weighted blanket with very soft pillows, or take a quiet, warm, candlelit bath (Zeff 2004, 44). I've gained a greater sense of peace by keeping a pair of noise-canceling earbuds and sunglasses with me to wear if my environment gets unexpectedly loud or bright.

There's also a one-size-fits-all option for rest that is mentally, emotionally, physically, and sensually restful: mindfulness practice (Aron 2013, 112). My scatterbrain loves to be anywhere *but* the present moment: instead, it's thinking ahead and making plans. When I stop and focus on what I'm doing in the moment, on the sensations I am feeling and how I am breathing, I give my brain a break from its nonstop chatter. When I feel overwhelmed, stopping, breathing, and existing in that moment gives me a moment of rest.

Adding another layer to this, you can try a mindful gratitude practice. While many of us keep gratitude journals or try to mentally list things we're grateful for, it's important to incorporate mindfulness into that practice by pausing to actually *feel* gratitude, to incorporate that sense of gratitude with a mindful pause as we consider how we feel. This is another way to rest the brain for a moment. Don't worry about *why* you're grateful or all the specifics surrounding it. Don't overanalyze it. Just… feel it. Let the sense of gratitude integrate within your whole self. Let the feeling of gratitude fully express itself within you.

These are all ideas, but there are many more ways to rest, to balance all the input your body is receiving and all the work your body and mind are doing. I encourage you to take an inventory of the types of rest you need and carve out a bit of time, even just ten minutes a day, to experiment with different ways to rest and see what feels good. For example, one December, I tried a thirty-day, thirty-minute morning yoga challenge on YouTube. I found my quality of sleep improved, my chronic joint pain reduced, and I started more days with a clear mind, rested and ready to work, so I decided to continue the practice. I've also had success with smartphone apps that track and reward daily meditation and mindfulness practices. You may find something similar that works well for you. Intentional rest is well worth including in any daily practice.

Rest Is Radical

One of the things I love about making rest part of my daily practice is that it's a radical act of self-preservation. Really, the whole concept of the Wheel of the Year is radical when framed against modern culture: it teaches us that everything has its season, and not every season is about planting or reaping. The season of Yule is a time for rest. Capitalism doesn't place much value on reflective time, so when we incorporate practices of rest and reflection into our spirituality and value them as equal to or more important than working, we are taking radical action and stepping into a healing relationship of bodily and energetic sovereignty. We are our own selves, and we can choose to honor all that we are, all that we need, and all we can do.

I'm not suggesting you stop shopping, giving gifts, and baking for Yule if you get a lot out of doing those things. I do, however, encourage you to note when you are approaching physical, emotional, mental, and sensory overwhelm, and consider what kind of rest your body needs in that moment. How can you balance your energetic output and input?

Confession: I'm probably going to keep project-managing my Yule, but there's an important benefit of that I didn't mention earlier: it lets me spread the work over a greater period of time, so instead of spending two weeks madly shopping, wrapping, and shipping, I can work on it for two months at a more leisurely pace. That way, I'm done with gift shopping and shipping by early to mid-December and can relax for the last two weeks of the year. That works for me, but it's not going to work for everyone. Some people may find rest in the Yule season by saying "no" to extra obligations. Others may find that they are rejuvenated by social activities, so they can prioritize those types of obligations over other expectations of the season. It's important to reflect on what works best for you and to find your own bliss, relaxation, comfort, and balance in your own unique ways.

May your Yule be blessed … with radical rest.

References

Aron, Elaine N. *The Highly Sensitive Person: How to Thrive When the World Overwhelms You.* New York: Citadel Press, 2013.

Dalton-Smith, Saundra. *Sacred Rest: Recover Your Life, Renew Your Energy, Restore Your Sanity.* New York: FaithWords, 2017.

Zeff, Ted. *The Highly Sensitive Person's Survival Guide: Essential Skills for Living Well in an Overstimulating World.* Oakland, CA: New Harbinger, 2004.

Cosmic Sway

Bernadette Evans

YULE, OR THE WINTER solstice, is the longest night of the year. Even though the days are shorter and there's more dark than light, there is hope that light will return. Traditionally, a tree was cut down and burned in the hearth for twelve days to coax the sun to come back. It's still comforting to sit around a fire when it's dark outside.

Many of the traditions that we take part in today date back to customs from years past. Caroling, decorating the tree, and many other traditions have been passed down from one generation to another. Take time to honor the goddesses, gods, Mother Earth, and your ancestors for all they've done. Raise a glass of mulled cider to them to say thank you.

Capricorn Season

On December 21, the Sun enters the sign of Capricorn at 10:27 p.m. Capricorn is an earth sign and associated with mundane matters, such as work. You feel ambitious and ready to put in the hard work to accomplish your goals. This energy supports you by helping you get the practical details ironed out to complete your tasks. It's an excellent time to organize and plan for the future.

There is a lot happening in the sky today. When Venus opposes Uranus, you may be greeted by an unexpected visitor to your home. Meanwhile, Mars will quincunx Uranus, and you could be making some adjustments or needing to compromise to keep the peace. The Mercury-Saturn sextile may emphasize you going over every last detail in your mind. It's good to be organized, but remember to enjoy yourself and don't sweat the small stuff. The last aspect of the day is the Moon-Sun trine. Everything should go over without a hitch. You'll enjoy the celebrations and so will your friends.

Christmas

The Moon will enter into the sign of Gemini on December 24 at 3:15 a.m. This Moon is all about communicating and sharing stories with friends and family who've come to visit. Venus will trine Neptune at 12:15 p.m. on Christmas Day, casting a lovely glow of friendship and spirituality over your celebrations. You might want to make an early night of it though, as the Moon will oppose Mars at 9:08 p.m. Libations, relatives, and the Moon-Mars aspect could bring out the worst in people. They may say or do something that irritates you, or you're the one to stick your foot in your mouth. The Moon will stay in chatty Gemini until 2:55 a.m. on December 26 before it moves into the sign of Cancer at 10:15 a.m.

Full Moon

The first Full Moon of the winter season is called the Full Cold Moon. It's on December 26 at 4 degrees of Cancer at 7:33 p.m. The Cancer Moon feels it all. Take time to do what nurtures you—whether that's curling up with a good book, cooking something that's yummy and nourishing, or spending quality time surrounded by the people you love. Find a nice balance between time spent at work or working on projects and quality time at home. Find your happy place and share your joy with others.

New Year's

The Moon will enter the sign of Virgo at 6:53 a.m. on December 31 and will be in Virgo January 1 as well. If you're planning a party, the energy of the Virgo Moon will come in handy. You'll be able to see what details need to be tweaked and organize appropriately. Remember to let your hair down and have fun too! On January 1, Mercury stations direct at 10:08 p.m. It will be in its shadow for approximately ten days before it gets back up to speed.

Dark Moon

The first New Moon of 2024 is on January 11 at 6:57 a.m. at 20 degrees of Capricorn. The energy of this Moon is about formulating a plan for the coming months. Write down your dreams and goals on a piece of paper, as this will help manifest them. The North Node squares the Sun and Moon, so it may feel like you're pushing a rock uphill and it keeps rolling back down. Focus on what you want to create and release having to know exactly how it will happen. Give it over to the universe.

Aquarius Season

The Sun enters the sign of Aquarius on January 20 at 9:07 a.m. This is an air sign that loves staying connected by sharing interesting ideas. You're able to think outside of the box to come up with innovative solutions. Now you just have to turn those genius theories into tangible results. All air signs are focused on communication in one way or another. Getting together with groups of friends to hear a multitude of concepts is more appealing than delving into deep, personal, one-to-one conversations. There's more of a detached air associated with Aquarius. You want more freedom to come and go and do what you want. Enjoy playing with this unique energy.

Full Moon

There's a Full Moon at 5 degrees of Leo on January 25 at 12:54 p.m. This Moon is often called the Full Wolf Moon. The energy of this Moon likes to play and enjoy life, but how do you balance having fun with what other people want and need? There's a push and pull between what's best for the collective and what satisfies the individual. Start by showing yourself some love, and then you can give to others with an authentic heart.

Reference

"Full Moon Names for 2023." *The Old Farmer's Almanac.* Yankee Publishing, Inc. January 5, 2023. https://www.almanac.com /full-moon-names.

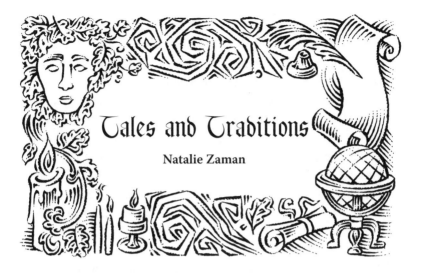

Tales and Traditions

Natalie Zaman

YULE. THE WINTER SOLSTICE. The longest night of the year.

You've probably felt the growing darkness. It started back in September, but it's really been kicking in since sometime in late October as the light fades earlier and earlier, subtly, only by minutes each day. But the end of the year is a busy time, so it's easy not to be put off by it. Come January, however, when all holiday trappings are stowed away, you may have the sense that there is more night than day, more darkness than light. Yule, though, is a bright spot. While winter technically begins on this day, it is at this time that the darkness starts to subside subtly and slowly. Spring is on its way—just like in Narnia.

The White Witch: The Queen of Winter

When I was in the fifth grade, a portion of class time, usually the end of the day, was devoted to reading aloud. (These were the days that pre-date audiobooks.) My whole class looked forward to this, partly because my teacher was an excellent narrator, reading with feeling and acting out the voices of all of the characters, and partly because of her choice of books: *Jennifer, Hecate, Macbeth, William McKinley, and Me, Elizabeth*; *The Phantom Tollbooth*; and *The Lion, the Witch, and the Wardrobe.* After we finished the books, she'd roll out the two-reel projector, and we'd watch the movie if it was available. These three books were my first encounters with witches and magic, and I especially loved the White Witch of Narnia.

There's no denying that Jadis is a witch who does many wicked things, but she definitely had drive, glamour, and guts—things for which my ten-year-old self longed. Over the course of time, I began to understand the subtleties in characters like her, who I originally perceived as one dimensional, good or evil. But that is just not so.

It's been said that well-behaved women rarely make history (Ulrich 2007, xiii). The White Witch illustrates this principle. At the beginning of *The Lion, the Witch and the Wardrobe*, she was in charge of Narnia and intended to stay as such. She didn't want things to change and did everything in her power to accomplish this, even freezing time and crowning herself the Queen of Winter. Is this not something that everyone can relate to? Who wants change if things are going well? But, as every sabbat imparts to us, change is inevitable. The story of Narnia's White Witch is a reflection of the unavoidable changes that happen at the Winter Solstice:

- Yule is the longest night of the year, and during Jadis's tenure, Narnia experienced its longest winter. But, just as the light returns at Yule, it is only a matter of time before spring comes to Narnia. The White Witch's fatal flaw is one that we all experience from time to time: fear of change. Sometimes we, like Jadis, fight to prevent it. Yet, it comes.
- Yule celebrates the birth of the god. In Narnia, the White Witch kills the god (Aslan) only for him to be reborn. C. S. Lewis's Narnia is based on the Christian paradigm, but this is only one retelling of the age-old story of death and rebirth. The White Witch is the catalyst by which Narnia is reborn. It's interesting that she initiates the change she fought so hard to control.

- Whatever mistakes she makes, it is notable that the White Witch is beautiful, as is the world she created. It certainly filled the Pevensie children with wonder. Yule is the season of cold and quiet beauty; the chaos of nature is, for the moment, at rest. The disturbing aspect of the White Witch's tale is the stasis she weaves with her magic. However powerful she is, nature and life are more powerful still and possess deeper magic. Life finds a way, and change finds the White Witch.

Yule *prêt-à-porter par* Narnia

Narnia's White Witch is a powerful and glamorous figure. Clothe yourself in the beautiful and fanciful aspects of her story for your Yule celebrations:

- **White:** White is the color of snow and mist. The White Witch dresses herself in white fur and velvet, and the lands of Narnia in snow. White is also the color of pure light reborn at Yule and hearkens to the hope of spring. Don white to embody winter's mystery and hope.
- **Turkish delight:** When the White Witch entices Edmund Pevensie into her sleigh, she does so with a warming cordial and a silver casket filled with the most perfect and delicious Turkish delight—a confection that is as pretty as it is sweet. A dusting of sugar hides brightly colored gel beneath, sometimes smooth, sometimes studded with nuts. Wearing candy might be a little tricky, but you can put on the fragrances of Turkish delight: rose water, orange, bergamot, lemon, and cinnamon. These are the scents of the season. Wear them to warm up, courtesy of the White Witch. (And no need to turn in any Sons of Adam and Daughters of Eve in exchange!)
- **Bells:** The White Witch travels about Narnia in a sleigh drawn by reindeer, their harness jingling with silver bells. Bells have long been a symbol of Yule and a tool to signal,

summon, and mark moments and passages. Wear a bell pendant on a chain or add bell trims to handbags and footwear. These will make music as you move and beckon spring, light, and warmth. I wonder if Jadis knew this is what she might have been doing every time she went out in her sleigh?

Books and Films to Read, View, and Inspire

Lewis, C. S. *The Lion, the Witch and the Wardrobe.* Mass market paperback edition. New York: Harper Trophy, 2002.

Lewis, C. S. *The Magician's Nephew.* Mass market paperback edition. New York: Harper Trophy, 2008.

Melendez, Bill, dir. *The Lion, the Witch & the Wardrobe.* 1979; New York: Children's Television Workshop.

Reference

Ulrich, Laurel Thatcher. *Well-Behaved Women Seldom Make History.* New York: Alfred A. Knopf, 2007.

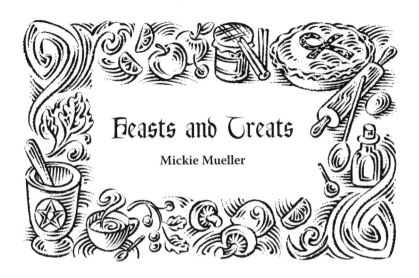

Feasts and Treats

Mickie Mueller

THE TIMING OF BIG holiday feasts can be daunting. Make most of these dishes ahead of time and take back your precious energy for a more relaxing Yuletide celebration. This menu combines traditional flavors and beautiful presentation!

Chicken and Cranberry Stuffing Casserole

This easy casserole has all the nostalgic flavors of a traditional winter feast in one dish. It's easy to adjust it to be gluten or dairy free, and you can make it vegetarian by using cream of mushroom soup and tempeh or seitan chicken. I put this one together the day before, so on Yule I just need to bake it.

Prep time: 15 minutes
Cooking time: 1 hour
Servings: 8

Nonstick cooking spray
2 8-ounce boxes instant stuffing (You can use chicken, vegan, or gluten free and prepare according to box, or six cups of home-made stuffing.)
1½ pounds boneless skinless chicken breasts (about 3 or 4 breasts)

2 10.5-ounce cans condensed cream of chicken or mushroom soup, unprepared (Vivian's Live Again makes gluten and dairy free with instructions for use in recipes on the package.)

8 slices (about ½ pound) Swiss or Monterey Jack cheese (Substitute vegan cheese if you're dairy free; I recommend Chao or Earth Grown.)

Optional additions:

½ cup dried cranberries

A few sprigs of fresh herbs: rosemary, thyme, and sage

Preheat the oven to 350°F and spray a 13 × 9-inch baking dish with cooking spray. Prepare the stuffing and mix in the cranberries and fresh herbs if you're using those options. Spread the raw chicken evenly across the pan, then pour the unprepared soup over the chicken. Layer the cheese on next and then top with the prepared stuffing. Cover with foil. Bake 45 minutes, remove the foil, and return to the oven for 15 minutes more. Prepare this up to 24 hours in advance and keep it in the refrigerator until ready to bake.

Crispy Veggies with Garlic

This is a quick and elevated alternative to steamed or microwaved vegetables. They're tender on the inside, a little crispy on the outside, and full of flavor. Your air fryer is good for more than just French fries; it's a great way to free up your oven for that casserole. If you don't have an air fryer, no worries; you can duplicate this one in the oven.

Prep time: 10 minutes
Cooking time: 15–20 minutes
Servings: 8

½ head of each: broccoli and cauliflower, cut into florets

2 cups brussels sprouts

2 tablespoons olive oil

½ teaspoon garlic powder

½ teaspoon pepper

½ teaspoon salt
Optional: ¼ cup fresh grated Parmesan

Preheat your air fryer to 400°F. I've used fresh veggies here; you can also use frozen. If you do, don't thaw them first, just proceed with the frozen vegetables as if they're fresh and add 1–2 minutes to the air fryer cook time, 8 minutes to standard oven.

In a large bowl, toss the vegetables in olive oil and spices. Cook in single-layer batches for 8–10 minutes, shaking the basket halfway through. After shaking, sprinkle with a little Parmesan if you're using the Parmesan.

Oven method: preheat oven to 425°F and bake 15–20 minutes; add Parmesan last 3 minutes.

Yule Log Cake

This one is naturally gluten free and can be made dairy free too. It's a beautiful presentation piece and easier to make than you might think with my pro tips! I made this the year I went gluten free and brought one to each holiday gathering I went to; everyone gobbled them up!

Prep time: 30 minutes
Cooking time: 15 minutes
Servings: 14

Cake

Butter or plant butter for buttering the pan
6 eggs at room temperature, separated into whites and yolks
¾ cup sugar
1 teaspoon vanilla extract
Pinch of salt
⅓ cup unsweetened cocoa
Powdered sugar
1 tub chocolate icing

Filling

Tub of dairy whipped topping, or dairy-free whipped topping
1 tablespoon cornstarch
2 teaspoons powdered instant coffee

Preheat oven to 375°F. Butter a 15 × 10 × 1-inch jelly roll pan, then line the pan with baking parchment, clipping the corners so that it fits nicely in the pan, and butter the parchment too. Separate the egg whites and yolks into two large mixing bowls.

To the yolks, add ½ cup sugar, 1 teaspoon vanilla, and pinch of salt. Beat the egg yolk mixture on high speed about 4 minutes until it's thick and doubled. Add cocoa powder to egg yolks and mix on low speed until smooth. Clean the beaters well and dry them.

Beat the egg whites on high speed until soft peaks form. Test this by removing a beater, dip it into the mixture, and hold it upright. "Soft peaks" means it will loop over at the top a bit. Return the beater and turn the mixer back on, then slowly sprinkle in ¼ cup of sugar, 2 tablespoons at a time, and mix until the egg whites form stiff peaks using the testing method described above. This time, the peak should stand straight up. Overbeating the egg whites will cause them to deflate.

Using a rubber spatula, add one scoop of beaten egg whites to the bowl of the chocolate mixture and gently stir. Slide the rest of the egg whites into the chocolate batter and fold in by slicing downward through the center with your spatula, flattening it across the bottom of the bowl and lifting it back up. You can find videos of this technique if you feel you need to see it done first. Repeat this motion of lifting the chocolate mixture up through the egg whites and turning it over at the top as you rotate the bowl a quarter turn at a time as you go. Continue this lifting motion until the whites are incorporated and the mixture is light and airy. Don't overdo it or the air will go out of the batter; mix until blended. Spread the batter gently and evenly into your prepared jelly roll pan and bake for 15 minutes or until the top springs back up when gently pressed.

While the cake is still hot, spread a clean linen kitchen towel on your counter and sprinkle with powdered sugar. Turn out the cake onto the towel and peel off the paper. Roll up the cake and towel (yes, both together) starting with the short side; this will train the cake and keep it from cracking when you roll it with filling. Place the cake seam-side down and allow to cool.

Filling: Put whipped topping, cornstarch, and instant coffee powder in a bowl and beat on high just until well blended. Chill in refrigerator.

Unroll the cake and cover the cake with filling 1 inch from the edges. Roll the cake back up but this time use the towel to help guide the rolling. Wrap the rolled cake in plastic wrap and refrigerate for 1 hour.

Place the cake on a serving platter and trim a bit off both ends so that they look neat and you can see the swirl. Using a spatula, cover everything except the ends with the chocolate icing. Drag a fork from one end to the other to simulate bark. A dusting of powdered sugar for snow looks beautiful, and you can decorate the top with Sugared Rosemary Sprigs (recipe below) and cranberries. I also like to add meringue mushrooms or Meiji Chocorooms.

Yule Mules

This cheery combination of ginger beer, cranberry juice, vodka, and lime includes a festive garnish. Serve in a traditional copper mug or a highball glass. I'll include a mocktail option as well.

Prep time: 5 minutes
Servings: 1

4 ounces cranberry juice
4 ounces ginger beer
2 ounces vodka (or sparkling water to make a mocktail)
1 lime, cut in half
Fresh or frozen cranberries
Ice
Optional: Sugared Rosemary Sprigs

Fill a cup or glass of your choice three-quarters full with ice. Add cranberry juice, ginger beer, vodka (or sparkling water if you're making it nonalcoholic), and the juice of half a lime and stir. Top with 3–5 cranberries, a slice of lime, and a Sugared Rosemary Sprig.

Sugared Rosemary Sprigs

A perfect garnish for cakes and drinks. They look like magical icy pine branches! You can make these up to three days in advance and keep them in a dish with a lid in the refrigerator.

Prep time: 5 minutes
Setting time: 1 hour 30 minutes
Servings: 20

½ cup water
1 cup sugar (½ cup for simple syrup, ½ cup for decorating with)
10 rosemary sprigs

In a small pan, add ½ cup water and ½ cup sugar and cook on medium heat, stirring occasionally until sugar is dissolved. Simmer for about 5 more minutes. Allow to cool.

Dip each rosemary sprig into the cooled syrup and leave them on a cooling rack in a clean sink for about ½ hour until the syrup sets a bit but is still sticky to the touch. Roll each sprig in the sugar and allow them to dry on wax paper. Set for 1 hour.

Crafty Crafts

Lupa

WINTERTIME IS NAP TIME for a lot of animals! From bears and some squirrels to snakes and frogs, many species hibernate or otherwise go dormant as a way to survive the season's cold temperatures and lack of food. Some of them burrow into the ground, while others create nests of leaves and other plant materials. It's a cozy way to get through the toughest season until spring returns.

It's also a good reminder to us that sometimes the best thing we can do in tough times is nothing at all. If there's not a good solution to a problem you're facing, don't waste energy on fruitless efforts. Instead, focus on conserving your energy and resting up for when the situation may be more favorable to change.

Hibernation Den

If you'd like to represent this part of the year on your altar, you can create your own den and animals to "hibernate" in it. In addition to being a nice Yuletide decoration, the den can also act as a reminder of the importance of stillness and rest, especially if you're like me and not very good at being patient!

Materials

Choice of clay

Materials for the den: yarn and sticks, or choice of clay

Materials for bedding: fur, wool, fabric, etc.

Optional: animal figurines, acrylic paint, acrylic spray sealant, acorns and seeds

Cost: $10–$100, depending on how elaborate you make it and whether you make or buy your own animal figurines

Time spent: 1–3 hours

First, decide how many animals you'd like to tuck into your den. While in nature most species will hibernate separately, you can combine whatever ones you like. Maybe some of the animal spirits you work with are hibernators, or perhaps you want to call on certain species for help with being quiet and patient or to mark the Yule season. You could even add species that don't technically hibernate but who might like a nice, quiet place to rest for a while. Remember that these will be little sculpted animals, not real ones, so you don't necessarily have to play strictly by nature's rules. (After all, look at all the holiday cards depicting lots of forest animals together in the snow!)

You might make your den out of twigs and sticks woven together with yarn or string. To make a wall, tie a piece of yarn to one end of a stick. Then lay out however many sticks you want to weave together. Weave the yarn under the next stick, and then over the one after that, and then under the next, and so forth until you get to the end. Then wrap the yarn around the stick on the other end and weave the yarn back through, weaving it over the sticks it previously went under, and under the ones it already went over. Repeat back and forth until you have woven them together. You can tie three of these together with more yarn in a triangle like a small tent, or make a box out of four or five with an open end.

Or you might try making your den out of clay; the craft articles for Imbolc and Samhain both have information on easy-to-use clays that don't require a kiln. You can make it look like a cave in a

mountain, a burrow in the ground, or whatever shape you like best. Make sure that your den is big enough for all the animals you want to include.

Speaking of animals, it's okay if you just want to use little animal figurines made of ceramic, plastic, glass, or other materials. Sometimes these can be purchased inexpensively from thrift stores or yard sales. But you can also make them yourself out of clay. The Imbolc article has tips on sculpting animals, as well as adding "hair" to them using cotton or wool. You can paint them with acrylic paints if you like, or if you're using polymer clays, you can choose appropriate clay colors.

Remember that this isn't about how skilled you are artistically, but about the act of creation. Your animals don't need to be in scale to each other, and they don't have to be completely realistic, either. Some people have animal spirits that show up in more fantastic colors or with unusual features, and it's okay to make your sculptures look more like those forms than the living, physical species. Try sculpting your animals to look like they're asleep. Or maybe make two sculptures per animal, one awake and one asleep, that you can change around with the seasons.

Your animals might like to have something nice to sleep on during their hibernation. Collect little bits of fur, wool, or nice, soft fabric. If you're feeling really ambitious, try making each animal its own little bed or sleeping bag! If the figurines are for individual spirits, you might try asking them what they prefer for their little representatives.

Some animals wake up every so often through their hibernation so that they can get a little snack, especially if there's a bit of a warm spell. Try adding some "food" to the den. Some items, like acorns and other seeds, may be available outside. But you can also sculpt different things each animal might like to eat during their winter retreat.

It's nice to have this as a meditative focus in your home, but let's say you need to take some of that patient, quiet energy with you out into the world. One option is to make another set to take to work with you if you have your own desk, locker, or other dedicated space that other people won't mess with. Or sew a small pouch out of soft fabric or leather that you can wear around your neck or carry unobtrusively. Tuck one of the animals into that pouch and keep it with you as a reminder of the need to slow things down and rest as you're able to.

While this is a great tool for Yule and winter's rest, you can make use of it year-round. There are animals associated with all of the seasons and sabbats. Consider making a representative for each one and tuck them all into the den. Then, when it's a particular animal's sabbat, bring them out of the den when it's their time to shine and tuck them back in when the season turns again.

Another option is to let the den be a representation of your circle or other sacred space during rituals. Create or acquire figurines for each of the animal spirits that you might call on. As you invoke them for your ritual, place their figurines in the den and then remove them at the end of the ritual when you thank them for their help and say farewell for now.

Finally, you can even create a den for an individual animal spirit's shrine. Even if that's all you have for them, it can make a nice, dedicated spot for them in your home. Add whatever decorations and offerings you give them to the den and let it be their special place.

The Natural Magic of Safety

Dallas Jennifer Cobb

IN THE NORTHERN HEMISPHERE, the earth is cooling; winter is arriving and settling in. Yule invites a celebration of safety and the element of earth or stone.

As the sun retreats toward the Southern Hemisphere (where seasons are reversed), we withdraw into the safety of home and hearth. Whether you have a fireplace, wood stove, or gas or electric stove, consider wherever you cook your meals to be the sacred "hearth," the heart of the home. Know that this place warms and sustains you.

Let us consecrate our hearths for Yule by practicing basic energy magic with a focus on safety. Not only is this a magical spell, but new neuroscience research supports and affirms its deep and abiding effects. Let's quickly understand how we affect our nervous system when we undertake energy basics like grounding and shielding.

Like many of you, I like to know *how* something works. And while I practice magic, there is more and more intersection between *science* and *magic*, so I include some information on how science confirms this specific magic works.

When we feel fright, flight, freeze, or fawn—the reactive states that often arise from fear, shock, or trauma—our ancient brain, the sympathetic nervous system, is activated. To consciously slow the heart rate, calm the nervous system, and relax the muscles—reversing the stress reaction—we need to engage the parasympathetic nervous system (Grande 2018).

Simple energy work can enable you to interact directly with your nervous system, developing ways to calm and restore a sense of safety after shock or upset. Energy work can also help to amplify your good feelings of safety and social connection if you practice them proactively when you are not activated in shock or fear.

Slow, deep breathing enables us to affect change within the body systems by engaging the ventral vagal complex, or vagus nerve. A longer exhale stimulates the vagus nerve, resulting in a slower heart rate and lower blood pressure, and it can trigger a gentle relaxation of muscles.

The process of "grounding" invites an exchange of energy between our body and the earth. The practice of "earthing" (standing with your bare feet on the earth) literally affects our energy state and often results in a feeling of relief from pent-up energy as the electrically held stress charge of our physical body is literally "grounded" (Menigoz et al. 2020).

Enough science, let's get to the magic. The following spell will engage your vagus nerve, establishing conscious control over your stress or fear responses, and take you through a physical and metaphysical process of grounding and self-protection.

The Natural Magic of Grounding Spell

There is a sacred association with earth at Yule, so let us celebrate it with a grounding spell to invoke and establish safety.

You need a stone. Not a crystal or a purchased stone. You need a found stone, a natural stone, a real stone. If you don't already have a stone, or hundreds of stones, in your house, you can easily gather one from the waterfront of a nearby lake, river, or stream; find one in an empty lot; or scoop one from your garden or just down the block. I like to use bigger stones because they hold more electromagnetic resonance and seem to work better. If you have a stone fireplace or hearth, or slate (stone) floor, lucky you! You can work directly with them.

Place your stone on the floor by your hearth. Put on a kettle or a pot of soup. Or heat up the oven and bake or roast something. Preparing a meal will warm your kitchen, warm your hearth, warm your house, and warm your heart.

While the kitchen is warming and the food is cooking (it can be as simple or complicated as you choose—the whole point is to "warm" your hearth), place your bare feet on your stone.

Say: "Earth" as though greeting it, and breathe deeply, pulling energy up from the earth below. This stone is part of the earth and holds its resonance.

Say: "Hearth" and feel the earthy energy reaching up through the foundation of your home, up and into your kitchen/hearth.

Say: "Heart" and pull the grounding energy of earth and hearth up into your heart. Feel the quiet solidity of rock and the support of earth flow up and into you.

Say: "Art" and let that earthy, grounding energy flow up and out the top of your head, cascading around you, surrounding you in earthy, dark, magical, mystical, and powerful energy.

As your kitchen hearth warms, chant softly: "Earth, hearth, heart, art. Earth, hearth, heart, art. Earth, hearth, heart, art." Over and over again, call out the sacred names and cycle the energy of the earth up and through your feet, your hearth, and your heart to gush out of your head as sacred possibility.

Speak quietly to yourself, inside or outside of your head:

Earth, the sacred home of all beings.
Hearth, my sacred home.
Heart, the sacred home of my feelings.
Art, the living spirit of creativity.
Connect me with the Divine.

I call in the safety nature provides, earth.
I call in the safety my home provides, hearth.
I call in the safety of my deepest feelings, heart.
And I call in the safety to create
A life worth living, a life worth loving,
A sacred life grounded in nature and art.
And in these lives the Divine.

Earth
Hearth
Heart
Art

Yule Nature Magic Ritual

Use the spell above to build a Yule-specific ritual of blessing and consecration.

Chant these words of the spell out loud, using them to cast a circle. In sacred space, run a power circuit of protective energy over and over until you begin to feel the warm flush of safety and feel secure in the power of earth as it is anchored and welcomed in your hearth, your heart, and your creative dreams.

Call on the Great Mother, earth, to hold you in her divine safety. You can ritually call on this safety anytime by weaving this magic practice of grounding and protecting whenever you need to. Remember how to use this basic energy technique so you can draw a warm blanket of safety over your ritual circle, your home, your heart, and your brilliantly creative life.

After the ritual, feast on whatever you created to warm your hearth. Sip tea and feel warmed. Eat cookies and laugh. Slurp soup and feel filled. Celebrate safety. These simple foods are symbolic of the resources needed to survive the winter. So let this little feast nourish and sustain you.

References

Grande, Dianne. "The Neuroscience of Feeling Safe and Connected." Psychology Today. September 24, 2018. https://www.psychologytoday.com/us/blog/in-it-together/201809/the-neuroscience-feeling-safe-and-connected.

Menigoz, Wendy, Tracy T. Latz, Robin A. Ely, Cimone Kamei, Gregory Melvin, Drew Sinatra. "Integrative and Lifestyle Medicine Strategies Should Include Earthing (Grounding): Review of Research Evidence and Clincal Observations." *Explore* 16, no. 3 (May–June 2020): 152–160. https://doi.org/10.1016/j.explore.2019.10.005.

Yule Ritual

Enfys J. Book

YULE IS A LIMINAL moment between the waning and waxing year, when the days stop becoming shorter and start getting longer. The sun begins to strengthen with each day following the solstice. It is also the darkest day of the year, which gives us the opportunity to pause, reflect, reconnect, and offer gratitude for our bodies, our minds, our wills, our hearts, and our spirits. We step into our own power, our own sovereignty, and build and reinforce the relationships between all our parts of self.

A Midwinter Reconnection and Grounding Ritual

This is a ritual to sow peace within yourself and to connect and ground to the slumbering earth and awakening sun while practicing mindful gratitude and awareness.

Start your preparation for the ritual by physically and energetically clearing your ritual space. Clean up any clutter; dust, vacuum, or sweep if it is an indoor space; and energetically cleanse with singing bowls, bells, or sacred smoke. Use whatever cleansing tools you prefer in your practice, and don't be afraid to try something new.

Supplies

A bell or singing bowl

A white jar candle or tealight

Cinnamon, frankincense, juniper, or rosemary incense

Incense holder

A lighter or match

Blessing oil (Feel free to make your own by adding 1–2 drops of a non-skin-irritating and pleasant-smelling essential oil to 1–2 tablespoons or so of olive oil or almond oil.)

Set up your supplies in the ritual space. Make sure the candle and incense holder are on stable surfaces away from anything flammable.

The ritual space needs to be dark and quiet. I recommend doing this ritual after sunset. Ensure your ritual space won't be disturbed by housemates, children, or pets until the ritual is complete. You may also want to cover any small lights on electronics or appliances in your ritual space.

To begin, take a shower or bath. While you bathe, acknowledge all the elements present in the water that are blessing you: the earth element is the minerals in the water and the surface you stand or sit on, the fire element is the heat in the water, the air element is the air and steam surrounding the water, and the water element is the water itself. Clean yourself with mindfulness and intention. Stay in the moment and feel the water on your skin. Notice the scent of any soap or shampoo you use. Feel your own hands touching your skin. Feel the air and steam entering your lungs as you breathe. Close your eyes, maybe even turn out the lights, and focus on the various sensations, smells, and sounds surrounding you. If you find your mind wandering, gently bring it back to the present moment by focusing on the feeling of the water on your skin and breathing deeply.

After your bath or shower, dry off and proceed to your ritual space. You may wear ritual clothing or work skyclad if you like.

Light the incense and place it on or in the incense holder. Feel yourself sink deeper into ritual headspace as the scent fills you. If you are indoors and haven't already done so, close the door, pull curtains over the windows, and turn off the lights. Make the room as dark as possible.

Stand in the center of your ritual space and slowly ring the bell or singing bowl three times to acknowledge the above, the below, and the center. Take a deep breath and say aloud, with conviction:

I call to myself the powers of peace
For worries and concerns to cease.
The things I don't need, I release
So love and contentment can increase.

Pause, breathe, and feel any distractions or concerns melt away, like slipping off a heavy backpack. Feel the darkness around you. Imagine roots growing from the bottoms of your feet down deep into the dark, cool earth. Feel the stability of the earth holding you. Breathe in and feel the energy of the slumbering earth wrapping around you like a cool, comforting shawl. Stay here and breathe for a few moments.

Place your dominant hand over your blessing oil and visualize pushing that cool, comforting, stable energy into it.

Light the candle. Notice how bright the flame looks after your eyes have become accustomed to the dark. Inhale and visualize yourself breathing in that bright, clear, warm light. Exhale and feel the light grow brighter inside you. Inhale to breathe in more light. Exhale to feel it grow brighter and stronger inside you. Feel yourself enveloped in the warmth and brightness of the sun as it begins to grow stronger in the coming days.

Place your dominant hand over your blessing oil and visualize pushing that warm, clear, bright energy into it. Visualize that energy mixing with the cool, comforting, stable energy you previously put there.

Dip a finger into the blessing oil and apply the oil to the crown of your head, the middle of your forehead, and your heart. As you do so, chant once more:

I call to myself the powers of peace
For worries and concerns to cease.
The things I don't need, I release
So love and contentment can increase.

Pause and breathe a few more moments. Give your body, your mind, your soul, your heart, and your spirit gratitude for everything they do to keep you alive and make you the person you are. Spend several minutes on this: offer at least one specific gratitude to each part individually.

When you feel the ritual is complete, ring the bell again three times, bowing in respect to the powers above, below, and center. Blow out the candle and snuff the incense. Say:

This ritual is at an end.
It is done, and it is well done.
So mote it be.

Save the remaining blessing oil and use it to bless yourself anytime you meditate or take a mindful walk in the coming months. Remember the peace and comfort it holds and how you can call that feeling into yourself.

Notes

Notes

Imbolc

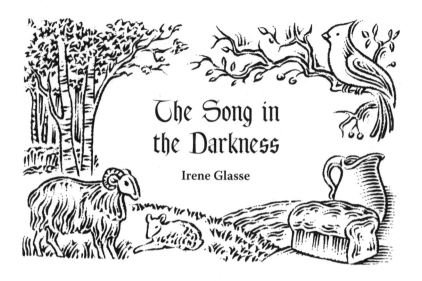

The Song in the Darkness

Irene Glasse

THE RHYTHM OF THE Old World still lives in our bones, in the memories of the ancestors that dwell within us. The Western world and its constant cycle of productivity and complete detachment from natural cycles remains *new*. Electric light did not become common in homes until the 1920s, a mere one hundred years ago. To compare, recognizable human civilization is believed to have begun roughly six thousand years ago. The pattern of our current lifestyle is a short flash compared to that expanse of time.

During the dark part of the year in earlier times, the rhythm of life turned inward. Long winter nights were spent gathered around the hearth fire for warmth and light. Our ancestors did not have streaming media to amuse them or bright electric lights to keep them working late. They had the fire with its inconsistent illumination and each other.

Winter was the time of telling stories and singing songs. It was a time for the art and creativity that the growing and harvest seasons' needs shunted aside. Without bright light, our ancestors were left with fewer ways to create. The tools left to them were the most basic ones: voice, imagination, rhythm.

At Imbolc, we are only just beginning to see the hope of spring to come. Snow still covers the ground in many places and only the hardiest of plants and animals are stirring toward spring. Although there is more daylight, the warmth of the growing season remains a dream on the horizon. Our ancient kin had already spent a few months huddled around the hearth fire and had another one or two yet to go.

It is no surprise that the goddess Brigid, an Irish deity celebrated at Imbolc, is associated with poetic arts as well as fire. Her full list of attributes can be viewed as the encapsulation of the work of winter in the old days: healing, smithcraft, sacred poetry, music, divination, sacred wells, and fire. To this day, the goddess Brigid and Saint Brigid (who are largely regarded as faces of one being) are honored through the keeping of a sacred flame and the tending of holy wells. Keeping the hearth fire burning and ensuring enough liquid water to drink, bathe in, and cook with when snow covered the land was a vitally important task.

Brigid as sacred poet and songstress reminds us that poetry and music are deeply resonant on a spiritual level. Imagine it for a moment: you sit by the fire, warm against the cold winds blowing outside. Your small home is lit only by the flames of the hearth. Against this backdrop, music rises. Perhaps just one person singing and tapping their chair along with their melody. Perhaps they have a simple instrument like a lyre, and the shimmering notes from it support the voice that sings. One by one, your family all join in the song. It is one you know. Perhaps it is one you wrote. Your voices blend and flow as the snow falls out in the darkness.

Ceremony and ritual should access as many physical senses as possible. If light is the visual representation of hope in the darkness, music is the audible version. We're usually good at vision and scent: we create altars and light candles, and incense is ubiquitous among Pagan practice. But music? We draw from this well less frequently, and it is just as potent and sacred as our statues and stones.

The peoples of the goddess Brigid were far from the only culture that valued music and poetry. The skalds, or bards, in ancient Scandinavian society were highly sought after and traveled widely. It is not surprising that a culture living so far to the north prized poetry whether sung or spoken. Rich rewards were offered to skalds in exchange for their compositions. The subject matter of the time varied greatly: stories of the gods and spirits, songs of praise for kings and jarls, funerary poems, love songs, genealogical recitations, and even structured slander and parodies were all part of a skald's repertoire.

These echoes of the ancient world show us a way to connect to the light in the darkness, the warmth within the cold, and the sacred creativity that informs so much music. The days of traveling skalds and quiet songs by the fire have transformed, offering us a wealth of music at our fingertips. We have almost instant access to the finest contemporary skalds, bards, and mystic poets. The world of Pagan music continues to expand, with wonderful groups like Faun, Wardruna, and Heilung releasing ever more Pagan music into the universe. One excellent way to curate that wealth of music into more focused and specific soundscapes is playlists.

Building a Magical Playlist

My magical playlists fall into two categories: atmosphere support and ritual support. Atmosphere-supporting playlists connect to a specific mood or feeling: confidence, calm, spiritual connection, happiness, etc. One of my most potent atmosphere-supporting playlists is my deep winter playlist. Like many people, I find a lot of the music we associate with winter, and particularly the holidays that occur around Yule, very trying. Although older winter holiday songs are slower and calmer, modern winter holiday music tends to be a bit frenetic. As a result, I've cultivated a playlist that connects me to the rhythm of the winter season.

Creating a good winter playlist means sitting with the images and feelings you associate with the season and then finding music that supports those feelings. I live in the mid-Atlantic and for me, winter is a cold season—we get snow and ice, the nights are long and dark, and warmth and comfort become incredibly important. There's a feeling of space and openness during winter here. My region is lush with greenery during the growing season, but winter sees the land laid bare.

For me, winter music has an openness and simplicity to it. I prefer acoustic instruments for my winter playlist—harps, lyres, acoustic guitars, hammered dulcimers, and hurdy-gurdies. Rather than lushly produced recordings, I love just one or two singers on a given song, when there are vocals at all. I seek music that reminds me of the falling snow, windows illuminated against the night, and the sharp feeling of the cold air against my skin.

Some of the artists on my winter playlist are Loreena McKennitt (her album *To Drive the Cold Winter Away* is lovely winter music), Anonymous Four, Mediaeval Baebes, Wardruna (from the album *Skald*), and Kellianna. Remember, there's no wrong way to connect to deep winter through music—your tastes may be completely different than mine, and that's totally okay. Start with one song that reminds you of winter and explore more songs by that artist and similar artists. Many playlist apps will suggest songs and artists based on your previous selections. Before long, you'll find you have a playlist of excellent music that fits your needs.

I use seasonal playlists like my deep winter collection to reconnect to the season when I feel like I've become detached. Where winter was once a season of quiet, rest, contemplation, and creativity, we are now pressured by our culture to continue as though the season is meaningless. Putting my winter playlist on reminds me to slow down, to allow the Imbolc season's hope amidst the cold and darkness to settle into my soul.

Ritual support playlists are specific to the working at hand as opposed to the general mood or theme of atmospheric playlists. Although my Imbolc playlist might contain some of the same songs as my deep winter playlist, it will also contain some variation. For me, ritual music needs to have the right tone but also be unobtrusive, which means I tend to use instrumental pieces. The instruments vary a lot depending on the ritual's focus. Litha or Midsummer ritual playlists will contain tracks that focus on drumming: high-energy music that makes me want to move or dance. My Imbolc playlist features calmer, slower songs with more fluid instrumentation. I find that singing bowl tracks work well for my own Imbolc workings.

Here are some tips and tricks for getting the most out of using a ritual support playlist:

- Make your playlist much longer than you think it needs to be, even if it means repeating songs. It's better to have too much music than too little.

- Leave the device controlling your playlist available to you during the ritual. Most of us try to leave electronic devices outside our circles, but every now and then a song that seemed good in theory just doesn't fit the moment. Being able to hit "skip" is incredibly helpful. Likewise, being able to control the volume of a playlist is very helpful, particularly if you have noisy neighbors.

- If you are using your phone to control your playlist, place it on "do not disturb" or airplane mode to reduce distractions. I also physically place my phone in a place I can reach easily that isn't in my field of sight. Some good options are underneath the altar, in a back pocket, or underneath your chair if you're using one.

- If you have a song that you wish to actively use during the ritual (to chant along with, for example) as opposed to just play in the background, set it to repeat several times on the playlist. I usually arrange for it to run five or six times in a row, then just manually skip to the next song when I'm finished with that portion of the ritual. This way, even if your timing is a little fluid, you still have plenty of time with that particular song.

- Arrange your playlist in the same kind of arc you experience in your rituals: preparing yourself and your space, welcoming the gods and powers you are working with, performing the ritual, integrating afterward, and closing the space. In my playlists, this looks like calmer, less directly focused music in the beginning and end and more potent tracks in the middle.

Creating Your Own Songs and Chants

If you like to sing and chant, what better way to honor Brigid and Imbolc than to craft your own chant or song? Although the idea of creating your own music can seem daunting, there are some techniques that make it much easier.

Contemporary music focuses on entirely original compositions, from instrumentation and melody to vocals and flourishes. However, for large spans of human history, it was common practice to take an existing melody or song and write new lyrics for it. Even the national anthem of the United States was created this way—the music for "The Star-Spangled Banner" comes from an older English song: "To Anacreon in Heaven."

To use this technique, try to choose a song or melody that is public domain. In the United States, most songs ninety-five years or older are public domain. Most folk tunes fall into this category: "Greensleeves," "Swing Low, Sweet Chariot," and "Auld Lang Syne" are some examples. For those of us who came to Paganism from Christianity, most hymns are also public domain and can be wonderful templates to work from. Choose a melody that fits the feeling or tone you're trying to access. For example, I use a Brigid chant that is designed to bless my home with light and hope. The tone of a chant like that is quite different from a chant or song designed to raise energy or to banish discordant influences.

There are some other tools that make crafting the words to your song or chant easier as well. When I'm writing a new song or chant, I have two windows open on my computer: one to an online thesaurus and one to an online rhyming dictionary. Both are available for free on the internet. The combination of using my own words and accessing those two databases as needed means that the writing process is smooth and my end result fits my desired outcome.

I write my best chants and songs when I have a clear vision of the ritual or working I'm writing for. Before you begin wordsmithing, contemplate what you want your song or chant to do. Is it an offering of praise to Brigid? A celebration of the return of light? A song to purify your space? Choose one main theme to create your song or chant around. Remember that if you are using an existing song as your melody, you do not need to rewrite the entire song. You can focus on just one part of the song and repeat it as needed.

Remember, this is *your* offering. Your own chant or song. You can change things, such as adjusting the melody to fit your voice, and it doesn't need to be perfect. It just needs to be yours.

Cosmic Sway

Bernadette Evans

IMBOLC IS THE HALFWAY point between the Yule season and the spring equinox. The earth is starting to warm up, and there is an anticipation of spring and warmer weather. You may want to think about what you'd like to plant in the coming months and get the seedlings started. The Moon moves into the sign of Scorpio on February 1 at 3:37 p.m. and will be there until February 3 at 10:24 p.m. It's a waning Moon and will be in its last quarter on February 2 for Imbolc. All of this points to going within. You're sensitive to your surroundings and other people. Mercury will sextile Neptune, which can magnify your intuition. Be conscious of your surroundings and listen for messages from the universe.

Dark Moon

The New Moon is at 20 degrees of Aquarius on February 9 at 5:59 p.m. This New Moon emphasizes thinking outside the box and being inventive when it comes to projects. It could also be easier to be more detached from people and situations and be the observer. Conversely, an Aquarian Moon likes groups of friends rather than one-on-one conversations.

Lunar New Year (Dragon)

On February 10, you get to say Happy New Year, again! It's the Lunar New Year, and this year it's the Year of the Dragon. The dragon is the one sign of the Chinese zodiac that's a mythical creature. Dragons are powerful creatures that command attention and are strong and irresistible. If you have a dragon in your corner, you are very lucky indeed. The element this year is wood, which emphasizes growth, stability, and creativity.

Today the Moon moves into the sign of Pisces at 8:42 a.m. Have fun and enjoy the festivities. Pay attention to your surroundings, as you could be picking up everyone's energy, which can be exhausting.

Valentine's Day

The universe keeps a wonderful schedule, as the Moon enters the sensual sign of Taurus on Valentine's Day. Slow down and spend some time outdoors soaking up the energies of nature. Enjoy a sumptuous meal or give your partner or loved one a massage. There may be some hiccups, as Mars will conjoin Pluto, and the Moon is making some tense aspects today, so things may not go quite as smoothly as you'd like. Be patient with yourself and others, and allow any irritations to drift away.

Pisces Season

The Sun enters the sign of Pisces on February 18 at 11:13 p.m. This is a water sign, which suggests your intuition can be accentuated. Pay attention to your hunches. If you need time alone to sit with your feelings or to just sit and be… do it; make time for yourself. There's nothing wrong with wanting to withdraw from the company of others to recharge your batteries. Swimming in these waters can be fun and special, but it can also tire you out.

You could be drawn to a metaphysical pursuit. Go purchase a tarot deck, a pendulum, or an astrology book. These tools can help you tune in to your intuition, and they're fun!

Full Moon

There's a Full Moon on February 24 at 5 degrees of Virgo at 7:30 a.m. This Moon is often referred to as the Full Snow Moon, as there's usually quite a bit of snow on the ground in February, at least in certain parts of North America. The energy of this Full Moon asks you to find the balance between being of service to others and following your own intuition and dreams. Have you been too critical of yourself or others? Maybe you've been downplaying your abilities and being really humble. Let go of any perfectionist tendencies and remember to give yourself a pat on the back once in a while. You're good at your job, and you should acknowledge your skills and gifts.

Dark Moon

Leading up to the New Moon that happens on March 10, Mercury will conjoin Neptune in Pisces at 10:06 a.m. on March 8. Your sensitivity, intuition, and creativity can be a real gift at this time. You may decide to study a subject that has a mystical or spiritual element to it. Chances are good it will feel like a natural fit for you.

Pay attention to how you communicate with others today. They may not understand what you're saying. There's confusion, so you want to be very clear when speaking.

Then the Moon will enter the sign of Pisces at 8:03 p.m. Whenever the Moon is in this sign, your psychic radar is highly receptive, and not only are you more sensitive, but your empathy for others is also increased. Be aware of the energies so you don't unconsciously take on other people's stuff. Doing so could leave you exhausted, and if you're not paying attention, you'll be confused as to why you feel the way you do.

The New Moon is on March 10 at 20 degrees of Pisces at 5:00 a.m. What seeds are you trying to grow with this Piscean New Moon? This Moon is about tapping into your imagination and dreams. It's a lovely state to float about in. Get quiet and go inward to hear what your still voice wants to create. Meditation, qigong, or yoga are exercises where you can let go and ease into a stance or mindset, surrendering to the process. You never know where the energy will lead you; that's part of the fun.

Reference

"Full Moon Names for 2023." *The Old Farmer's Almanac.* Yankee Publishing, Inc. January 5, 2023. https://www.almanac.com /full-moon-names.

Tales and Traditions

Natalie Zaman

I'VE ALWAYS BEEN FASCINATED by the Candlemas aspect of Imbolc: all those candles, a much-needed light in the darkness…a reminder that spring is on its way, really. Mary Poppins also fulfills this role: she is a light when there are (seemingly) no other lights.

Mary Poppins: The Spring Witch

My first introduction to Mary Poppins was through Julie Andrews's portrayal in the Disney film. Later in life, when I read the books, I found that the original Mary Poppins is a far darker, more complex character than her cheerful, chipper counterpart (though I love her as well!). She is more witch than woman—a wise one who knows much and reveals just enough.

Mary blows into town on the east wind in what I have determined is February. The first Mary Poppins book is divided into twelve chapters, one for each month of the year. If you consider that the penultimate chapter is "Christmas Shopping," and so, December, that would make chapter one, "East Wind," February. In other words, Mary Poppins arrives just in time for Imbolc. The Banks children are having a dark night of the soul before she comes, but Mary's arrival ushers in a period of enlightenment. Like the candle that lights a dark winter night, Mary Poppins brightens the lives of the Banks children through a series of adventures "till the wind changes" (Travers 1934, 14). After that, they're prepared to face whatever comes next. (Although she does return in subsequent books.)

- At Imbolc, we're reminded that spring is coming. Indeed, it's here even though we might not be able to see it. Chapter by chapter, Mary Poppins shows her young charges the magic that exists right under their noses. Before Neil Gaiman's *Neverwhere* and J. K. Rowling's Harry Potter series, P. L. Travers's Jane and Michael Banks have direct encounters with talking animals (in chapters "Miss Lark's Andrew" and "Full Moon"), sentient stars (in "Christmas Shopping"), and a magical sweet shop (in "Mrs. Corry"). All of these adventures exist in their home city of London—but they only find them with Mary Poppins as their guide.

- At Imbolc, we stand at the halfway point between Yule and Ostara—a time of betwixt and between, as all sabbats are. Mary Poppins has one foot in the "real" world and the other in a magical one. These worlds coexist and can be seen—if you're in the right company. In "The Day Out," Mary and her friend Bert travel into one of his chalk pictures for tea—but who makes the picture come to life? Mary? Or Bert?

- Imbolc is a feast of water and wells, and of course, Mary Poppins, always prepared, gets around via a watery device: her ubiquitous umbrella.

Imbolc *prêt-à-porter par* Poppins...

Sometimes getting into character is *what you do* as well as what you put on. Mary Poppins is described by P. L. Travers as prim and tidy with everything in place. Because Imbolc centers on the first stirrings of spring, it is an excellent time to get everything in order so that you're prepared for the work ahead when spring arrives. So take time to channel Mary Poppins (and maybe a bit of Marie Kondo) to put your wardrobe in order. Clear out your closets, dressers, and makeup caddies, and purge those things that no longer serve you.

- **Snakeskin and serpent textures:** The unexpected happens when Mary Poppins takes Jane and Michael on an outing to the zoo. There, her cousin, one of the snakes—revealed as the true king of the animals—gives her a freshly shed snakeskin belt as a birthday gift. Snakes symbolize immortality and transformation, qualities Mary Poppins brings to the story; her mortality is questionable, and she certainly transforms the lives of the Banks family. Snakes are also creatures of Imbolc. By the time February rolls around, snakes have been in hibernation under the ground, but it is time for them to begin to stir. In volume I of Alexander Carmichael's *Carmina Gadelica*, he translates folk poetry and songs, including the *"Sloinntireachd Bhride,"* where there is a song to honor this moment for the serpent:

  Early on Bride's morn
  The serpent shall come from the hole,
  I will not molest the serpent,
  Nor will the serpent molest me (Carmichael, 1900, 169).

  Honor Mary, her family, and this Imbolc tradition with snake-print clothing and accessories.
- **Carpetbag:** Mary Poppins's magical carpetbag is a doorway to another world. (No surprise, as carpets have long had a reputation for being magical.) The Victorian carpetbag was a cheaply made piece of luggage (and upcycled to boot, as it was made principally of repurposed carpet). It gained a rather bad reputation in the nineteenth century: it was said that people who carried carpetbags (carpetbaggers) had little to offer but sought to gain much. The opposite could be said of Mary Poppins, whose carpetbag held quite a lot! Touches of tapestry or carpet fabric—maybe a vest or Moroccan-style slippers—provide the still-much-needed warmth at Imbolc (with Mary's flare).

- **Umbrella:** No one should leave the house without an umbrella. P. L. Travers carried a green umbrella with a carved parrot handle and based Mary's famous umbrella on her original. Parrots are communicators and truth-talkers—a fitting familiar for Mary Poppins, who is glib and always quick to make an observance. The umbrella is also a nod to the power of water, held sacred at Imbolc.

Books and Films to Read, View and Inspire

Stevenson, Robert, dir. *Mary Poppins*. 1964; Burbank, CA: Walt Disney Productions.

Travers, P. L. *Mary Poppins*. Illustrated by Mary Shepard. BooksLibrary. UK: Gerald Howe Ltd., 1934.

References

Carmichael, Alexander. *Carmina Gadelica: Hymns and Incantations with Illustrative Notes* [...]. Vol. 1. Edinburgh: T. and A. Constable, 1900. https://www.sacred-texts.com/neu/celt/cg1/cg1074.htm.

Travers, P. L. *Mary Poppins*. Illustrated by Mary Shepard. UK: Gerald Howe Ltd., 1934.

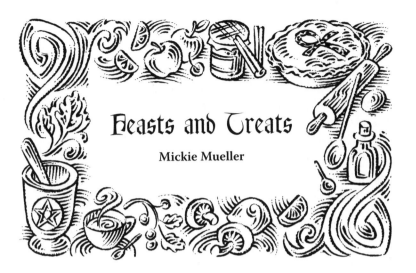

Feasts and Treats

Mickie Mueller

THIS TIME OF THE year makes me think of the goddess Brigid, who I honor with a regular flame-keeping practice, so Imbolc is very special at my house. I like to think about my Celtic ancestors when I honor the day, and that comes up in the menu I plan as well. I'm glad to share these family favorites from my hearth to yours!

Hearty Stout Chicken

This recipe uses your favorite stout beer (or substitute gluten-free or alcohol-free beer) and a store-bought rotisserie chicken to make it really easy. Substitute cauliflower steaks, tempeh, or seitan chicken to make it vegan.

Prep time: 15 minutes
Cooking time: 1 hour
Servings: 4

2 tablespoons olive oil
1 medium onion, chopped
3 garlic cloves, minced
1 teaspoon dried thyme, or 3–4 sprigs fresh thyme
1 teaspoon dried rosemary, or 2 sprigs fresh rosemary

1 teaspoon salt

1 teaspoon pepper

1 rotisserie chicken separated into legs, wings, thighs, and breasts

1 bottle stout beer (like Guinness), or gluten-free beer of your choice (Red Barn is good)

4 carrots, peeled and chopped into 1-inch pieces, or 1-pound bag of baby carrots

2 parsnips, peeled and chopped into 1-inch pieces

½ pound fresh small button mushrooms, or large ones quartered

¾ cup frozen peas

In a deep skillet or Dutch oven that can go on the stove, heat oil and add onion. Cook about 3 minutes or until tender and then add the garlic and cook about 1 minute, stirring and being careful not to burn it. Put the thyme, rosemary, salt, and pepper in for about 1 minute. Arrange the chicken pieces in one layer skin-side up in the pan and pour the bottle of beer over the top. Add the carrots and parsnips around the chicken and bring to a boil, then reduce to simmer and cover for 35 minutes or until the vegetables are tender. Add mushrooms and peas to the pan and cook 10 minutes uncovered, allowing the sauce to reduce slightly. I like to serve it in a shallow pasta bowl so that you get the piece of chicken, vegetables, and some of the sauce.

Spinach Artichoke Dip

Warm and melty, this is great served with tortilla or pita chips. This can be a dish that celebrates dairy or, with a few tweaks, one that uses no dairy at all.

Prep time: 15 minutes

Cooking time: 25 minutes

Servings: 4–6

1 6-ounce bag frozen spinach, thawed

8 ounces cream cheese or dairy-free cream cheese (I like Daiya Plain Cream Cheese Style Spread.)

¼ cup Greek yogurt, or dairy-free coconut milk or almond milk yo-
     gurt plus ¼ teaspoon corn starch
¼ cup mayonnaise
2 garlic cloves, minced
½ teaspoon salt
½ teaspoon pepper
½ cup mozzarella cheese, divided into ¼ cups, or vegan mozzarella
     cheese
1 14-ounce can of artichoke hearts, drained

Preheat oven to 350°F. Squeeze spinach to remove all excess liquid. If using fresh spinach, blanch it first and squeeze the extra liquid out. Add all ingredients to a big bowl, but reserve ¼ cup of the
mozzarella cheese. Spray a small casserole dish (one quart size or
two half-quart size) with cooking spray. Spread the dip evenly in the
baking dish, cover with foil, and bake for 20 minutes. Remove foil,
add remaining cheese, and return to the oven for 5 minutes or until
the cheese on top is melted. Serve with pita chips, tortilla chips, or
toasted crusty bread.

Boxty (Irish Potato Pancakes)

Boxties are traditional Irish potato pancakes. These hashbrown-like
treats use both mashed potatoes and grated potatoes and make a
lovely side dish.

Prep time: 15 minutes
Cooking time: 14 minutes
Servings: 4–6

½ cup all-purpose flour or gluten-free flour blend
1 teaspoon baking powder
1½ teaspoons salt
1 teaspoon pepper
1½ cups grated raw potatoes

1 cup mashed potatoes (Leftover mashed potatoes are best, but you can also make them from boxed in a pinch, just make them extra thick and don't tell my Aunt Catherine.)

1 cup milk of your choice

2 eggs

3 green onions or scallions, thinly sliced

Oil or cooking spray for frying

Add dry ingredients to a large bowl and mix well. Put the grated potatoes in a clean linen tea towel and squeeze until you've removed all the water you can from them. Put them in a sieve or colander and toss with the salt to remove more liquid for about 5 minutes. Add the mashed potatoes, grated potatoes, milk, eggs, and green onion to the bowl and mix well into a thick batter. Heat up a large skillet or griddle and coat with cooking spray or oil. Spoon the batter into 4-inch rounds in the skillet and cook until golden brown; turn and repeat on the other side. Drain on paper towels.

Almond Flour Orange and Cinnamon Shortbread

I love to bake traditional shortbread, but my body can't tolerate gluten, so when I find a gluten-free recipe that my whole family loves, I have to share it. This is based on one I found on Power Hungry and messed with until it morphed into these yummy cinnamon gems I present here. Sometimes baking with gluten-free ingredients requires different techniques than you're used to, and this recipe is a good example of that—less steps but great results.

Prep time: 10 minutes

Cooking time: 10 minutes

Servings: 16 cookies

1 teaspoon orange zest

2 cups blanched almond flour (not almond meal)

5 tablespoons sugar

1 teaspoon cinnamon

⅛ teaspoon salt

4 tablespoons melted butter, plant butter, or coconut oil

2 tablespoons water

Begin by preheating the oven to 350°F. Zest the orange by grating just the orange-colored surface with a small grater. Add all ingredients to a mixing bowl and mix by hand with a spoon. Roll into 16 balls and place on two parchment-lined cookie sheets. Using the bottom of a cup or a cookie stamp, press each one to about ⅓ inch thick. Bake 10–12 minutes until the edges are golden brown and the center looks dry. Cool for 10 minutes on the cookie sheet (trust me, waiting is key), then move to a wire cooling rack. I have also used a ceramic shortbread pan to make this recipe, and it works well; you may need to bake it a bit longer and just be sure to let it cool thoroughly before trying to remove them.

Reference

Camilla. "3-Ingredient Almond Flour Shortbread Cookies (Vegan, Paleo, Keto Option)." Power Hungry. August 20, 2019. https://www.powerhungry.com/2019/08/almond-flour-shortbread/.

Crafty Crafts

Lupa

THE ETYMOLOGY OF IMBOLC is rather contentious. Old Irish "im-bolg" means "in the belly" and is usually thought of as a reference to the rounded abdomens of ewes about to give birth in lambing season. However, it may also be connected to the Proto-Indo-European word $h_2mel\hat{g}$, which is thought to mean "milk." This was also the time of the Roman celebration of Lupercalia, in which people are ritually purified as winter prepares to turn into spring. And we can bring that back around to sheep as we consider the "cleansing" that occurs when the ewe passes her afterbirth once her last lamb has been born.

Sheep Sculpture

Regardless of the actual origin of the term, Imbolc is a celebration that is closely related to these domestic ovines. Sheep are among the first species to be domesticated by humans, and while they aren't as common in the United States as they used to be, there are still over a billion worldwide, with about five million in this country alone. Most Pagans don't have direct experience with these animals, as we've become quite urbanized. We can still draw on them as symbols for this time of year, though, and the following craft is directly influenced by my own time spent caring for a small flock of St. Croix sheep.

Materials

Sculpting clay

Sculpting tools (or general items to sculpt with)

Optional: bendable wire, aluminum foil, reference photos of sheep, acrylic paint, acrylic spray sealant, cotton balls, glue, yarn or ribbon, any other extra materials for decorating the sculpture

Cost: $10–$75

Time spent: 1–2 hours not including drying time for clay and glue

First, you're going to need some sort of sculpting clay. I recommend something that doesn't require a kiln if you're a beginner. Polymer clay (such as FIMO or Sculpey) is a great option that comes in many colors and can be cured in a regular kitchen oven. You can also get air-drying clay, though its working time is, of course, limited before it gets too dry and hard. I work a lot with epoxy putty such as Apoxie Sculpt. This one can cause skin sensitivities in some people, so I recommend putting a barrier cream like Gloves In A Bottle on your hands before working with it, wearing rubber gloves when mixing the epoxy and the hardener, and washing your hands thoroughly afterward. Epoxy putty will cure hard on its own in about twenty-four hours; however, that means you only have an hour or two at the most before it begins to harden.

If you're just going to sculpt a small sheep, you shouldn't need an armature; however, if you're going to make one that's more than a few inches tall, you may wish to get some bendable but sturdy wire to create a "skeleton" to sculpt your sheep onto. Just form it into the very basic shape of your sheep and then apply the clay in layers to the frame. If you're sculpting an especially large sheep, you may need to add bulk to the frame with aluminum foil so that you're not using as much clay.

It's also very useful to have reference photos of sheep if you want to be particularly realistic, though you can also just sculpt however your heart tells you to. A great place to find reference photos is http://commons.wikimedia.org; you can even find public domain photos there.

Finally, if you don't already have a set of sculpting tools, many craft stores will have an inexpensive beginner's set. However, many sculptors, even professionals, will sometimes use whatever they have on hand! I've used everything from dull pencil tips to the ends of paper clips to sculpt clay.

When I'm sculpting, I like to start with the body since it's the biggest part, and then I add the neck and head, and finally legs, hooves, and tail (don't forget horns if you're sculpting a breed of ram that has them!). Don't try to get all the details in place first; get the basic shape of your sheep in place and then add the details in afterward. Keep in mind that you may have to handle the uncured or wet clay as you move the sculpture around, which can squish any detailing you've done to the part you're touching. Try to move it by only one part, like a leg or the head, and then add the details to that part last. Some people will put their sculpture on a lazy Susan so they can rotate it around without touching the clay.

Once you've finished sculpting your sheep, it's time to cure it according to the instructions included with the clay you've chosen. Then, when it has fully cured, it's time for decoration! Acrylic paints work great for painting clay sculptures; they're inexpensive and easy to clean up. You can seal them with a clear acrylic spray sealant.

Maybe you want your sheep to be woolly! Pull apart a few cotton balls until you have several wool-textured pieces, then cut them into ¼-inch long lengths. Get craft glue or tacky glue and apply a layer of it to a small area of your sheep (an old paintbrush is helpful here). Using either your fingers or a set of tweezers, carefully apply small bits of cotton to the glued area, sticking one end of the cotton into the glue so the cotton appears to be "growing" out of the sheep;

you can use your reference photos if you want to make sure the cotton goes in the same direction and manner as a sheep's wool. Alternately, you can cut the cotton even finer into the consistency of flocking; then sprinkle this cotton flocking onto the glued area. This latter option is especially good if you already sculpted wool onto your sheep, since the flocking just coats whatever you've sculpted without obscuring details. Make sure you only cover a small area of the sheep with glue at a time so that it doesn't dry before you finish adding cotton to each section. (By the way, if you happen to have wool roving or batting, you can use them instead of cotton if you prefer.)

Finally, you may wish to decorate your sheep further with other symbols of the season. You could use red, orange, and yellow yarn or ribbon to create a halter or necklace for the sheep that reflects Brigid's flame. Or use clay, paper, or another material to craft miniature flowers like snowdrops and crocuses, which often bloom while snow is still on the ground. Maybe your sheep needs a lamb to go with it too or a corn husk Brigid's doll to watch over it!

The Natural Magic of Attunement

Dallas Jennifer Cobb

DEEP WITHIN THE EARTH, the first stirrings of spring are occurring. Like the stirring of purpose or natural instinct within a seed buried deep in the ground, much of the magic that happens now takes place out of visual sight.

A traditional time for cleaning the home and hearth, ritual purification, and pledging oneself to one's Craft, many Pagans use this time to rededicate themselves.

Called Imbolc by the Celts, the festival is associated with lambs' milk and lactation, the early indicators of spring lambs soon to be born. Imbolc celebrates the invisible, early, and interior signs of great things to come. Like the seed dreaming of being a flower or the ewe ready with milk for the new lamb to come, we learn to attune to the sometimes quiet, sometimes invisible signs that foretell the annual cycle of new life.

Attuned to Awakening Ritual

Drawing on sound, we can use the energy of the invisible to cleanse the hearth and home, purifying and sanctifying it with vibration. We have been inside a lot more during the long, dark nights, and it makes sense to bring a breath of something fresh here.

There is no need to buy anything. Simply look around your space and find things that make sounds, whether they are actual musical instruments like bells, chimes, or drums, or everyday items that produce a sound like pots, crystal glasses, or jars with shells or sand in them. Sound is a naturally occurring healing power, which is free and easy to access. Whether you have instruments in the house or not, or choose to use your own instrument (voice) to hum, sing, chant, or drone, the power of sound is something we can all use to attune our body, space, and environment.

Brain World magazine describes the earth's electromagnetic energy as "a gigantic electric circuit. Its electromagnetic field surrounds and protects all living things with a natural frequency pulsation of 7.83 hertz on average—the so-called 'Schumann resonance,' named after physicist Dr. Winfried Otto Schumann, who predicted it mathematically in 1952" (Guzman, 2017).

By earthing (see the Yule Natural Magic section for more information on earthing), we connect to the 7.83 Hz of the earth and become part of the resonant field of protection.

Using sound, we awaken the opportunity to affect the energy in all objects, people, and spaces, promoting the attunement process, bringing everything consciously into the field of earth's protection.

Start in the furthest reaches of your home, as far from the main entrance and exit as you can. Clap, thump, ring, or tone and let the sound clear out the space invisibly, connecting it to the mystery.

After clearing each room vibrationally, clear the energy out the main door, ringing or shaking it out and away.

Close the door and say:

Attuned to the Great Mother, I am like a seed dreaming in the protected dark, part of the sacred mystery. New potential is seeded within me.

In Tune Spell

The human body is made up of around 60 percent water, and sound is able to travel five times faster through water. In *The Healing*

Power of Sound, Jeffrey Thompson claims that, "direct stimulation of living cellular tissue using sound frequency vibration has shown marked cellular metabolism and therefore a possible mobilization of a cellular healing response" (Gaynor 2022, 140–141).

What does it mean in plain language? We can use sound to change energy wherever it exists, including within each cell of our body. Sound can be used to cleanse a space, purify a magical tool, neutralize a crystal, and heal and bless another person. Today we will use simple sounds to "tune up" our body and its surrounding energy bodies.

Sit quietly in a space in your home that feels uplifting and that you would like to further uplift or attune. Perhaps it is your hearth or kitchen, the heart of your home. Or maybe it's the room where you have your most-used magical altar. In the midst of winter, it could well be the room with the best natural lighting, where a south-facing window invites the short hours of bright light from the sun in.

I usually do this spell in daytime hours, so the chance of working with sunlight is increased, but really, you can do it at any time.

Place a hand on your heart and a hand on your belly button.

Inhale fully, first belly, then chest.

Exhale and hum. Feel how your belly, your chest, and even your vocal cords vibrate. Allow the vibration to loosen up your throat, creeping into your ears and head.

Open your mouth and release the hum with the sound "ah." Like the sound of satisfaction. Breathe and release the hum through your mouth with the sound "oh." Like with comprehension. Breathe and release the hum through your closed mouth with the sound "mmm." Like when something is delicious.

Breathe in quietly, feeling your system settle.

Continue. Breathe in, chant "ah," breathe in, chant "oh," breathe in, chant "mmm," and breathe in sweet silence. These are the three sounds that make up the word *Aum* (also written as *Om*). Aum is considered to be the sound of the universe: "Patañjali, a sage who wrote and taught the first and most comprehensive yoga scriptures, interprets these three stages as the beginning, middle, and end of all other sounds in the universe" ("Meaning of Om" 2021). These sounds are followed by the "pure silence" in which you inhale ("Meaning of Om" 2021).

Putting these three sounds together, breathe in, connect them, and say them in one long exhale: "Ahhohhmmm." Enjoy silence as you inhale.

Repeat. "Ahhohhmmm." Silence. And then five more times, for a total of seven. "Ahhohhmmm."

The auricular (ear) branches, which are part of the vagus nerve, are stimulated by chanting Aum. And research shows a strong correlation between chanting Aum and a deactivation of the amygdala, the part of the brain responsible for fight, flight, freeze, and fawn responses (Kalyani et al. 2011).

Today we will use it as strong preventative magic. We can clear away stress responses and stimulate the feelings of attuned safety, security, and connection. Held in the embrace of the Great Mother, we are filled with all possibility.

Reference

Gaynor, Mitchell L. *The Healing Power of Sound: Recovery from Life-Threatening Illness Using Sound, Voice, and Music.* Boston: Shambhala Publications, 2002.

Guzman, Isabel Pastor. "Tuning In to the Earth's Natural Rhythm." *Brain World Magazine.* October 4, 2017. https://brainworldmagazine.com/tuning-in-to-the-earths-natural-rhythm/.

Kalyani, Bangalore G., Ganesan Venkatasubramanian, Rashmi Arasappa, Naren P. Rao, Sunil V. Kalmady, Rishikesh V. Behere, Hariprasad Rao, Mandapati K. Vasudey, and Bangalore N. Gangadhar. "Neurohemodynamic Correlates of 'OM' Chanting:

A Pilot Functional Magnetic Resonance Imaging Study."
International Journal of Yoga 4, no. 1 (Jan.–Jun. 2011): 3–6.
https://doi.org/https://doi.org/10.4103%2F0973-6131.78171.

"The Meaning of Om: How to Use Om in Your Yoga Practice."
Masterclass. June 7, 2021. https://www.masterclass.com
/articles/what-does-om-mean-explained.

Imbolc Ritual

Irene Glasse

THIS IMBOLC RITUAL TAPS into the power of music and movement to welcome the growing light of early spring. Through curating two playlists, one for purification and one for dance, we access the transforming qualities of music. Candlelight and water support connection with the goddess Brigid, welcoming her blessing upon our homes.

Music and Flame

What is it you want or need? What do you want more of in your life? What would you like to begin or perhaps get better at? How could your days be richer or full of meaning? What would help you quiet yourself and feel the joys of this life more deeply? Sit quietly and spend time asking yourself these questions before you go any further. And then... Begin!

You Will Need

Two playlists: one that contains music you associate with purification and one that focuses on music that makes you want to dance

A candle or battery-powered flickering tealight for each room of
your home

A central altar holding one large candle, a bowl of water, and a lighter
if you are using flame candles rather than battery-powered ones.
Additional altar decorations are lovely but optional and entirely
up to you.

A snack and drink for after the ritual to help you ground and recharge. For Imbolc, I like to use sheep's milk cheese, fresh bread,
and cool water.

Journaling supplies if writing down your reflections is part of your
practice

Prepare for the ritual by bathing and dressing for it in the way
you prefer. I like to wear white or light colors for Imbolc, and I include a Brigid's Cross pendant in my jewelry. If you have particular
purification practices (saining with smoke, anointing, self-blessing,
etc.), perform those as well.

Place one unlit candle or flickering tealight in each room of
your home. If you are using flame candles, remember to put them
somewhere they can safely burn without risk of being knocked over.
Small lanterns or nonflammable dishes are wonderful for this.

Set up your altar in the "heart" of your home. This place varies
a bit from home to home but is where people end up gathering for
conversation. It is the hearth space, whether it contains a physical
hearth or not. For many people, this space is the kitchen or living
room, but the needs of each household vary, so choose the space
that feels like the center, hearth, or heart of your home.

Take a few centering breaths, then light the big central candle on
your altar.

Starting at the room farthest away from your altar, turn off all
the lights in the house. Make your way back to the altar once the
lights are out and sit or stand directly in front of it. If you are using
a flame candle, place the lighter so that you can reach it without
needing to see it. Then, blow out or turn off the central candle.

Connect to the darkness and quiet around you. Direct your awareness down into the earth beneath you. Become aware of the sleeping life all around—the seeds waiting to germinate and grow, the deep tree roots pulsing slowly in their winter rhythm, the hibernating fauna sleeping deeply. Take a moment to curl into the restful darkness of deep winter night.

Then, connect to the small, subtle shifts happening around you. Notice the stirring of early spring—the little movements, the seeds beginning to swell, the roots drinking more deeply of the water beneath the ground, the soil becoming just a little bit warmer. Feel the way the earth is preparing for the growing season. Feel the anticipation building all around you.

Concentrate on that feeling of anticipation. Allow the excitement for spring, growth, and movement to fill you. Breathe deeply and draw in that quickening energy. When you feel full, pick up the big central candle on your altar. Channel that wonderful early spring energy into the candle. Then, set the candle down and light it. This is your sacred flame, your connection to Brigid's holy fire.

Start your purification playlist. As the music plays, pick up the candle and begin to walk through your home. Do so slowly and mindfully, carrying the light of early spring with you wherever you go. In each room, light the candle you placed there before the ritual began. For flame candles, light the room candles from the large one. For battery-powered candles, simply turn them on as you draw near. Watch the spreading light illuminate your home with purifying energy.

When you have finished walking through your home and all the candles are lit, return to your altar. Set the central candle down and allow the song currently playing on your playlist to finish or simply stop the playlist. Pick up the bowl of water, your connection to Brigid's holy wells and sacred springs. Using these words or your own, make an offering to the goddess Brigid:

Hail, Brigid, Bright One! Sacred smith, songstress, sparking flame! Healer, seer, dancer divine! Bless my home with your touch. I offer you clear water in honor of your sacred wells. Be welcome here, Brigid. May your grace awaken the sleeping earth. Hail, Brigid!

Set the bowl of water down. After the ritual, you can pour it out onto the ground outside or use it to water plants within your home.

Switch to your dancing playlist. Start it playing and turn the volume up. Connect once more to the growing, quickening energy of early spring. Begin to dance. Allow your body to move in whatever way feels best to you. Let joy and light fill you as you move. Dance through your home, carrying that brightness and happiness with you.

When you feel finished, return to the altar and turn off your playlist. Sit down and enjoy the food and drink you set out for yourself. Eat mindfully, concentrating on the textures and flavors of your food. Allow the act of nourishment to draw you fully back into your body.

After you have finished your food, return to the furthest point in your home from your altar. Turn on the lights in that room and snuff the candle. Walk through your home once more, turning on the lights and blowing out (or turning off) the candles as you find them. Make your way back to the heart of your home and turn on the lights in that room. Sit or stand in front of the altar. Using these words or similar, close the ritual:

The wheel turns and the light grows. Now is the time of quickening, of lengthening days, and of the first hints of spring to come. May Brigid's blessing be upon this home and all who dwell within it. This rite is ended.

Blow out the candle. You can remain in contemplation for a while, write down any reflections, or simply begin to clean up your ritual supplies and return your living space to its usual form.

May the growing light illuminate your life with joy, creativity, and healing. Blessed Imbolc!

Notes

Notes

Notes

Ostara

Ostara + Easter = Everything's All Right

Deborah Castellano

Most of all I imitate the behaviour of Mary Magdalene,
for her amazing—or, rather, loving—audacity which delighted
the heart of Jesus, has cast its spell upon mine.
—St. Therese of Lisieux

WHEN I FIRST STARTED practicing witchcraft over twenty years ago, I had zero intention of becoming a witch with folk Catholicism leanings. But over the years, I was asked to become a godmother, I went to the "Mother Noodle" (Sicily), and the edges around my wheel started to softly blur together. For me now, Ostara is about the days getting longer, the last of the bitter cold in New Jersey, and the smell of defrosting mud; it's about the Empress tarot card but also about putting gravel in my holy water font because I'm waiting with Mary Magdalene for the resurrection; and it's veiling my Black Madonna in black silk on Good Friday and unveiling her on Easter because the resurrection happened.

My interest in Mary Magdalene was simple: (1) Her argument with her sister was so important that it's in the Bible, unlike my arguments with my sister. (2) Jesus would not let the apostles shame her. (3) While no one had ever witnessed a resurrection before, she was open to the possibility and willing to hang out in a burial cave to see what happened.

More personally, I wonder where Catholicism would have gone if we kept her book in the Bible and had more than a few Sapphic-esque fragments to look at ("Then Mary stood up, greeted them all, and said to her brethren, 'Do not weep and do not grieve nor be irresolute, for his grace will be entirely with you and will protect you.'"), especially where she reveals secret teachings to the rest of the apostles (*Nag Hammadi Library* 1984, 472). What if we talked more about Mary Magdalene as the "apostle to the apostles," a role that's still often downplayed in Catholicism? Her words "turned [the apostles'] hearts to the Good" (*Nag Hammadi Library*, 472). What if we talked about how she had visions of what to do for the movement and that she was closest to their teacher and his teachings, which made her fit to teach the apostles? She demanded justice for their dead teacher when no one else would or could.

She resonates with me because her love for her teacher was so big and so complicated that we still don't understand it. It always reminds me of part of a song that talks about holding onto love when you get it and letting go of love when you give it. Control has always been something I've struggled with, wanting too much or too little. It took me a long time to get to a place where I could understand letting go of love when I give it. It's incredibly difficult to love like that, to love without expectation of reciprocation and unending talks of *but what does this mean*? It requires patience that I try (mostly unsuccessfully) to learn from her. She never backed down, no matter what names she was called; she kept herself focused on the movement and the message of her teacher even when she was tired, even when she was down, which is admirable to me as a fellow activist. I was inspired to become a self-taught perfumer while studying about her, a part of my profession for the last decade.

My favorite story about Mary Magadelene is when she asks for justice for Jesus's death. Knowing her own worth and merit, she had no problem marching straight up to Emperor Tiberius Caesar himself. Knowing she would need a little ritual drama to make her point, she flourished an egg and proclaimed, "He is risen!" The emperor rolled his eyes and said, "Yeah, okay, and your egg is red." Eggs during that time did not come in red, as you may recall. So the joke was on him when that egg turned scarlet in her hand. She then said that Pilate (a key figure in Jesus's death) was the *worst*, and the emperor was like, "Oh, right. I had forgotten? But now I remember. So, he's getting banished. Sorry about all this, lady." She turned on her heel and left, counting it enough of a win in the standing up to tyrants category.

It's Not an Ending; It's a Beginning

One of the best Easters in my memory is the year I got an unexpected divorce. It was a surprise for me, so I was not in the stablest place emotionally (I felt like I was hit by a bus on the daily), physically (in addition to all my preexisting conditions, I was also graced with super fun aura migraines, new and exciting skin conditions, and other shiny new ailments), financially (what finances?), and spiritually (*Are you there God? It's me, Deb.*).

That particular Easter, I was shaking and trying to get ready for festivities with the more conservative side of my family, feeling sick to my stomach. I would be the only one of the cousins who could not stick the landing on her marriage. All I could think about were their seemingly perfect lives. I knew they weren't perfect, but all I could see were their steady marriages, their adorable children, their solid career paths, their nice cars and houses. They all made it very clear that they supported me and would help me in any way I needed, but when I looked in the mirror, all I saw were all of my shortcomings—my broken body, no kids, my failed marriage, my unstable career, my even less stable finances, and a dying car and expensive rent. I knew they would be nothing but kind, but I felt like I was drowning in my own failure.

I tried to think about Mary Magdalene—all I had to do was try to slap on some makeup and maybe attempt a smile and eat some food. She must have felt even sicker than I did, watching Jesus get crucified in front of her, a gory scene I always try to somewhat gloss over. It's a level of body horror I'm okay without dwelling in much. It's part of the point, but not the main point, at least not to me. For me, it's always been about the radical concept of love and acceptance, a concept we still struggle with today as a society and still causes adversity, especially for those in oppressed communities.

My circles talk a lot about adjusting each other's crowns as (gender-inclusive) queens. It's a way to hold each other up when we're falling down from our own difficulties. Mary Magdalene would be the first to fix a (gender-inclusive) fellow sister's crown when she was falling. I didn't feel like a queen at that point in my life, though I do now. I was too broken to see my crown at all, let alone that it was in danger of falling off my head completely. I know Mary Magdalene would have seen it, as she saw it on everyone's head. Mary Magdalene who bought the alabaster jar of myrrh because the world will always burn anyway. It's burning right now. It was burning when she walked the earth herself. It was burning when we talked about the goddess Ostara, birds that turn into rabbits, when YHWH's wife had a name. Her name is Asherah; she is the Queen of Heaven.

We have been taught to forget about the Queens of Heaven, these sky goddesses who spilled stars from themselves, who dealt in love and war, who were austere and terrifying with storm clouds in their hair and sacrifice in their eyes. We once baked tiny honeyed cakes for their favor, to the Marys, to Astarte, to Inanna, to Venus, to Isis, to Asherah. We pleaded with raw voices for our hearts' desire: *I need her to love me*; *I need a baby*; *I need to marry into this family*; *I must be made priestess of this temple*; *I need to create art.*

My mother, MamaFran, my own local Queen of Heaven, came to pick me up that day and took one look at me and knew. Perhaps she couldn't command stars and storms, but she knew I couldn't articulate the mix of anxiety, shame, and otherness that I was feeling. She was there to adjust my crown.

She immediately claimed a migraine and made our regrets and decided we would go to a local restaurant. It was Easter, so it was jammed full of people with reservations. I immediately became despondent. It was my fault we couldn't even be with our family. But she decided we would sit at the bar and have a glass of wine and eat there. You have to understand, my mom is equal parts rebel and Italian-American Martha Stewart. I don't think she had eaten at a bar in her life. She had probably sat at a bar, period, less than ten times ever. But we sat at the bar, exiles in our homeland. I think about how my mother had the patience and foresight to know that maybe she didn't know *exactly* what I would become, but she knew it would be better than these dark days of ruin. I think about her rebellious streak, like Mother Mary who was going to do what she thought was best for her child, try and stop her, as she took me shopping for small cosmetics, tiny tokens of glamour that would set me on my path to connect with the Queen of Heaven myself.

I think about my sister, laughing and doing dishes after a party at my house and how we sometimes fight as only sisters can. She always adjusts my crown just so, and she will tame any dragon she needs to for her family. She will plot a course, right by my side, dragon in tow. My tiny nephew, her child, who is becoming less and less tiny every day, our Lazurus with the kindest heart who sees past all veils and adds all the right garlands to my crown, garlands I didn't even know I needed until he adds them.

Mary Magdalene, my own Queen of Heaven, teaching me how to be brave and move forward in uncertain times like this never-ending pandemic full of loss, even when there's no approved map of what to do when you can't give funeral rites because the body is gone, how to navigate speaking with (possibly terrifying) angels for the first time, and what to do when your guru has come back from the dead. She made her own map with her own landmarks and boundaries, and if that map included visiting fangirls in France, *c'est bon, n'est-ce pas*? Or as I like to say, why not her?

Reference

The Nag Hammadi Library in English. Translated by Members of the Coptic Gnostic Library Project of the Institute of Antiquity and Christianity. 2nd ed. Leiden, The Netherlands: Brill, 1984.

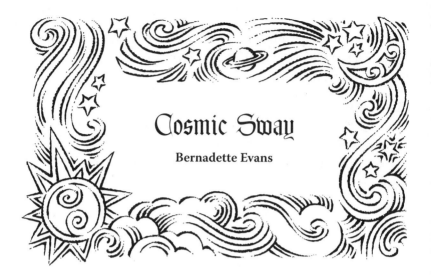

Cosmic Sway

Bernadette Evans

ON MARCH 19, IT'S time to celebrate the holiday of Ostara. This is a celebration of our earth getting warmer (in the Northern Hemisphere). It's a season of renewal and rebirth. Whether you're a farmer who is getting ready to seed his crop or a person with a small backyard garden, it's time to think about seeding, planting, and growing.

This is also the time of the spring equinox, when there's an equal amount of daylight and evening hours in both hemispheres. Astrology received its own day to celebrate all things astrology-related in 1993. It's a great time to hear some wonderful astrologers speak on different astrological themes.

In the morning and early afternoon, the Moon is in the last degrees of Cancer. Doing activities that are comforting and nourishing is good for your spirit. The Moon will trine the Sun at 2:52 p.m., the last aspect before the Moon is void-of-course. With this flowing energy, you may feel your relationships and any activities you're engaged in seem to be moving along beautifully. The Moon will enter the sign of Leo at 3:33 p.m., which can give you more energy. Whenever Leo enters the room, expect to have more fun as well.

Aries Season

The Sun will enter the sign of Aries at 11:06 p.m. This is the beginning of the Western tropical zodiacal year. Aries is a fire sign and is symbolized by a ram. The energy is enthusiastic, excited, and sometimes can be a little pushy. Enjoy the burst of energy that propels you forward. Your confidence and leadership qualities will help you win over friends and coworkers.

Full Moon

There's a Full Moon on March 25 at 3:00 a.m. This Moon is often referred to as the Full Worm Moon. This is no ordinary Full Moon: it's a lunar eclipse at 5 degrees of Libra. This is the first of two eclipses in this series of eclipses, with the second one being a solar eclipse on April 8. Eclipses are extremely potent, bringing with them changes that can be felt up to six months after they took place. Of course, if it contacts a personal planet in your chart or an angle, it will have even more of an impact. A Libra Full Moon puts the focus on relationships, partnerships, and who you are in the mix. Are you more attentive to what other people want and always put their needs ahead of yours? Maybe it's the other way around. Either way, Libra is about balance. Sometimes the scale may tip to one side more than the other, but if you recognize the imbalance, you can set it right again. Find the equilibrium between you and someone else.

The Full Moon is also when we perform a ceremony where we release what no longer works for us. Maybe it's time to let go of an old way of being. Whatever you decide to say goodbye to, it can feel liberating and free up some energetic space.

Mercury Retrograde

On April 1, Mercury will station retrograde at 6:14 p.m. at 27 degrees of Aries. It will station direct on April 25 at 8:54 a.m. at 15 degrees of Aries. Aries energy wants to keep moving—full steam ahead! Unfortunately, it may not be that easy. You could become frustrated at the lack of movement or momentum. Instead of banging your head against the wall, try another tactic. Think before you speak or act (always a good idea), and get your plans ready to go once Mercury stations direct. Use this time to pull back, look at the bigger picture, and revise your plans. I know it can be difficult being patient, but it will pay dividends. You'll feel more confident when you launch your project.

Dark Moon

This is the second eclipse in this set of eclipses. It's a New Moon solar eclipse at 19 degrees of Aries on April 8 at 2:21 p.m. This is the first sign of the zodiac, and it boldly proclaims its arrival; you're ready to go … or are you? Because of Mercury retrograde in Aries, it's almost as if things are stalled for a while. Make a list of what you'd like to accomplish in the next six months or year. What are you excited about and ready to be at the forefront of? Mars is still in the sign of Pisces, which can dampen or soften the energy somewhat, but it's still Martian go-getter energy.

Taurus Season

The Sun enters the sign of Taurus on April 19 at 10:00 a.m. This is an earth energy, which means it's slower and more relaxed than Aries energy. A good way to embody this energy is by getting outdoors. Spend some time in nature, taking walks through the park or getting your gardens ready for planting. Taurus is ruled by the planet Venus. It's still in the energetic sign of Aries until the twenty-ninth, when she sighs and moves into the sign of Taurus. This is when you can maybe slow down a little and put your feet up; unwind outside with a cup of tea and a good book.

Earth Day is on April 22. How do you want to look after the planet? Find a way that speaks to you so you can show your appreciation for Mother Earth.

Full Moon

The Full Moon is on April 23 at 4 degrees of Scorpio at 7:49 p.m. This Full Moon often goes by the name of Full Pink Moon. Whenever there is a Scorpio Full Moon you can expect situations and encounters to have an element of intensity to them. Possible tensions could arise out of jealousy or possessiveness. How can you work with this energy in a less heavy manner and lighten up? Do a Full Moon release ceremony where you let go of anything that you feel is weighing or pulling you down.

Reference

"Full Moon Names for 2023." *The Old Farmer's Almanac.* Yankee Publishing, Inc. January 5, 2023. https://www.almanac.com /full-moon-names.

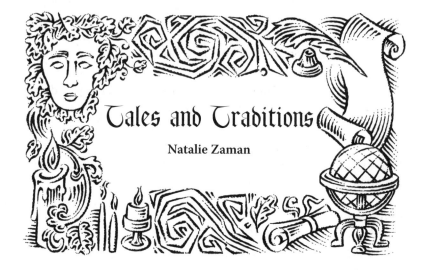

Tales and Traditions

Natalie Zaman

THE DAYS HAVE BEEN lengthening since Yule, and at the Spring Equinox, it is the first time in the year when we have a day of equal light and darkness. The stirrings felt at Imbolc have burst forth. The weather warms up, flowers show their faces, and baby animals take their first awkward steps. Ostara is a season of youth, a season personified in the character of Dorothy Gale of *The Wonderful Wizard of Oz*.

Dorothy Gale: The Princess Grows Up

Is it a coincidence that I was introduced to this story around the time of the Spring Equinox? April *is* the windiest month in Dorothy's home state of Kansas, but that had nothing to do with the fact that when I was a child, *The Wizard of Oz* aired during Easter week. It aired between Thanksgiving and Christmas from 1959 through 1967. After that, NBC acquired the rights and for a little over thirty years it was an Eastertide tradition for many families.

Later in life I read the book that inspired the film and was surprised (as I always am) at the many differences between book and movie, the choices made by writers and directors about what elements of the original story to keep or discard, and what they decide to change. But it was when I was teaching English full-time and attended a professional development workshop about literary criticism (over twenty years ago—so it really stuck with me!) that my perspective about the story really changed. We discussed Dorothy's journey to the Emerald City as an exercise in growing up. The friends she meets along the way and their desires—Scarecrow and his want of a brain (knowledge), the Tin Man and his wish for a heart (passion), and the Cowardly Lion who wants courage—are all things she develops as she makes her way down the Yellow Brick Road. While she starts out as an innocent child, by the end of the story (and even throughout), Dorothy shows that she has all the makings of a modern-day princess—at least, if Harper's Bazaar is to be believed: Dorothy is confident, diplomatic, down to earth, adaptable, and balanced (Davis 2018).

Ostara *prêt-à-porter par* Oz...

At Ostara we begin the journey through the year in earnest. Up to this point, all has been preparation. We are all very young for a spell, and as the wheel turns and inevitable change follows, we must grow or wither. Putting on a bit of Oz will help.

- **A smile:** Both in the book and the film, Dorothy's time in Kansas is portrayed in dull monochrome (gray in the book, sepia in the movie). L. Frank Baum chalks this up to the hard times experienced by the adults in the story. However, Dorothy's ability to smile saves her from being drained of color like everyone else:

  When Aunt Em came there to live she was a young, pretty wife. The sun and wind had changed her... They had taken the sparkle from her eyes and left them a sober gray; they had taken the red from her cheeks and lips, and they were gray also. She was thin and gaunt, and never smiled now... It was Toto that made Dorothy laugh, and saved her from growing as gray as her other surroundings (Baum 1900).

Turning back the clock and appearing youthful is an obsession in our world. I feel that what people are *really* trying to recapture is the innocent joy that is the feeling of youth. You can capture this feeling in a simple smile, which far outweighs appearances. Smiling is an accessory that costs nothing, fits everyone, and is guaranteed to lift any look at any time, in any place, and anywhere. Smiling releases serotonin and helps the body heal from stress, and it's contagious. Try not to smile back when someone smiles at you.

- **Vibrant color:** The land of Oz is awash in color—the joy that lives in Dorothy's heart even in the midst of the gray prairie. Color can be armor and a means of self-expression that buoys us through our darkest days. I wear lots of black, but color is easy to incorporate in the form of glasses frames, nail varnish, jewelry, and accessories like scarves and socks. Pops of color are just as effective as huge swathes. It should be noted that color is not a preventative. Even in Oz, all things eventually fade; the Emerald City maintains its green glory by locking spectacles with green lenses over everyone's eyes. It is, however, an aid. Donning vibrant colors helps ease change as it happens.

- **Silver:** MGM studios has most folks convinced that Dorothy's fantastical shoes were red. However, her "ruby" slippers were, in fact, silver, as was the kiss that Glinda planted on her forehead at the start of her journey. While ruby slippers are great for Technicolor on the big screen, silver is protective and a perfect element to carry with you on your journey through the year. Charge your silver jewelry and accessories at Ostara for extra protection before wearing them.

Books and Films to Read, View, and Inspire

Baum, L. Frank. *The Wonderful Wizard of Oz*. Illustrated by W. W. Denslow. Chicago; New York: G. M. Hill Co., 1900.

Fleming, Victor, dir. *The Wizard of Oz*. 1939; Culver City, CA: MetroGoldwynMayer.

References

Baum, L. Frank. *The Wonderful Wizard of Oz*. Illustrated by W. W. Denslow. Chicago; New York: G. M. Hill Co., 1900.

Davis, Jessica. "6 Character Traits Needed to Be a Modern Princess." Harper's Bazaar. Hearst Magazine Media, Inc. May 17, 2018. https://www.harpersbazaar.com/uk/celebrities/news/a20695756/6-character-traits-needed-to-be-a-modern-princess/.

Harmetz, Aljean. *The Making of the Wizard of Oz*. Chicago: Chicago Review Press, 2013.

Feasts and Treats

Mickie Mueller

IT FEELS GREAT WHEN Ostara arrives; we're just coming out of the cold months, and the earth is awakening and stretching. We start seeing some lovely fresh produce this time of the year, and it can be really inspiring to start planning Ostara dishes that will be special to share on a bright table laden with spring blossoms. Flowers and eggs always make me think of the spring equinox, and I'm including both in this celebratory menu to warm your heart and focus on the potential of the season.

Scotch Eggs

On the day I'm writing this, I announced to the household that I was thinking about making Scotch eggs for dinner tonight, and my daughter Trish did a big, hilarious, audible stage gasp and nearly fell off the couch. That's an enthusiastic endorsement, and this recipe won't disappoint.

These classic hard- or soft-boiled eggs are baked in a sausage and breadcrumb crust. They're good served hot or cold, so they can be made ahead of time. This isn't health food, but it is delicious! Yes, I have gluten-free and vegetarian options.

Prep time: 15 minutes
Cooking time: 35 minutes
Servings: 4

¾ cup crushed gluten-free square rice cereal or panko
1 teaspoon olive oil
1 pound pork or turkey breakfast sausage (Substitute plant-based
  sausage that comes in a roll and behaves like raw sausage such as
  Beyond or Impossible.)
4 soft-boiled or hard-boiled eggs, peeled
1 egg, beaten

Heat oven to 400°F. Mix the crushed rice cereal or panko in a bowl with the olive oil using clean hands. Divide the sausage into four large, rectangular patties about ½ inch thick. Place an egg in the center of the patty. The rectangle patty should be horizontal so that you can wrap the longest part of the sausage around the middle of the egg like you're wrapping it in a blanket. Continue forming the sausage around the egg and pinch it together where it meets in the middle and at the top and bottom until it's completely covered. Roll in the egg mixture and then in the crushed cereal. Place each one on a baking sheet and bake 35 minutes, turning halfway through. They can also be cooked in a preheated air fryer at 400°F for 12–15 minutes. These are equally good served hot or cold.

Dipping Sauce

This dipping sauce is great to go with the Scotch Eggs, and I like it with the Oven-Roasted Fries (recipe below) as well.

Prep time: 3 minutes
Servings: 4

1 tablespoon mayonnaise
¼ cup Dijon mustard
1 tablespoon honey

Mix all ingredients well in a dish and serve.

Oven-Roasted Fries

The surprising part of this recipe is coating the potatoes in egg whites; it works amazingly well to make them crispy outside and tender inside. A vegan option is to coat them in olive oil. I include oven and air fryer versions here.

Prep time: 5 minutes
Cooking time: 30–35 minutes
Servings: 4

4 russet potatoes, cut into wedges
1 egg white, or olive oil
½ teaspoon salt
½ teaspoon black pepper
1 tablespoon minced garlic
1 tablespoon fresh-chopped rosemary, or 1 teaspoon ground rosemary

Preheat oven to 450°F or air fryer to 400°F. In a large bowl, toss the potato wedges in egg white and then drain excess egg white out of the bowl. Add the seasonings and toss to coat. For the oven version, spray baking sheet with cooking spray or use parchment paper. I cook these in the air fryer in one layer at a time for 15 minutes, shaking the basket halfway through. Alternately, roast in the oven for 30 minutes, turning them over halfway through.

Butterfly Pea Flower Color Changing Lemonade

Butterfly pea flower tea is naturally a beautiful blue, and when you add an acid like lemon to it, the color changes to a vivid purple! I'll share my old bartender's tip for making layers with the components in the glass so that your guests can mix up the magical transformation in their own glass!

Prep time: 10 minutes
Steeping time: 15 minutes
Cooling time: 30 minutes
Servings: 6–8

5 cups water

8–10 dried butterfly pea flowers, find these online or at a local health food store

1 52-ounce jug of natural lemonade (You can use homemade or store bought made with real lemons. I steer clear of the powdered kind.)

Ice

Tall clear glasses and a big metal spoon

Boil 5 cups of water and pour over 8–10 dried butterfly pea flowers and allow to brew. Once the flowers turn pale, remove them and allow the tea to cool. When you're ready to make your drinks, do it in the order given here for the best results. Different liquids have different "specific gravities," so to layer the liquid, they must be in the correct order. I also keep the lemonade off the ice that's at the top of the glass to keep the color change more dramatic at the end when they mix it.

First, fill the glass one-quarter of the way with lemonade. The lemonade goes on the bottom because it's made with sugar, making it heavier. Next, fill the glass to the top with ice. Grab a metal spoon—the ones that came with your cutlery set that we call a tablespoon is perfect. Hold the spoon bowl-side down right on top of the ice at the top of the glass and very slowly drizzle the butterfly pea tea over the back of the spoon until the glass is full. You should have three ombre-looking layers: pale yellow at the bottom, bright blue at the top, and a thin layer of purple in the middle where some of the butterfly pea has met the acidic lemonade. It's so pretty! Gently put a straw in (we like pretty paper ones) and serve your guests, encouraging everyone to stir it with their straws! The whole drink will turn a beautiful amethyst purple and is light and refreshing.

Crafty Crafts

Lupa

SPRING IS MIGRATION SEASON for many birds as they leave their wintering grounds and head for their summer breeding grounds. It's not just songbirds that make these long flights, either: shorebirds, raptors, waterfowl, and many others may fly hundreds or even thousands of miles on this vernal journey. (The single longest migration is the arctic tern, which flies back and forth from the Arctic Circle to the Antarctic every year!)

Perhaps you've seen groups of birds flying overhead as spring unfolds! Geese and other waterfowl are especially easy to notice, as they may make a lot of noise while they wing their way across the sky. Their cries and songs are a sign to me that spring is on its way, and I use that as one of my main focuses to celebrate the turning of the season.

Migration Mobile

One way to capture the energy and excitement of this time is by creating a migration mobile. A mobile is a hanging piece of art in which multiple decorative pieces are balanced in mid-air, usually by hanging from strings from a main support or several secondary supports. This migration mobile features cutouts of birds suspended from threads.

Materials

Items for the supports: thin sticks, wooden dowels, plastic straws, etc.

Thread or string (or both)

Cardstock or thin cardboard (a cereal box would work well)

Acrylic paint

Acrylic spray sealant

Paintbrushes

Scissors

Craft knife

Cutting mat or board

Optional: Clear tape, any other items to decorate the birds

Cost: $20–$120

Time spent: 2–3 hours

First, plan out your mobile. This craft will create a more complex mobile with one primary support that has several secondary ones tied to it, and each secondary support has a bird on either end balancing each other out. It can be very helpful to sketch out your mobile so that you have a plan and you make sure that one side isn't going to be heavier than the other.

Next, get some thin sticks, wooden dowels, or even plastic drinking straws, one for the primary support and enough for the secondary supports. Make sure the primary support is long enough that you can suspend all the secondary supports from it without having them bump into each other as they move and turn, and make sure your secondary supports are all about the same length and weight. You'll also need thread or string; sewing thread will work well for attaching your birds, though you may want something a little stronger for tying the primary and secondary supports together.

For your birds, either get some cardstock or use a cereal box. You'll also want paint (acrylics work well for this), paintbrushes, and anything else you want to use to decorate your birds. Keep in mind you want to keep them lightweight, so make sure your decorations aren't too heavy.

Next, decide what kind of birds you want to have in your mobile. Maybe there are particular species that you've seen migrating through during spring, especially those that like to stay for the summer and raise their young where you are. Or maybe you just want to pick your favorite birds, whatever they may be.

Now, get out your cardstock or cereal box. Draw the silhouette of each bird in flight from the side, but without the wings—just the head, body, and tail as though the bird was flying past. Then draw the two wings as one piece, as if you were looking at the bird in flight from overhead and could see its fully outstretched wingspan. You can be as detailed in these outlines as you want. Make sure you have enough birds that each secondary support has two, one for each end (you can put a third bird in the middle if you want too).

Cut out the drawings you've made. Then cut a slit in each bird's body that parallels the bird's back: using a sharp craft knife and a cutting mat or board, carefully make a slit about a quarter of the way down from the top edge of the back. The slit should be as long as the widest part of the wing piece when measured from front to back (not end to end!). Slide the wing piece through the slit so that the bird's body is centered in the middle of the wings. If you need to adjust the slit a little or enlarge it to allow the wings to slide through a little easier while still staying snug, now's the time to do so. You want the wings to be able to sit in the slit without either being warped or falling out. (If you've made the slit too large, that's okay! We'll fix that in a bit.)

Now, take the wings out of the bird and get out your paints. If you've used a cereal box or other cardstock that has printing on it, you may want to prime the cutouts with white paint first to cover up the printing. Then you can paint the cutouts to look like the birds you're trying to depict. You can make them lifelike or fanciful; it's entirely up to you! Let the paint dry thoroughly and then seal them with an acrylic spray sealant. Alternately, if you have white or light-colored cardstock, you can also decorate your birds with crayons, colored pencils, markers, or other media instead of or along with paint.

Once the paint or other media is completely dry, cut some lengths of thread a bit longer than how long you want them to be on the mobile. Run one end of the string through the slit and tie it around the top of the silhouette so the bird is hanging from the thread at its back. You may need to move the thread around a bit to get it to balance right. Then carefully slide the wings back into the slit, again adjusting the thread as needed to get the bird balanced. If the wings aren't staying put, you can tape the underside of the wings to the sides of the bird with a little clear tape.

After all your birds have been tied with thread, it's time to put your mobile together! Start by tying your heavier cord to the center of the primary support to create a loop to hang the mobile by. Then start tying the secondary supports to the primary support. Make sure they're evenly spaced to maintain balance, and leave enough room that they don't bump into each other. Finally, tie your birds, one at a time, to the ends of the secondary supports (and one in the center of each if you wish). Then hang the mobile where you can easily reach it so you can adjust where the supports and birds are all tied together to correct any imbalances. Finally, hang the migration mobile in its new home and enjoy the birds "flying" through your home!

The Natural Magic of Security

Dallas Jennifer Cobb

ASSOCIATED WITH THE DIRECTION of east, Ostara is aligned with the element of air. It is in the east that everything begins at sunrise, and it is with the first breath that the little lambs come to life.

Ostara celebrates the dance of light and dark, and as of today, with the equinox, we cross over the midpoint, the balance point, and the days become longer than the nights, with each day bringing more and more light from now through the solstice.

Suddenly we have something to believe in. The sun is returning slowly, and today the balance shifts. Now we have the security of knowing that everything will get easier and more abundant, that we will not starve, and that winter is surely over.

As lambs are born, the cycle of renewal is real. And in the abundance of the Great Mother we find security: the security to believe, to relax, and to see that we are infinitely loved and taken care of.

With the air of spring, we air out our homes, air out the duvets and winter blankets. And we breathe in the fresh air of new beginnings, inspiration, and much needed oxygen.

An Air of Belief Ritual

If you are like me, then you are probably a "Show me, prove it, and then I will believe" kind of person. So many of us are. If "the earth is our mother," let us look to her for our deepest assurances of security (Perry 1987, 528).

Today, be ready to develop an air of belief with this ritual. They say that what we focus on will grow. So let's focus on the possibility of spring by getting outside into nature and looking for it.

We go consciously looking for empirical data to support whatever it is we seek to believe in. So today you will look carefully at, and to, Mother Earth, who will show you the way to security. Like a good mother, the earth seeks to keep us close, connected, and secure.

Make a ritual of the sacred practice of going out looking for, and making note of, clear signs of spring. Like a small child who takes a few steps on their own, then turns and looks at the mother for security, go and look for the miraculous, the magical, and the mystical. Look to the Great Mother for confirmation. Look for the return of migrating birds or the tiny shoots of crocuses or snowdrops poking up through the snow. Listen for the drip of sap from warming trees and the new birdsongs that can be heard. Smell the petrichor (literally ancient Greek words for "rock" and "fluids of the gods" combined) present as the melting snow and ice soak into the soil. Feel the dance of a light breeze on your skin or the strength of the sunlight soaking through your closed eyelids.

These things we see, hear, feel, and smell are real. These are the proof we have sought—proof that the cold is being miraculously transformed into warmth and the dark is being mystically transmuted into light, and proof that magically the earth is alive and the Goddess is afoot. The more proof you witness, the easier it is to believe. Your Mother loves you securely.

When you witness these miracles, know that they not only confirm the renewal but inspire new life. We, too, breathe and feel renewed; we feel invincible, inspired, and ready for everything.

Witnessing these—the deepest mysteries, the balancing of the energies of day and night, dark and light, sullen and bright, depressed and all right—we stand precariously perched and in balance. We witness the mysteries of the Goddess, pregnant now with possibility and the miracles of new life. And we believe.

When you have walked and gathered enough evidence that you know it is true, return home. Light a candle on your altar dedicated to the growing light. Then quietly slip your hand into the hand of the Great Mother and say: "I believe."

An Ostara Security Spell

The word *Ostara* comes from the Anglo-Saxon goddess Eostre, a word that *Easter* surely evolved from. Celebrated on the spring equinox, Ostara is known for fertility and birth, new life, chicks hatching, lambs being born, and the return of the light. Represented by the element of air, Ostara is associated with the east where the sun rises, with thought, inspiration, and the craft of divination.

Like the practice of "seeing is believing," this spell will help us establish a renewed sense of security.

What you will need: the time of sunrise—consult an online source like Time and Date and plug in your location to find the time of sunrise where you are; an alarm clock—set for fifteen to twenty minutes before sunrise so you have time to brush your teeth and put on some warm clothes; and a sense of direction—you want to know which way is east so you can find it in the dark for a short sunrise ceremony.

Instructions

Go outdoors and find a private space where you can face east. Somewhere that allows for a view of the horizon is great because it enables you to see the sunrise quite quickly. Don't worry, there probably won't be many people out at this time, even if you live in a city. However, please practice common sense and scan your environment to be aware of any potential hazards.

Hold your hands together over your heart, where you can feel the rise and fall of your breath.

Face east and await the sunrise, looking for a filament of sun cresting above the surface of the earth. Draw a deep breath, as though inhaling the very sun itself. Incant:

I draw the magic of the Mother within me, each time I inspire.
Eternal Maiden, Mother, Crone, the earth is the security I desire.
I look to you Mother for inspiration
And listen now for divination.

Relax, let your mind soften, and listen for the message of inspiration to come to you. When we are sleepy, relaxed, and quiet, the Divine speaks within us.

Trust that the words you heard, the image that flashed before your eyes, the animal or bird that ran or flew by, or the particular shape of the clouds is a sign. It is. And from these take meaning and find your sacred inspiration.

The Earth Mother is with us and sends us signs and omens, portends and messages through nature every day. All we have to do is trust in the Great Mother.

Reference

Perry, Ted. "Version 3—Written by Ted Perry." Quoted in Rudolf Kaiser. "Chief Seattle's Speech(es): American Origins and European Reception." In *Recovering the Word: Essays on Native American Literature*, edited by Brian Swann and Arnold Krupat. Berkeley and Los Angeles, CA: University of California Press, 1987.

Ostara Ritual

Deborah Castellano

THERE ARE MOMENTS IN all of our lives where we feel like we are standing at a crossroads, where we feel bruised and battered, where we don't know which way to steer our internal ships. These moments are a great time to take a breath and be present with the uncertainty in front of you. It's an act of audious magic to chose to adjust your crown and recenter yourself to determine what your next steps will be on your path. Mary Magdalene is a perfect guide on this part of the path, though you can also always work with your own goddesses and spirits for this ritual.

Adjust Your Crown

Everyone connects with magic differently; for some it's the act of planning and preparing the ritual, for others it's creating something—a talisman, a drawing, a song, a piece of writing—and for still others it's communing with your goddesses and spirits. This is an opportunity to connect your will to magic using all of those aspects—planning, creation, and communing.

You Will Need

A crown for yourself
A crown for deity

An image of deity
White candle or tealight
White glitter
Rose petals
Rose water
Lighter or matches
Mirror of some kind
Offerings you think your deity will like
Optional: Paper and pen, novena chaplet

Find a crown for yourself prior to the ritual. It can be from a thrift shop, it can be bought online, it can be a crown you've made for yourself. You can make the crown out of paper, out of flowers, out of fabric from a beloved piece of clothing—whatever suits your journey. You can embroider your crown, you can draw words or sigils or make a collage, you can sew herbs or crystals that are important to your journey, you can weave ribbons with colors that are important to you into it, you can anoint it with oils to empower you. The important part of the crown is that it resonates with you. If a Queen of Heaven is part of your ritual, you will then need a small framed image of her that resonates with you. You can then either buy a small crown for this image that will fit on the frame or make one yourself. The smaller crown can match yours if you would like.

Sprinkle the glitter, rose petals, and rose water around the outside of your candle (a tealight can work too) before you start the ritual itself. Now all of your ritual components are ready to be used.

Kosmesis

It's one of the first makeover montages in history: in *The Iliad*, there's a big part where Zeus has had it up to his swan's neck in the goddesses meddling in the Trojan War. He thought it was much better left to the menfolk gods. But Aphrodite (A Queen of Heaven), Hera (another Queen of Heaven), and Athena (a case could be made for her as a Queen of Heaven as well) had already spent considerable time and energy on the war, including starting it with the whole squabble over the apple thrown by Eris. So it was probably about a hot three-and-a-half seconds before Athena said, "Okay what's the plan?" And then the whole makeover montage ensued. The Queens of Heaven resumed their domains in dealing with love and war and sociopolitical directing, Zeus was only a temporary detour, easily dealt with by the Queens of Heaven with glamour magic.

In Mary Magdalene's story, she dresses Jesus's hair with myrrh, she washes his feet with her own hair, and she was in charge of the funeral rites for his body—all comparable acts of glamour magic. Additionally, it's part of folk Catholicism to crown statues of Mary with fresh flower crowns, likely stemming from Beltane roots. Bringing flowers to Mary when you are getting married in the Catholic church is also a common practice. In theory, you're supposed to ask for *all* the babies. In practice, it's the bride's time with Mary to have whatever kind of chat she feels like having with her on her wedding day, as per my priest at the time of my second marriage. (I also scored bonus points with him by being good at ritual arrangement.)

Your crown needs adjusting, so you are likely in no mood to get all dolled up. But that's exactly why you need to bathe yourself, pull a brush through your hair, brush your teeth, and give yourself a little ritual bathing drama. You don't need to put on an evening gown if you don't want to. Maybe you have a very nice silk robe, maybe you have a knock around cashmere wrap, maybe you have a nap dress, maybe you have luxurious sweats that are nice and clean, maybe you have flowy linen pants. It doesn't really matter what you wear as long as it's something that makes you feel good and is clean. As I can very clearly and distinctly recall, I looked like a tangled-haired zombie in unwashed sweatpants when I needed a crown adjustment the most.

Put on some cosmetics if that's your bag, put on some moisturizer even if it isn't. You are performing a small ritual that has been embedded in our collective mythos since 700 BC for a reason. You are setting the stage for better times to come. You are likely doing a thing that will make your own personal Queens of Heaven happy because it's showing you want to adjust your crown in your troubled times and not be a depressed zombie with unwashed hair indefinitely. Allow yourself a little luxuriation, whether it's wearing a scent you usually wouldn't wear, moisturizing your hands, putting on a bold eyeliner that you save for special occasions—whatever.

Invoke

If you would like to invite Mary Magdalene or another Queen of Heaven to your Ostara rite, here is where you would do that. You can use traditional novenas if you like that kind of thing (at least a whole chaplet!), and if that's not your thing, that's okay too. If you are concerned the Queen of Heaven you want to invite may not come to your ritual, you can ask her prior to your ritual to give you a sign that she wants to be included (or doesn't; sometimes that's an equally strong message to receive). In my experience, Mary Magdalene is pretty freewheeling about ritual life, at least in my house. That said, not everyone likes everyone ever. Almost everyone I know can work with St. Expedite, but I received a very strongly worded return to sender message about my attempt. (Maybe he didn't like the pound cake?) If Mary declines, work with the universe or one of your own goddesses.

If you prefer to skip the novenas, you can always speak straight from your heart. Practice it once or twice in the shower or wherever you do your thinking. What comes out of your mouth in that moment may be something completely different than what you practiced, but the practicing opens the line between you and Mary Magdalene or your preferred Queen of Heaven. If the idea of doing that gives you heart palpitations, you can always write it (or sing it or dance it or draw it) ahead of time.

Offer

Offerings are generally a good idea when invoking. It's about showing care to your Queen of Heaven. Offerings that Mary Magdalene enjoys include white candles, perfumes, food made with eggs, red roses, fresh clean water, resin incense, white jars with myrrh or lavender or spikenard in them, figs, honey, olive oil, and bread. If you are offering to another Queen of Heaven, tiny honey cakes are a good idea, and it's hard to go wrong with fresh clean water, candles, and good incense. Arrange it as nicely as if you were serving it to the most important person in your life. When you make your offering, say all the things that you are giving out loud as if you are her divine waitress and you are reading her the specials.

Ask

Why do you need help with adjusting your crown? This is a good space to really open your heart to your Queen of Heaven or use it as a release for yourself. Talk about your circumstances, talk about your difficulties, talk about why you need help, and then ask for it.

Crown

Light your white candle or tealight. Focus on adjusting your crown as you light the candle. Say something like, "Please hear my plea, O Queen of Heaven, in the name of God Herself. Amen." Run the small crown over the flame of the candle. Say something like, "I crown you as Queen of Heaven in the name of God Herself. Amen." Place the crown on the frame.

Run your crown over the flame. Say something like, "I crown myself in your name, O Queen of Heaven. Amen." Make sure you put your crown on with confidence and that your crown is on your head straight. Make eye contact with yourself in a mirror. Say something like, "I am Queen of myself, in the name of the Queen of Heaven. I am power, I am glamour, I am love."

Divination

You have asked for help in your troubled times, now use your preferred method of divination to get the response. There's no such thing as a bad omen. I mean, there is. In the short term, that's part of Fortuna's wheel: *I have lost my kingdom.* But it's only a quarter of her wheel. Nothing is good forever and nothing is bad forever. If your omen is negative, keep pulling until you figure out how difficult that part of the wheel will be for you and what you can do to get to the next part of the wheel: *I will reign.*

Notes

Notes

Beltane

Shadow Comforts to Self-Care

Melissa Tipton

AS THE SEASONS SHIFT from spring to summer, and with new growth bursting into full bloom, Beltane celebrates the fertility of nature. On an internal level, this is a potent season to tend to our creative fires, the light within that's responsible for sparking new ideas and fueling growth and change. When we take time out of our busy schedules to stoke these inner flames, we move through life feeling more inspired, eager to engage, and focused on genuine priorities. If our connection to this fire has become a little shaky, this can leave us feeling directionless, lacking in energy to follow through on our intentions, or chasing goals that don't authentically light us up.

A wonderful way to support your creative fire is to perform a compassionate inventory of your self-care routine. Is it truly supportive or could it use a little makeover? A very common yet easy-to-miss energy drain is something author Jennifer Louden refers to as "shadow comforts" (Louden 2007, 41). These are things that feel good in the moment, like binge-watching a favorite show or venting to a friend about work drama, but they're actually siphoning away our energy. Now, to be clear, this isn't suggesting we should never Netflix and chill—sometimes that's precisely what we need! This is simply an invitation to look deeper and see if there are ways to support ourselves, and by extension our creative energy, even better.

While shadow comforts can take many forms, I've found three general categories to be quite useful in sussing out where these shadows might be hiding in our self-care practice. There is a degree of overlap between groupings, so there's no need to get caught up in "correctly" classifying your comforts, but they give us an excellent place to start as we assess our daily routines.

Distracting from Our Feelings

When life evokes challenging emotions, it's sometimes difficult to simply feel what we're feeling. Perhaps we fear that our emotions will become overwhelming, so it seems smarter to shove them aside and move on. Emotions also carry information—for instance, anger can alert us to what isn't working for us, such as unhealthy relationship dynamics—and we might harbor a belief that allowing this information in means we *have* to act on it right away, so again, better to shove it aside and stick to business as usual.

Ultimately, experiencing our feelings is a vital part of being alive, without which we might feel disconnected from ourselves, from others, and from our inner guidance. And much like water, which is a symbol of the emotions, damming our feelings creates a buildup of energy that can burst into our lives in unexpected ways, such as difficult moods that seem to come out of nowhere or snapping at someone even though we intended to be patient.

There are countless ways to distance ourselves from our feelings, but they often fall into two main categories: intellectualizing instead of feeling and distracting ourselves. With the first, we might find ourselves narrating internally or to others what we're feeling as opposed to allowing ourselves to experience the emotions. Or we might get caught up in explaining the feelings, perhaps by analyzing why so-and-so "made" us feel this way. Similarly, we might try to minimize what we're feeling by reasoning with ourselves: "Oh, c'mon, it could be worse! I should move on." All of these habits can be confused with genuinely supporting ourselves as we process what we're feeling.

In the second case, we can use all manner of activities to distract ourselves from feeling. Binging on *anything* is a common strategy (binge-watching, shopping, scrolling, etc.). While these activities can be nurturing at times, a good rule of thumb is if we feel super "zoned out" while doing them, these might be shadow comforts. We can also overfill our schedule, leaving scarcely a moment for ourselves, and this often goes hand-in-hand with prioritizing everyone else's needs, perhaps by saying yes to requests at the expense of our own well-being. Busyness can be explained away as just trying to get ahead on our goals or being a good friend, family member, or coworker, but if we have a hard time taking a break without feeling guilty, this is an invitation to explore whether we're prioritizing comfort over growth and genuine self-support.

Trying to Eradicate Uncertainty

Another category of shadow comforts is expending undue energy trying to iron out the natural uncertainty from our lives. There are so many things in life that we cannot know, but this doesn't stop us from trying! In fact, we can spend more energy trying to obtain certainty than we do on taking action, which only perpetuates the cycle, because it is often the action-taking that gives us real information and some measure of certainty. For instance, I can hypothesize until the cows come home what might happen if I accept a job offer, but I can only really know by experiencing what happens after I say yes.

Attempts to eradicate uncertainty tend to fall into one of three camps: perfectionism, overanalyzing, and forcing events. With the first, we're laboring under the belief that if only we can find the "right" way to do something, we can be assured of a good outcome. I couldn't tell you how many books I *haven't* written because of this belief, but I can say, without a doubt, the books from which I've reaped the greatest satisfaction are the ones I've actually (and imperfectly) written. Perfectionism keeps us from exploring what we have to offer, and it fools us into thinking we have less resilience than we actually do. For instance, does it feel good to get a bad book review? Nope. But it also isn't *nearly* as big a deal as perfectionist thoughts make it out to be.

Overanalyzing is another popular way to try and eradicate uncertainty, and we can spend massive amounts of time mulling over pros and cons, polling the opinions of our entire friend group, drawing endless tarot cards, and the list goes on. These activities can feel an awful lot like self-care (and sometimes they are!), but when we're blocking ourselves from taking action because we don't know everything there is to know, we've entered the territory of shadow comforts.

And finally, we can dispel uncertainty by forcing an outcome, even an outcome we don't like, just to get the waiting over with. When I was in my twenties, one of the (many) disastrous patterns I expressed in my dating life was bringing about the very rejection I feared. Instead of waiting for someone to break up with me (never mind if that was actually going to happen—my childhood wounds had me convinced it was inevitable), I would start fights with increasing frequency until my partner would get so fed up that they'd... wait for it... break up with me! As miserable as this felt, it seemed *less* miserable than being uncertain.

This pattern can show up anywhere we rush or pressure ourselves and others into making decisions. It can hide beneath the guise of being assertive, staying committed to our goals, or not wanting to play small when really we're pushing ourselves to do things at a pace that isn't supportive and that rejects factors beyond our control.

Projecting Our Stuff onto Others

Projection is an unconscious process that occurs within *everyone*—and I do mean everyone. Projection is when something that exists within our own unconscious gets projected onto other people (or groups, institutions, etc.) and we believe it exists solely "out there." For example, if I'm angry but I'm not in touch with those feelings—i.e., they're unconscious—I might find myself encountering a bunch of "angry people" everywhere. Over time, I might get the impression that the world is filled with angry jerks, not realizing that my disowned anger is being projected onto others. Now, this doesn't mean I never encounter angry people and it's all in my head, but when I'm projecting, my perception of how angry those people are is often exaggerated, and—here's the trippy bit—I am *more* likely to be drawn to angry people.

When we disown a quality within ourselves, we're apt to be drawn to this quality in others, as our unconscious seeks to create balance and wholeness. If that balance cannot be forged within, our psyche will seek it without. For instance, if I was taught to believe that thinking highly of oneself is arrogant and shameful, I will likely shun self-praise and deflect compliments, but I might find myself inexplicably drawn to people whom I perceive as boastful or excessively confident. Those people "carry" my disowned shadow qualities, and by keeping them close, even if they aggravate the heck out of me (as shadow carriers often do), I feel some measure of wholeness by having those qualities in my life, albeit within another person.

When we project our psychic content, we're more apt to feel disempowered because now it appears that the *only* way for things to get better is if other people or external circumstances change. Since we can't force change on someone else, it's easy to feel overwhelmed or even hopeless, and this can lead to chronic complaining and venting, which can feel so good in the moment but in reality keeps us stuck. Often, this venting involves getting other people to agree with our take on things—for instance, that things really *are* the other person's fault and we can only feel better if they change—which, again, can feel comforting and validating in the moment, but it doesn't support our growth and long-term happiness.

Tapping Into Deeper Nourishment

Recognizing any shadow comforts that have crept into our self-care practice is an important step in learning how to pivot and offer ourselves genuine support and nourishment. And bonus: as we practice this with ourselves, we hone our ability to better offer support and nourishment to the people we love. So, what do we do if we spot ourselves reaching for the temporary fix of shadow comforts? First of all, it's helpful to acknowledge that wanting comfort isn't wrong! The fact that we want soothing and respite from our cares is completely natural. Our aim isn't to deny ourselves comfort but to explore whether we're pursuing comfort in a way that carries unwanted consequences.

When I find myself wanting to binge-watch a show—or, more realistically, when I'm already midway through a binge-watching session and I notice I've been zoning out—I can pause and check in: What am I feeling right now? Often the simple act of noticing my feelings helps me get more grounded because I'm not unconsciously dissipating energy in service of walling off my emotions, which can leave me scattered and unfocused. Once I'm in touch with my feelings, can I create a little space to simply experience them? Perhaps I place one hand on my heart and one on my belly, closing my eyes for a few breaths and allowing the emotions to flow through me without judgment or the need to figure anything out. This might be all I need to come back to center.

Other times, I need to go a bit further, and I like to ask myself, what do I need right now? I tend to think best by writing out my thoughts, so I'll grab my journal and freewrite to help clarify what I need. Once I've identified this, I can check in: Is this activity truly meeting this need? Is there something else I could do that would address this need more directly? For instance, maybe you're grabbing your phone to hop on social media, but when you check in, what you're actually needing is connection, so you reach out to a friend to see if they want to talk. Or perhaps you started to stress-shop because you're hurting from a recent breakup, but you realize you're truly wanting physical comfort. So you might choose to give yourself a scalp massage, take a soothing bath, or cuddle with a pet.

Tending the Inner Fire

As we continue to refine our self-care practices and become skillful tenders of our inner fire, we'll find ourselves with more energy to pursue the things that matter most to us. And not only does our creative fire provide the energy to initiate and follow through on our goals, it also illuminates what our soul is most passionate about, what "lights us up." This is a win-win because now we have more energy *and* we know what we'd like to channel it into. This magical combo of motivation and purpose mirrors the explosion of growth as nature transitions into summer, expanding into fullness. This Beltane, let's tap into this astonishingly powerful current of creative power as we shed shadow comforts in favor of truly, deeply caring for ourselves.

Reference

Louden, Jennifer. *The Life Organizer: A Woman's Guide to a Mindful Year*. Novato, CA: New World Library, 2007.

Cosmic Sway

Bernadette Evans

MAY 1 IS THE celebration of Beltane, which is known for being the halfway point between the spring equinox and the summer solstice. The earth is warming up; the trees are growing buds and getting ready to blossom with leaves and flowers. Summer is just around the corner. With the increasing daylight, it brings with it expectancy, fun, optimism, and growth.

On May 1, Venus will square Pluto at 12:30 a.m. They are both in fixed signs, suggesting there may be some stubbornness or rigidity in your relationships. Try to see the other person's point of view and come to a compromise, or agree to disagree. You may have some intense conversations around what you each need from one another. Be up-front and don't manipulate or guilt the other person into doing what you want. That will only lead to bitterness or resentment instead of a loving partnership.

Pluto Retrograde

Pluto will station retrograde on May 2 at 1:46 p.m. Pluto retrograde is known for taking a deep dive into the unconscious realms and peering into the darker sides of yourself. When Pluto is retrograde, taking time to understand who you are and your unconscious desires is part of the journey. Should you choose to accept this mission, you could reach out to have someone (such as a psychologist) guide you through it. You can also spend time alone deciphering what it all means ... or at least what some of it means. Pluto will station direct on October 11 at 8:34 p.m.

The Moon also squares the Sun on May 1, and it is a fourth-quarter square. You could feel irritated and take it out on some poor soul who just happens to be in the vicinity. Don't. Is there an area of your life that you've been neglecting? Pay attention to a person or a situation to stop the downward spiral that could be happening.

Cinco de Mayo

May 5 is the celebration of Cinco de Mayo. A time to honor the Mexican people, their spirit, and their culture. You may want to spend some time educating yourself about the Mexican people and their way of life. Another way to commemorate the day is to visit an art gallery that showcases Mexican artists. However you choose to celebrate Cinco de Mayo, remember to have fun!

The Moon is in the sign of Aries today. This seems appropriate, as the Aries energy is about courage, leadership, and being bold and assertive. If you're celebrating today, enjoy and *salud*!

Dark Moon

On May 7 at 11:22 p.m., there is a New Moon at 18 degrees of Taurus. This is a good time to go over your finances and see if you need to do some fine-tuning. If you've been working too hard, this New Moon is asking you to slow down and breathe. Life is short; remember to take time to enjoy the simple pleasures. If you've been taking it easy for too long, maybe it's time to get back to work. Balance is always the key to everything. I love the saying "Slow and steady wins the race." Be consistent with your habits, and you'll see results. The Sun and Moon are sextile Saturn today. If you concentrate and do your work, you'll be rewarded.

On May 12, it's time to wish a happy Mother's Day to all the mothers and anyone else who nurtures others—human or animal. It seems appropriate that the Moon is in the sign of Cancer, which is about home, family, and nurturing. If you feel inclined, honor all those ancestors who've come before you and paved the way. Remember to do something loving that you enjoy. The aspects are all flowing today, presenting an opportunity for harmonious and loving connections. Enjoy the day, whatever you do.

Gemini Season

The Sun enters the sign of Gemini on May 20 at 8:59 a.m. Gemini is an air sign, so one of its main objectives is communication. Getting out to parties and socializing are part and parcel of this engaging energy. When the Sun is here, you enjoy lively discussions. You could want to learn a little bit of everything. Since this energy loves to learn and communicate, immerse yourself in a fascinating topic, then share what you've learned with others.

It's Victoria Day in Canada. No matter whether you're trying to enjoy a day off or you're at work, the Moon is making challenging aspects all day today, and you could run into some obstacles. At one moment you could feel like you're making progress and things are going great, and then in the next instant, you're backtracking and doing something over. Expect it so you're not upset if and when it happens. If it doesn't, fantastic!

Full Moon

There's a Full Moon on May 23 at 9:53 a.m. at 2 degrees of Sagittarius. This Moon is often called the Full Flower Moon. As you know, Full Moons always bring something to the surface for you to see. You're being asked to release what no longer serves you. Sagittarius likes to explore, have fun, travel, and study new philosophies and religions. At this time, you might want to re-examine your beliefs. Do they still fit with the person you are today? Don't be afraid to explore new ways of being. This energy desires freedom, but sometimes you may have to make a commitment to something, someone, or yourself.

The sky is very busy today with a lot of friendly action between the planets. Enjoy a fire with a group of friends or another type of get-together. Venus and Jupiter conjoin in the last degree of Taurus before Venus enters the sign of Gemini. With these two together, expect a lot of friends, fun, and laughter. You can work on yourself after you're worn out from playing.

Memorial Day

On May 25 at 11:36 a.m., the Moon will enter the hardworking, ambitious sign of Capricorn. It will do its best to make sure everyone is having a good time this Memorial Day weekend.

At 4:45 p.m. on May 27, the Moon will enter the sign of Aquarius. That evening, the focus is on what's best for the group. The Mercury-Saturn sextile gives you an eye for detail. Planning and arranging everything to make sure everyone is happy is great, but make sure to enjoy yourself as well. Try to relax and don't get too upset if someone forgets a salad. You're with friends, and that means everyone is happy to spend time together. Happy Memorial Day!

Dark Moon

The New Moon is on June 6 at 8:38 a.m. at 16 degrees of Gemini. This New Moon packs a powerful punch, with the Sun, Moon, Venus, Jupiter, and Mercury all in Gemini. The Sun, Moon, and Venus are especially chummy, as they're all at 16 degrees. This energy is asking you how you communicate with others. Are you engaged in lively conversations with friends, siblings, coworkers? With Venus in the mix, what do you value about your relationships? How do you relate to others? Is it easy to talk with them, or is it difficult to hold a conversation? What can you do to make it easier?

This is also a great time to learn something. Pick a subject and grab a book or two; that will give you something to chat about at the next party you go to. Is it time to go on a short road trip? Grab a buddy and go for a short drive and explore a new area.

On June 16, it's the day to say thank you and happy Father's Day to those who step in to nurture and support others. The Moon's in the sign of Libra and trines the Sun. This makes for a nice flowing energy, one where everyone is friendly and does their best to play nice and get along. Venus does square Neptune, which can manifest as having unrealistic expectations in your relationships. Enjoy your loved one's company and try not to put too much pressure on them or yourself.

Reference

"Full Moon Names for 2023." *The Old Farmer's Almanac.* Yankee Publishing, Inc. January 5, 2023. https://www.almanac.com /full-moon-names.

Tales and Traditions

Natalie Zaman

COEXISTING ON OPPOSITE SIDES of the calendar, Beltane and Samhain are partners in honoring the life force. At Samhain, we honor the shade, the coming darkness that will become the womb for life to begin again. At Beltane, we celebrate the opposite: life at the height of its power, its unbridled magnificence and majesty that creates as easily as it can crush.

Darth Vader: The Prince of Light and Darkness

The tale of Darth Vader is powerful and bittersweet, much like Beltane. Anakin Skywalker is a complex character with so much promise and just as many challenges. His physical makeup (those midi-chlorians) earmark him as godlike—the chosen one—but he is also flawed like any human. As Yoda successfully predicted: "Fear leads to anger. Anger leads to hate. Hate leads to suffering" (*The Phantom Menace* 1999).

In addition to what he was born with, Anakin's unique emotional history and talent stack make for chaos in the grand order of the Force. Whatever the plans of the Jedi or the Sith Lord Emperor, Padawan Anakin and Darth Vader defy predictability. The life force honored at Beltane embodies this same chaos. This power, the power of nature, is bright and beautiful—and difficult if not impossible to tame, and so, potentially dangerously destructive: The sea can be a place of peace and rest, but underneath the waves, tsunamis brew. Wildlife can be both gorgeous and majestic, but animals hunt and kill to live and assert dominance. Lightning is energy come to life—but it can also be the spark that ignites a forest fire, leaving scorched earth and death in its wake.

- On the exact opposite position on the calendar from Samhain, Beltane honors that same universal force embodied in the shadow of Darth Vader. He is a character of extremes: darkness and light, ecstasy and struggle, life and death. In many ways, "the Force" is what is honored at Beltane—the natural energy that is both life and death. Life is more prevalent at Beltane and death at Samhain. Anakin creates the lives of Luke and Leia with Padmé; his choices as Vader break her heart and bring death.

- Beltane is the next turning of the wheel that ushers us into a new phase of season, weather, work, light, and being. Similarly, reacting to the turning of events in his life, Anakin gives up his Padawan persona for a new life as a Sith. Symbolically he takes on the name of Vader, adding "Darth," the honorific taken on by the Sith to cast away their old lives. This is not the end for him, however. Looking at the full story as it has been presented thus far, the wheel continues to turn, and Vader comes full circle: repenting, redeeming, and returning to Anakin, though he is certainly a different Anakin than the one we met in Tatooine.

- Beltane is a fire festival. Jedi and Sith weapons of choice are lightsabers, blades of fire powered by crystals. The colors of Darth Vader's lightsabers reflect Beltane energy: white-blue when he was the Padawan Anakin, and then red, the color of all Sith lightsabers.

Beltane *prêt-à-porter par la* Sith

Take some fashion tips from Darth Vader to go against the grain and express the dark majesty, magic, and mystery of Beltane and its season:

- **Black:** Darth Vader is a presence in head-to-toe black—and of course, there's that billowing cape. Black might not be the first color that comes to mind when thinking of spring and the months of May and June, but it is highly protective and so an apropos color with which to garb oneself during the beautifully chaotic season of Beltane.

- **Technology:** "He's more machine now than man," said Obi-Wan Kenobi of his old friend and mentee, Anakin Skywalker (*Return of the Jedi* 1983). In his transition from Padawan to Sith, Darth Vader sustained injuries that he overcame with the help of technology (and the Force, of course). Many of us utilize technology daily, from Bluetooth connections to voice-controlled smart speakers. We use it to optimize our lives, manage our shopping habits, track everything from mileage to sleep, and operate devices in our homes. How many of us feel lost when we don't have an internet connection? This technology isn't merely a tool—it's in our homes and on our bodies. Besides being practical, it can also be a means of personal expression: statement headphones, sleek smartwatch bands, and personalized phone cases...the challenge is not to rely on them utterly. Use sparingly.

- **Prince Charming:** It could seem (at least at first) that the Anakin-Padmé love story is something out of a fairy tale—but Anakin/Darth Vader is no Prince Charming. In fact, he's not a prince, minor royalty, or even a person of means; we meet Anakin Skywalker as a poor human, a slave. What he does have is intelligence, those midi-chlorians, and charm. In *The Phantom Menace*, Anakin gives Padmé the gift of a carved *japor* snippet charm, a bit of Tatooine bone, or ivory, carved with symbols of luck. Anakin gives the gift in the hopes that Padmé will remember him; she keeps the amulet until her death. Charms can serve many purposes: they can be sentimental, they may incorporate symbols or be made of metals and stones with desirable attributes, or they can simply be pretty. You probably won't be able to get your hands on some authentic japor—but earthly materials will do just as well. Some crystals and symbols associated with Beltane are:

- Carnelian: good for stabilizing energy—a challenge at Beltane
- Ruby in fuchsite: represents male-female balance
- Amber: embodiment of life, especially if it contains fossils
- Malachite: brings abundance—the promise of Beltane
- Maypole: represents masculine energy
- Chalice: represents feminine energy
- Seed: represents beginnings, the life force
- Sword: represents the battle between the light and the darkness; some Beltane traditions include mock battles between the seasons where summer prevails. At the end of his life, Darth Vader renounces his Sithness and becomes Anakin again.

Books and Films to Read, View, and Inspire

Lucas, George, director. 1977–2005. *Star Wars: Episodes I–VI.* Lucasfilm Ltd.

References

Lucas, George, dir. *Star Wars: Episode I—The Phantom Menace.* 1999. San Francisco, CA: Lucasfilm Ltd.

Richard Marquand, dir. *Star Wars: Episode VI—Return of the Jedi.* 1983. San Francisco, CA: Lucasfilm Ltd.

Feasts and Treats

Mickie Mueller

BELTANE IS SO LOVELY and full of the magic of the blossoming of the land. The spirit of love and happiness is in the air, and I love to get outside and see what's blooming, enjoy fresh fruits, and celebrate. Even when it's on a weekday, marking the day with a few fun food traditions is a wonderful way to recognize the magic of the day.

Bannocks

Eating oatcakes known as bannocks on Beltane has been part of many old folk traditions. The original recipes were unleavened and made with animal fat, but this version is suitable for a modern palate. You can serve them right away or make them the night before so that they're ready in the morning to serve with my quick homemade mixed berry jam (recipe below). Take advantage of this bit of folk kitchen magic even on a weekday!

Prep time: 12 minutes
Cooking time: 25 minutes
Servings: 8 bannocks

1½ cups oat flour
1 cup all-purpose flour, or gluten-free flour blend
2 teaspoons baking powder

1 teaspoon salt
⅓ cup water, or choice of milk
5 tablespoons melted butter, or plant butter
Nonstick cooking spray

For oat flour, just blitz 1½ cup rolled oats in the food processor or blender until powdered. If you're gluten free, be sure to get gluten-free oats. Mix all dry ingredients in a large bowl with a wire whisk or fork. Add the milk and butter and mix with a wooden spoon until it comes together to form a soft ball of dough. If it's crumbly, add a little extra milk or water 1 teaspoon at a time until it's a good, workable texture. If it's too sticky, add a little flour. Knead the dough briefly and gently.

Heat up a skillet or griddle to medium-low heat with a little cooking spray while you cut the dough in half and, using your hands, press and shape each into a disk that's about 1 inch thick and will fit in your skillet. Try not to overwork the dough to keep it from being tough. Score across the top of the bannock in the shape of an X and transfer the first one into the skillet. Grill it low and slow on the first side, moving it a bit occasionally so it doesn't stick, until the bottom looks golden brown, about 12–15 minutes. Flip it over and finish it on the other side about 10 more minutes. When you tap it, it should sound hollow; that means it's done. Repeat with the second bannock; cut them along the score lines and serve.

Chia and Mixed Berry Quick Jam

This is super easy and sets quickly into a lovely homemade jam with the magical power of chia seeds! I love that this is low in sugar, and you know what went into it.

Cooking time: 5 minutes
Setting time: 5–10 minutes
Servings: 1 cup jam

1 cup of fresh or frozen mixed berries
Sugar or sweetener of your choice to taste
1 tablespoon chia seeds

Heat the fruit in the microwave or in a small saucepan on the stove. Mash them as you go with either a potato masher or the back of a spoon. I use a muddler that's used to bruise fruit, herbs, and spices in mixed drinks. Leave it chunky or mashed to oblivion; the choice is yours. Taste and add sweetener of your choice if it's needed. Stir in 1 tablespoon of chia seeds and mix well. Transfer to a small jar or bowl and put it in the fridge or freezer to cool 5–10 minutes. As it cools, the chia seeds will thicken the fruit into a beautiful jam—delicious served on biscuits or hot bannocks. Store in the refrigerator up to 1 week.

Beer Batter Fried Dandelion Blossoms

An old-time foraging recipe, these taste a bit like fried mushrooms! They're easy and delicious, full of nutrients including protein, calcium, iron, and vitamins A and C. It's important to only use dandelions that have not been treated with pesticides, and make sure that you know how to identify dandelions before you proceed.

Prep time: 10 minutes
Cooking time: 10 minutes
Servings: 4

2 cups dandelion blossoms, or as many as you can pick
1 cup all-purpose flour (You can use wheat or all-purpose gluten-free blend.)
¾ cup beer, or substitute nonalcoholic beer or sparkling water
¼ teaspoon salt
1 cup oil of your choice for frying

When you pick them, cut them where the stem meets the flower, including the green part that holds the petals together. Thoroughly rinse the blossoms and roll in a paper towel to dry. Mix flour, beer, and salt to make the batter. Put about an inch of oil in a skillet and heat over medium.

Dip each dandelion in the batter and then drop them in the skillet, yellow-flower-side down; this spreads out the blossoms as they begin to cook. I usually do no more than 10 at a time since they fry up quickly. After about 1–2 minutes, use a fork or chopsticks to flip them over and cook about a minute or two on the other side.

Drain them on a napkin-lined plate and sprinkle lightly with salt. If you have leftover batter, you can just drip it into the skillet and make "cracklins"! These are delicious dipped in a sauce like spicy mayo or eaten on their own.

Crab Stuffed Flounder

This is a very fancy presentation that looks like it was a lot of work, but it's easy to make. This one has even won over people whose favorite fish was square and breaded!

Prep time: 10 minutes

Cooking time: 20 minutes

Servings: 6–8 fillets depending on size

1 pound flaked crabmeat, drained (A budget substitute is a 1-pound pack of imitation crabmeat, chopped.)

2 teaspoons ground dry mustard

1½ teaspoons Worcestershire sauce

¼ teaspoon salt

½ cup crushed rice cereal

1½ teaspoons Old Bay or Cajun seasoning

2 green onions (scallions), thinly sliced

1 tablespoon mayonnaise

1 egg

Olive oil spray

1½ pounds Pacific flounder fillets (Check your labels; do not use cheap Arrowtooth flounder. It's mushy and terrible.)

Preheat oven to 400°F. Combine crab, ground mustard, Worcestershire, salt, crushed rice cereal, Old Bay or Cajun seasoning, and green onion and mix well. Add mayonnaise and egg and combine until mixture is moist throughout. Spray both sides of each fillet with olive oil. Spoon about ¼–½ cup of crab mixture onto the wide end of the fillet and roll it up; place on baking pan with the seam-side down, and repeat with all the fillets. Sprinkle the top with a little more Old Bay or Cajun seasoning and bake for 20 minutes.

Sweet Potato Gnocchi and Asparagus

These savory pillows of yumminess are easier to make than you might think. Sautéed with asparagus, it makes a beautiful side dish. The gnocchi can be made in advance and boiled when you're ready to make dinner.

Prep time: 1 hour
Cooking time: 10 minutes
Servings: 4

Sweet Potato Gnocchi

3 medium-sized sweet potatoes, baked in microwave until fork tender
1 egg
1½ cups all-purpose flour, or gluten-free blend

Asparagus and Butter Sauce

2 tablespoons butter, or plant butter
1 tablespoon olive oil
Bundle of fresh asparagus, trimmed and cut into 1-inch sections
3 cloves minced garlic
Salt
Pepper
Optional: 5–6 leaves of thinly sliced fresh basil or 1 teaspoon dried basil, and fresh-grated Parmesan

Slice sweet potatoes in half lengthwise, and once they're cool enough, use a large metal spoon to scoop the insides away from the peel. In a large bowl, mash the sweet potatoes until smooth. Measure out 3 cups of the sweet potatoes, then stir in the egg. Next, gently stir in the flour and add a bit more flour if needed until it becomes a loose ball of dough, firm but a bit sticky. Be careful not to overwork the dough, or it will be heavy instead of puffy.

Turn the dough out onto a clean, floured cutting board and take sections of the dough and roll each into 1-inch ropes. Cut each rope into ½-inch pieces and score one side of each with the tines of a fork for the traditional shape. Bring a pot of lightly salted water to a boil. Boil the gnocchi 5 minutes or until they float to the top, and strain.

In a medium-high skillet, heat 2 tablespoons of butter or plant butter and 1 tablespoon of olive oil. Sauté the asparagus and garlic until the asparagus is tender and remove from the skillet, keeping the butter and oil in the pan. Now add the gnocchi and sauté until the surfaces of the gnocchi become seared and a bit crispy. Return the asparagus to the pan and toss together. Salt and pepper to taste and remove from heat. Top with fresh basil and Parmesan if you wish.

Crafty Crafts

Lupa

SPRING IS WELL UNDERWAY, and flowers are blooming all over the place! You know what goes really well with flowers? Junk mail!

No, really!

Many of us toss junk mail into the trash. If it ends up in a recycling bin in the United States, it still has a one-in-three chance of ending up in the landfill, since only about 67 percent of paper here ends up funneled back into recycled goods. Thankfully, paper is one of the easiest materials to repurpose at home.

Floral Paper

We can do our own recycling—or, rather, reusing—on a small scale by making paper by hand. There are hobby papermaking kits available through many craft stores, but you may also wish to consider also making some of the supplies yourself. Here's what you'll need:

Materials
Mold and deckle
Two plastic tubs
Blender
Flower petals

Junk mail or wastepaper
Food coloring
Old towels
Sponge
Optional: Supplies for making your own mold and deckle
   Cost: $10–$130
   Time spent: 2–3 hours, not including drying time; add another 30–60 minutes if making your own mold and deckle

Let's talk more in depth about the supplies you'll need for this craft, and then we'll get into how to use them. Some of these may be found inexpensively at thrift stores or yard sales.

A mold and deckle: These are two wooden frames of the same size; in many kits they're fairly small, about 6 × 8 inches or so. One has metal screening, similar to that used on windows, across one side of it. You can make frames out of scrap wood or get two plain rectangular picture frames of the same dimensions. Go to a hardware store that sells window screen by the foot and get a section large enough to cover one side of one of the frames. Then staple the screen securely to the frame, similar to stretching an artist's canvas over a frame. Around one side of the other frame, glue some foam weather stripping; some types may already have their own adhesive on the back.

Two plastic tubs: One of these needs to be large enough that you can easily fit the mold and deckle into it. You're going to be filling this tub with paper pulp, and you need to be able to fully submerge the mold and deckle into the pulp, with room for your hands as well. The other one will be used as a soaking tub for paper to be turned into pulp.

A blender: You're not going to want to use this for food after you've made your first batch of paper with it, so consider going to a thrift store for a cheap secondhand one. You don't need anything super fancy, just a basic blender with an on and off button and maybe a couple different speeds. (Make sure it has a lid!)

Flower petals: You can acquire these in your yard, open lots, along roadsides, etc. (be careful of places where herbicides or pesticides may have been recently used). Bonus points if you pick the flowers of invasive or other non-native species; in the United States we have plenty of those, from dandelions to Queen Anne's lace to periwinkle and many species more. Or head to a florist if you have one in the area. You might see if they'll sell you wilting flowers at a discount or even give them away!

Junk mail and other wastepaper: Again, most folks have plenty of this and sometimes newspapers as well. Keep in mind that the more colors and inks there are on the paper, the more it will stain your paper, so if you want to primarily stick to white paper with just

some words on it, that will give you the best results. On the other hand, you can always experiment with…

Food coloring: While you can use liquid food coloring, powdered food coloring is more concentrated and you need less of it to get a good color to your paper. Even if you're dealing with a rather grayish pulp thanks to printing with inks, you can still get some darker colors to help cover it over some, though you may need to experiment with proportions to get the colors you really like. You can also experiment with things like fabric dyes and diluted acrylic paints, but since these are not biodegradable, food coloring or natural dyes are best. Please be mindful that you aren't going to get the vivid colors of, say, construction paper this way, but this will add just a tint to the paper you make.

Several old towels: Again, make sure these are ones you aren't especially attached to, as the paper pulp can stay stuck to the fibers even after going through the wash.

Sponge: Any good, clean sponge will do; again, this should be dedicated only to papermaking.

To make your paper pulp, start by tearing up your junk mail into pieces about 1 inch square, or run it through a paper shredder. Put some water in the plastic soaking tub with the paper, enough to thoroughly soak the paper. Leave it to soak overnight. The next day, start putting the soaked paper into the blender along with water until the blender is about half full. Blend until pulpy. Again, you'll need to experiment with proportions until you get a consistency you like; the thicker the pulp, the heavier and thicker the paper. Empty the blender into the pulp tub (the one big enough for your mold and deckle) and repeat the process until you have as much pulp as you want.

Now's the time to add in the flower petals. You can toss entire petals in there or tear apart larger ones; leaves can go in there as well. Try not to add thicker portions of the plant, as they can affect the thickness of your paper. If you want to dye the entire batch of paper, add dye to the pulp until the desired color is achieved. You may wish to wear rubber gloves, especially if working with anything stronger than food coloring.

Next, put the mold screen-side up and then place the deckle over it, weather stripping–side down. Holding them firmly together, submerge them into the pulp at about a forty-five degree angle and then flatten them out as you bring them back up, now filled with pulp. Shake the mold and deckle back and forth and then side to side to make sure the pulp is evenly distributed on the screen.

Now here's the tricky part. Remove the deckle so you just have the pulp sitting on the screen of the mold. Lay out a few towels on a flat, level surface. Then quickly and smoothly flip the mold over and press the pulp into a towel. Remove the mold and continue to press water out of the paper with your sponge, flattening the paper as you go. You can also further flatten it with a smooth board or a rolling pin if you wish. Repeat until you've run out of pulp or made as many pieces of paper as you wish.

Leave the paper to dry on the towels. It should be completely dry within a few days depending on temperature and humidity. You can use this paper for spells, artwork, and more!

One more note: you can also make paper with seeds too! Just make sure they're plants native to your area, avoid adding chemical dyes to your paper, and don't use heat to dry it.

The Natural Magic
of Attachment

Dallas Jennifer Cobb

Psychiatrist John Bowlby is considered to be the founder of attachment theory, which holds that a safe and secure relationship between a child and their primary caregiver lays the groundwork for a relationship of attachment, which is probably the most important relationship, leading to subsequent "social, emotional, and cognitive development" (McLeod 2022). Attachment is characterized by the "universal need to seek close proximity with their caregiver when under stress or threatened" (McLeod 2022).

While many of us haven't necessarily benefited from secure attachment, it is never too late to address attachment wounds and heal them. A recent article in *Counseling Today* states that attachment wounds can be healed by "being cared for and caring for others" (Baruch and Higgins 2020).

Many of us find attachment healing through close personal relationships with children, partners, and spouses, even if our parent relationships were not attachment based. Attachment can also be experienced in relationship to our familiars and animal companions. A therapist or counsellor can be a "stand-in good parent" and enable the client to experience appropriate attachment. And cultivating a strong, committed, and two-way relationship with nature can enable us to care for and feel cared for by the earth, our Great Mother.

Because Beltane historically celebrated the beginning of the pasture season, it was a time of returning to sleeping out of doors in nature. In Ireland fires were lit and livestock was herded between the fires as a blessing as they went out to pasture. Maypoles were erected and slow, ribbon-weaving dances took place, celebrating fertility. Known as the time of sacred sex between Goddess and God, lovers consider Beltane sex to be a sacred act.

With the union of lovers, of Goddess and God, Beltane is a time to honor the internal union of sacred masculine and sacred feminine natures. It is a time for us to be nurturing and supportive of ourselves, honoring our feminine capacity, and to extend good boundaries and be self-protective, honoring our masculine ways.

The Ritual of Attachment

We all know that spending time in nature can help to relieve and reduce stress, but did you know that time in nature can produce feelings of being connected to something much larger than yourself? It can also help you to feel "part of" (Mayer et al. 2009).

In honor of Beltane, plan a lovers' night outdoors by yourself. Why are we so hypnotized to believe that we can only be attached to another? What if we regularly planned dates and sacred time alone to build our self-love and strong attachment? Tonight, we turn to ourselves to feel attached, wanted, connected, and held.

Remember, safety is the most important factor, so if you live in a city the plan may be to open your windows wider tonight or to sleep on your balcony or rooftop. If you live in a rural area, you might retreat to your garden, yard, or back forty. Camping is a great choice too; sleeping in a tent can put you in close contact with nature.

Set up your safe nature setting and make a healing pledge:

I mend what's broken inside of me,
I choose healing and unity,
No longer divided, I am whole,
Earth Mother blesses my heart and soul.
Here in nature with my loving Mother,
From now on, there is no other,
I am wanted, cherished, and loved,
From now on I am my own beloved.

By ensuring you are in a safe environment, you have invoked the sacred masculine. By laying out soft blankets, duvets, and pillows, and draping your bed in bright-colored cloth, you invite the sacred feminine. Understand the necessity of both energies and see how they twine together perfectly. As you slip into your bed, imagine your own duality, as if you are two people, God and Goddess, in one. Held in this sacred dual embrace, quietly list one positive feminine quality paired with one positive masculine quality. Keep it equal, and let each one be attached to the other, perfectly partnered. Tell yourself what your wonderful qualities are, like a lover whispering compliments to you:

I am a capable employee and a devoted mother.
I earn good money, and I have a beautiful home.
I maintain good boundaries and love my friends dearly.
I am ferociously protective and tenderly loving.

When you run out of pairs of masculine and feminine traits, pause and acknowledge the sacred union:

Sacred energies unite in me,
From external clamouring set me free,
I am attached and feel at ease.
I am complete and it sets me free.
So mote it be.

Sleep in the safe and nurturing space you have created and celebrate the union of the sacred energies of masculine and feminine within you.

Simple Love Spell

Do you feel a need to attract a lover, partner, or mate? Use the magnetic energy of Beltane to work this simple love spell. Call on Venus (Roman) or Aphrodite (Greek) to aid you in what you seek.

Take a pen and paper and write: "I am…" and fill in some of your strong feminine qualities; "I am…" and write down some of your strong masculine qualities. Aloud, say:

Great Goddesses of love, alive within me, help me to see:
I am the one that I seek.

Keep your list and add to it over time, knowing that the greatest love connection you can form is that of self-love and secure attachment with the Mother of us all, earth. When these bonds have grown and become secure attachment, you will radiate and draw your right partner to you.

Reference

Baruch, Adele, and Ashley Higgins. "Healing Attachment Wounds by Being Cared for and Caring for Others." *Counseling Today.* American Counseling Association. October 29, 2020. https://ct.counseling.org/2020/10/healing-attachment-wounds-by-being-cared-for-and-caring-for-others/.

Mayer, Stephan Fl., Cynthia McPherson Frantz, Emma Bruehlman-Senecal, Kyffin Dolliver. "Why Is Nature Beneficial?: The Role of Connectedness to Nature." *Environment and Behavior* 41, no. 5 (September 2009): 607–643. https://doi.org/10.1177/0013916508319745.

McLeod, Saul. "What Is Attachment Theory?" Simply Psychology. Updated August 18, 2022. https://www.simplypsychology.org/attachment.html#:~:text=Attachment%20can%20be%20defined%20as,appropriately%20to%20the%20child's%20needs.

Beltane Ritual

Melissa Tipton

LEARNING HOW TO GENUINELY nourish and support ourselves so we can create the life that we desire requires identifying habits that might appear, on the surface, to be acts of self-care, but that serve as temporary distractions, draining our energy and keeping us stuck in limiting patterns.

Igniting Creative Energy

In this ritual, we'll surrender shadow comforts to the purifying fires of Beltane so we can genuinely support ourselves, paving the way for growth, change, and greater access to creative flow.

Items Needed
Frankincense or dragon's blood incense
Two candles in heatproof containers
Optional: journal

Before beginning, read through the ritual to make sure the space you've chosen allows you sufficient room to move, and then energetically prepare your space by lighting the incense and wafting it around, making sure to send smoke into any nooks or corners.

Which incense should you use? Ultimately, trust your intuition, but two suggestions are frankincense and dragon's blood. While both have cleansing properties, I tend to experience frankincense more as a purifying, elevating agent (the energy is transformed into a more helpful vibration), whereas dragon's blood seems very effective at banishing negativity (the unwanted energy is expelled from the space). If you have both, you might experiment with using dragon's blood first, almost like an energetic broom, followed by frankincense to raise the vibe.

Cast the Magic Circle

Start in the direction of your choice (I typically begin in the north), facing outward. Feel your feet firmly rooted in the earth as you invite energy to rise from the earth's core, through the soles of your feet, traveling up your body, streaming out through the crown of your head.

Allowing the earth energy stream to continue flowing, shift your awareness to the cosmos above you. Feel a cascade of sky energy spilling down into your crown, washing through your body, down and out through the soles of your feet. You now have twin flows of energy moving through you, connecting you to the above and below. Breathe here for a moment, enjoying the connection to all that is.

Now, pointing your dominant hand's index finger (or using a wand, if that's part of your practice), feel these twin flows coursing down your arm and out through your finger in a vibrant ribbon of energy. Use this ribbon to draw a circle, moving clockwise, returning back to your starting point. Repeat, moving around the circle twice more.

Standing in the center of the space, close your eyes and feel the circle of energy around you. Sense as the line of energy expands above and below, forming a sphere. You might notice a shift in how the space feels, or perhaps sounds from beyond the sphere will be slightly muffled. It's magical, isn't it! Release the flows of energy from earth and sky, letting them naturally subside.

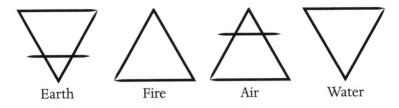

| Earth | Fire | Air | Water |

If it's part of your practice, you can now welcome the four elements, also known as "calling the quarters." Depending on your tradition and preferences, you'll situate an element in each of the four cardinal directions. I often pair earth with north, fire with east, air with south, and water with west, but do what feels best to you.

To call the quarters, visualize a door with an engraving of the element's alchemical symbol, and as you call in that element, see the door open. Stand facing the appropriate direction as you say the following aloud. (Adjust these evocations as needed to match your starting point and elemental-directional pairings.)

To the north, I call upon the element of earth! Earth, please guide and aid me in my magic. Hail and welcome!

To the east, I call upon the element of fire! Fire, please guide and aid me in my magic. Hail and welcome!

To the south, I call upon the element of air! Air, please guide and aid me in my magic. Hail and welcome!

To the west, I call upon the element of water! Water, please guide and aid me in my magic. Hail and welcome!

Construct the Energetic Portal

Your circle is cast and anchored by the four directions. Now it's time to create an energetic "power source" for your candles. First, choose where you'll be placing the candles, making sure there's enough space for you to walk in between them. I like to orient one candle in the east and one in the west. Make sure they're safely situated away from anything flammable.

Working with the two candle placements individually, focus your attention on the floor or ground where you'll be setting the candle. Use your index finger in a slow, clockwise circling motion, hovering an inch or two above the ground, and keep circling your finger through the air as you focus on activating the energies of purification and release. You should get a felt sense or see in your mind's eye a little vortex of energy taking shape, aligned with the intention of purification and release. When it feels ready, place your candle on this vortex, "plugging it into" the energy. Repeat for the second candle.

Standing with the candles in front of you, sense the energetic space between them. You might even see it take shape in your mind's eye as a shimmering curtain through which you will pass.

Now, to help gather the energy you'll be releasing, create an energetic bubble in front of you. I like to hold my hands about a foot apart, palms facing, and sense the bubble taking shape between my hands. Call to mind the shadow comforts you wish to release. You might envision one comfort at a time, perhaps imagining yourself engaging in that activity, getting in touch with what it feels like, and then send all of that energy into the bubble. Repeat for any shadow comforts you're ready to release.

Dissolve Shadow Energy

Holding the energetic bubble, slowly and with intention walk between the candles. Feel and envision the energy dissolving and diffusing, like fine glitter being blown from your energy field by a strong fan, returning to the greater cosmic cycle.

Once you've passed through the candles and the energy has been released, take a moment to notice how you feel. Perhaps you feel lighter—your body might feel a little more mobile and flexible; or maybe your mind seems clearer, less cluttered. Allow yourself to enjoy this new energetic experience.

If any insights or intuitive messages arise, such as guidance on how to deeply nourish and support yourself in daily life, you might spend some time within this sacred space journaling so you can carry the energy of this ritual into your lived experience.

Release the Circle

When you're ready, snuff out the candles and give thanks. Use your index finger in a circling, counterclockwise motion to close the two vortices of energy underneath the candles. Then release the four quarters. Start where you began when calling the quarters, but this time, move counterclockwise.

To the north, I thank and release the element of earth! I'm grateful for your guidance and aid, earth. Hail and farewell!

To the west, I thank and release the element of water! I'm grateful for your guidance and aid, water. Hail and farewell!

To the south, I thank and release the element of air! I'm grateful for your guidance and aid, air. Hail and farewell!

To the east, I thank and release the element of fire! I'm grateful for your guidance and aid, fire. Hail and farewell!

Back in the north, reach out your index finger and imagine you're hooking the edge of an energetic curtain, and as you move around the circle counterclockwise, peel open this curtain and say:

Open now this sacred space,
All energies find their proper place.
Fare thee well and safe return,
Let my magick unfold as the wheel doth turn.

This circle is undone but never broken. Beltane blessings!

Notes

Notes

Notes

Litha

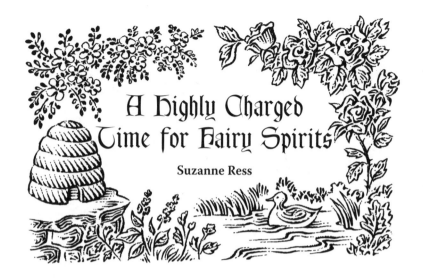

A Highly Charged Time for Fairy Spirits

Suzanne Ress

LITHA IS A HIGHLY charged time when summer fairy spirits are most likely to appear to humans. This year could show to be especially fruitful in this regard, as the powerful Midsummer moon will reach its full, most powerful state on June 22, two days after the official solstice.

Fairies, or faeries, named such in medieval England, have their origins further back in time, when they were known by the Greeks as nymphs. There were nymphs of water, trees, meadows, forests—all females. They were considered protectors of their element but were not as powerful as gods. In Latin as well as in modern Italian, a fairy is a *fata*, or Fate. Even in older English versions of "Sleeping Beauty," the three fairies are known as the three Fates. That is, *fate* as in preordained outcome or the forces of nature.

A Greek satyr was a male nymph, with horse or goat ears, legs, and tail, goat horns, and a permanent erection. The ancient Roman version of the satyr was the faun. Both the satyr and the faun were fertility spirits, and they were both believed to have unquenchable sexual appetites. With time, this aspect of their being faded to create Pan, a boyish fairy. Pan wasn't sexless; he was male, but he was more a playful companion to the nymphs than were the fauns and satyrs.

Robin Goodfellow, hobgoblin, pooka, devil, brownie, hobbit, imp, and *demon* are all English names for household prankish "folk," inhabitants of "enchanted" lakes, springs, wooded areas, and meadows. Although they may sometimes have a playfully malicious intent, they do not have enough power to do great harm to humans, so they must content themselves with jokes, jests, fun, and trickery. They are solitary fairies and tend to stay in a favored locale, once they find one they like, forever.

Puck can shape-shift, becoming animal form, usually a horse, but also a goat, dog, rabbit, or man. In Irish folklore, the *pooka* often appears as a dark horse with golden eyes.

Some years ago, I had my mare bred for the first time, and eleven months later, she gave birth alone at night to a little red colt. He was full of energy and so small that he could walk back and forth underneath his dam's belly. His ears were long and curled slightly inward, and he had two whorls on his white blaze, which, according to horse folklore, signifies either a genius or a crazy horse. His amber-colored eyes had a mischievous look. I proudly showed him off to my friends. One of them commented that he looked like a character from a Shakespeare play, and immediately I knew who she was referring to: Puck from *A Midsummer Night's Dream.*

He grew quickly, and his red coat darkened. He loved playing, battles with the wheelbarrow, running, and bucking full vertical for joy.

In Shakespeare's *A Midsummer Night's Dream*, which takes place at Litha in Athens, the most vivid character is Puck, a companion and helper to the king and queen of fairies, Oberon and Titania. I had read the play in high school under the tutelage of an excellent English teacher, and I loved it. Many years later I attended a very well-done summer theatrical performance of the play, which deepened my understanding and love of it. The costumes for the fairies and Puck really stood out in that performance, and they stuck in my mind so that, come fall and Samhain, I made similar Halloween costumes for myself and my family.

Puck's costume consisted of brown fake fur pants with a yarn horse tail, a sparkling blue-green-silvery top, and a headpiece with vines and flowers and little horns. What were we dressed up as? Fairy creatures!

A Midsummer Night's Dream, written around 1595, creates a vivid picture of the fairy world that most people believed in at the time. This portrayal has had a strong influence on people's conceptions of fairies and the fairy world to this day. We are first shown the fairy world of the play in an enchanted wood outside the city, where Puck speaks, referring to an ongoing argument between Oberon and Titania. As a punishment to Titania, Puck says, Oberon has commanded him to play a trick on her by sprinkling magical flower drops in her eyes as she sleeps in the forest. These drops will cause her to fall in love with the first being she lays eyes on when she awakes. The being "happens" to be a lowly weaver named Bottom, escaped to the enchanted woods to practice a play with his friends. Puck has bestowed Bottom with a donkey's head in place of a man's.

In addition, Oberon has ordered Puck to drop some of the flower juice into the eyes of a certain young Athenian man to make him fall in love with the woman chosen for him. Puck "mistakenly" puts the magic drops into the eyes of the wrong man as he naps in the enchanted forest. The result is a wild, romping lovers' mix-up through the woods.

At one point in the play, Puck admits to his shape-shifting ability, saying, "Sometime a horse I'll be, sometime a hound, / A hog, a headless bear, sometime a fire / And neigh and bark and grunt and roar and burn, / Like horse, hound, hog, bear, fire, at every turn" (Shakespeare).

Litha, which falls on the summer solstice, also called Midsummer, is on June 20 in 2024 in the Northern Hemisphere. It celebrates the longest day of the year and the beginning of summer. Litha is about the relationship between darkness and light. In ancient pagan celebrations, the Oak King represented light and ruled all the lengthening days between Yule and Litha. After Litha, the Holly King was in charge when nights began to grow steadily longer. Litha is an excellent time for love magic, love spells, handfasting rituals, and the charging of love potions and amulets.

Puck shares some similarities with the Green Man or the Greek Pan. At Litha, oak men, or green men, guard the oak, or "duir" (druid), trees, the strongest in the forest. It was thought that oak trees and water gathered from oak hollows had magical power. If you find some of the water, it can be supercharged as in ancient times under the waxing moon at Litha.

The summer solstice marks the longest day of the year, meaning that for the entire summer, the days will grow shorter. This shortening of days happens gradually at first until Mabon, when it speeds up. Because of the tilt of the earth's axis in relation to the sun, after Litha and into July the time of sunrise comes only a few minutes later per week, and the sunset time remains almost steady, so the shortening of days is barely noticeable. By November and until Yule, sunrise is a couple of minutes later and sunset a couple of minutes earlier every day, so the nights grow longer very quickly.

My colt was born on the night of the spring equinox, and by Litha, he was joyously romping in the fields and woods of my property with my other horses.

Between Mabon and Samhain, the veterinarian suggested it was time to wean my Puckish colt from his dam's milk. Until then, they had been sharing a large stable at night, but I had a smaller one empty and ready for him.

I had divided the large terraced fields with electric fence for grass management purposes. The day I decided to begin the weaning process, I let Puck out into the highest fenced terrace and then let his dam and my other horse into the lowest terrace so there was a field between them. They could see each other, but they couldn't have physical contact.

All day long, they called to each other. Puck continually trotted or walk-trotted back and forth along the fence line, calling frantically for Plica, who, between chomps of the season's final grass, trotted back and forth along the lower fence line, calling nervously back to him.

By late afternoon, when it was finally time for them to go back to the stables for the evening, I first put his dam into her usual large stable, luring her with food, then closed it shut tight before leading the still very excited Puck to the empty stable and closing him in. Now they were within smelling distance of each other, and they could clearly see each other's faces, but no matter how long Puck stretched out his neck, he could not reach his mother. The calling and crying continued, and I could even hear it from inside the closed house.

By the next morning, they'd both relaxed a little bit, and the calling, though it did not stop, was less frantic when they were out in the fields.

By the fourth day there was no more calling, and after another couple weeks, I let Puck join the other two horses in the field again. By then Plica's milk had dried up, and that was that.

Yule passed, and the days began slowly to lengthen, and I realized that Puck had grown taller than his dam.

By Imbolc, he was exhibiting very stallion-like behaviour, such as rearing up while on the lead and chasing me in the paddock, and the veterinarian, coming to bring routine wormer pastes, noticed this and suggested it was time to have him gelded (remove the testicles).

For most domestic stallions, life can be pretty lonely, as they must be kept separated from other horses, and, as riding horses, stallions can be challenging. I did not intend to breed on from Puck, so the best choice for everyone was to have him gelded. The vet returned with his assistant on a sunny spring day between Imbolc and Ostara and performed the fairly simple operation in my field. Afterward, I buried Puck's testicles in my rosemary garden.

Puck turned a year old at the spring equinox, and, as his red fur shed out, I noticed that his summer coat was coming in nearly black. Around this time, he discovered how to open his stable door from the inside. One morning I came down as usual at sunrise to feed the horses, and Puck was waiting for me at the fence. I thought I must not have latched it tightly the evening before, but, when it happened again the next day and the next, I understood. After several nights of his escapes, I decided to put him in his dam's larger stable and put her into the smaller one at night. The larger one had a different, more complicated closure.

For a while this worked, and Puck stayed inside the larger stable until morning. But then he figured out how to open that one too. Not only did he open up the stable door and go out into the paddock, but he sometimes let out the other horses too! I had to wonder what sort of nighttime high jinks they were up to!

My next solution was to place a clip, like one at the end of a dog or cat leash, on the stable door closure as a lock. It wasn't long before Puck figured out how to remove the clip and, of course, open the door. For a while I thought, what the heck, he might as well stay out at night, but then he took to regularly letting out the other horses as well, and, with all their walking around in the paddock, the mud got churned up, making it difficult to push a wheelbarrow through, to say the least.

Finally, I decided to buy a small padlock. In order to open or close the door to his stable, this dark, golden-eyed, mischievous horse would need the key, which I kept on top of the saddle locker in the service box.

For a few weeks, it worked.

Then, on Midsummer's Day, when I came down in the morning with the feed, Puck was not in his stable. He came trotting out from behind the fragrantly flowering linden trees for his breakfast.

I looked at the padlock. It was still on the closure of the stable door but open, unlocked, and not broken. There was no way he could have found the padlock key, unlocked it, and let himself out—no, no way at all … unless he had shape-shifted!

Reference

Shakespeare, William. *A Midsummer Night's Dream*. The Folger Shakespeare Library. Accessed July 22, 2022. https://shakespeare.folger.edu/shakespeares-works/a-midsummer-nights-dream/.

Cosmic Sway

Bernadette Evans

JUNE 20 IN THE Northern Hemisphere is the celebration of Litha, also known as Midsummer. It's the summer solstice, a time when we experience the most amount of daylight. The days will begin to slowly get shorter, but for now, it's time to revel in the Sun and all the bounty it brings us. Get outside and enjoy the warmth and the fresh air.

You may want to celebrate this day with a bonfire. Everyone usually enjoys a beautiful fire. Maybe you want to just sit and look into the flames; that can be mesmerizing in itself. You could sit around the fire visiting good friends and telling stories. Maybe there are roasted marshmallows in your future. Decisions, decisions.

Today when you experience the heat from the Sun and the longest amount of daylight for the year, the Moon will be in the sign of Sagittarius. This fiery energy loves to travel and hear about adventure and other cultures. Understanding other people, their thoughts, and their perspectives can widen your outlook. So, not only are you figuratively experiencing more light, but you could be shining the light on your beliefs.

Cancer Season

The Sun enters the sign of Cancer at 4:51 p.m. on June 20. This is the sign of home and hearth, family and nurturing. This energy can magnify emotions, making you more sensitive to your environment and those around you. Sometimes it's nice to hide from the world and curl up in the corner with a cup of tea and a book. Maybe you enjoy spending time baking something yummy for your loved ones. It could be that your love language is something else entirely. Pick something that appeals to you—an activity that helps you feel centered and comforted when you engage in it.

Full Moon

On June 21 at 9:08 p.m., right after the celebration of Litha, there's a Full Moon that goes by the name of the Full Strawberry Moon. This Full Moon's at 1 degree of Capricorn. This energy asks you to find the balance between work and home. Have you been working too much? Are you so focused on your career that you've forgotten about making time for home and maybe self-care? It's wonderful having work that fulfills you; just remember to take time to play and relax as well. It's good for your spirit.

Saturn Retrograde

Saturn is often given a bad rap, which is why it's called the "great malefic." It's the planet of work, responsibilities, authority, and boundaries. It also brings rewards after putting in the time and effort. This planet will station retrograde on June 29 at 3:07 p.m. at 19 degrees of Pisces. It stations direct on November 15 at 9:20 a.m. at 12 degrees of Pisces.

Since Saturn rules order and hard work, when it's retrograde, it may feel like you get a little reprieve because the energy has let up. Whenever a planet retrogrades, it gives us time to review and revise. Saturn retrograde can help you see where you need improvement and how to achieve it. It's possible an older or wiser person appears and gives you guidance. Maybe you're that mentor to someone else. Time on earth is limited, and what you do with it while you're here matters. Passing on knowledge to the next generation is a valuable and honorable task.

On July 1, it's time to say happy Canada Day to our friends and neighbors north of us. The Moon is in the sign of Taurus. The Cancer Sun and Taurus Moon encourage you to look after yourself. Take things slow; actually stop and smell the roses. Picture yourself relaxing in a hammock or having a yummy picnic. This is the kind of day where you should be carefree and just go wherever the wind takes you.

Neptune Retrograde

Neptune is known for its spirituality, vision, and ideals, as well as illusions and deceit. This nebulous planet stations retrograde on July 2 at 6:40 a.m. at 29 degrees of Pisces. It will station direct on December 7 at 6:43 p.m. at 27 degrees of Pisces.

When Neptune is direct, it's easy to wear your rose-colored glasses and ignore what you don't want to see. When Neptune retrogrades, you could be in for a shock: what you thought was real was just an illusion. Seeing clearly is a good thing. It helps you distinguish between reality and fantasy. Your dreams may actually become clearer, more in focus.

On July 4, while many people celebrate Independence Day, the Moon will enter the sign of Cancer at 4:51 p.m. This energy is concerned with nurturing yourself, your family, and those you care about. You may want to plan a get-together and enjoy the day. Some of you may have been partying for a few days and need time to rest and recharge your batteries. Have a wonderful day, however you choose to spend it.

Dark Moon

On July 5, there's a New Moon at 6:57 p.m. at 14 degrees of Cancer. Since Cancer is a water sign, it's time to dive in, either figuratively or metaphorically. Stroll to a lake or walk by a river or stream. If that's not possible, you can always enjoy a nice bath or shower. If you didn't have a chance to connect with family during the holiday, this New Moon invites you to call them and see how they're doing. During this month with the Cancerian energy, remember to care for yourself. Feed your body, mind, and spirit nourishing foods, information, and silence. Connect with Source or spirit. When you're in tune, you'll feel right at home.

Full Moon

On July 21 at 6:17 a.m., there's a Capricorn Full Moon at 29 degrees. This Full Moon is often called the Full Buck Moon, and this year it's the second Capricorn Full Moon, with the first one being last month at 1 degree! The twenty-ninth degree is about finishing up tasks related to that sign. You've become adept and proficient at work and zip through your tasks with ease. Since Full Moons are about releasing energy, maybe you're ready to let go of a workload that's been taking you away from family. Follow the trail that leads to your heart; tap into what soothes you, what calms your nervous system, mind, and heart. If you're not sure, just get quiet and listen.

Leo Season

You can hear the roar of the lion on July 22. The Sun entered the sign of Leo at 3:44 a.m. Whenever the Sun is in this sign, it's time to stand out and shine! What brings you joy? Remember what you used to love to do as a child? If you can't ride your bike at breakneck speed anymore (please don't), remember the feeling. Bring that childlike abandon and freedom into your experiences, and take some time to laugh and play. You're here to have fun ... so go for it!

Reference

"Full Moon Names for 2023." *The Old Farmer's Almanac.* Yankee Publishing, Inc. January 5, 2023. https://www.almanac.com /full-moon-names.

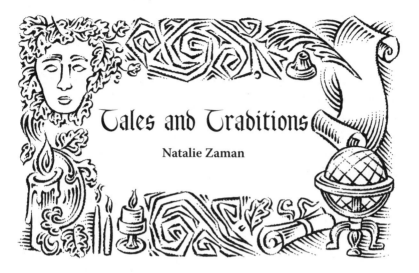

Tales and Traditions

Natalie Zaman

JUST AS WE MARKED the longest night at Yule months ago, we now do the same for the longest day at Litha. At Yule, the sun was re-born. Now at the Summer Solstice, the sun is at the zenith of its power. You can feel its intensity and endurance. Summer afternoons in New Jersey were, and are, notoriously hot and sticky. Unless you are waterside or dancing through a sprinkler, the outdoors is not the place to be. Did the local TV networks consider this when planning their summer lineup years ago? Many a summer afternoon was de-voted to hours of what were then ten- to twenty-year-old monster flicks. My particular favorites were the Hammer *Dracula* films and the Japanese *Godzilla* series. A wonderful representation of Litha and its season is (almost) everyone's favorite monster.

Godzilla: Wizard of the Waves

Japan's thirty-two Toho (a production company) *Godzilla* movies were made between 1954 and 2018 and are of a genre called *kaiju*—great monster stories. It's one of the oldest and longest-running film franchises in the world, and its wizardry with special effects has kept audiences returning for decades. Many of the kaiju films featured that unmistakable sea monster-come-dragon, Gojira (a combination of two Japanese words: *gorira*, gorilla, and *kujira*, whale). While themes for these films varied, in just about every one, Godzilla emerges from the sea and proceeds to wreak havoc, either as a purely destructive force or as a hero, especially to children. (Perhaps he can be forgiven for the cities he crushed.)

The sabbat of Litha centers on the sun and its power. Though a watery creature, Godzilla has firepower, breathing a powerful stream of flame to smite his enemies. He is a fitting ambassador for this turn of the wheel in many ways.

- Godzilla resides in the sea, a typical summer retreat. In just about every film, he makes a dramatic entrance, emerging from bubbling, churning, steaming ocean waters. Each time he breaks the waves, a world is saved or a problem is solved and everyone can begin again. Among the traditions celebrated on or around the Summer Solstice is the feast of St. John's Eve. While this day, Midsummer, is sacred in many cultures and traditions, one of the most dynamic celebrations I have witnessed is the Voudou headwashing ceremony where celebrants are reborn through the power of water. Once they emerge, they are ready for a fresh start.

- Dragons are one of the magical creatures associated with the Summer Solstice, perhaps because of their close association with fire and light. Surely Godzilla is dragon-like enough to be an ambassador of Litha. If not, maybe one of his kaiju counterparts might do, such as the giant crab creature Ganimes—the Summer Solstice does usher in Cancer season after all!

- The Summer Solstice is a time of troubleshooting. Think about it: Samhain began the year (it is the Witches' New Year, and its accompanying darkness is both tomb and womb); Yule marked the first spark of life and light. At Imbolc, that sparked life began to stir, and we became aware of the work to come as the environment changed, and at Ostara, that work commenced. At Beltane, we tended to that work, and now, before the harvest begins, what can we do to correct anything that has gone awry? Godzilla stories are the Summer Solstice chapter of the Wheel of the Year—issues arise, and the kaiju arrive to assist.

Litha *prêt-à-porter par* Kaiju

Who wouldn't want to put on a Godzilla suit and trample a model city? (I can only imagine the satisfaction.) If you can't do that, consider incorporating Japanese elements into your current rotation. (Please note that this is not cultural appropriation but an acknowledgment of Japan, Japanese designers, and street style's significant contribution to fashion. Be sure to acknowledge this—know what you wear!)

- **Supersize it!:** Many Japanese silhouettes are bold and often oversized (such as those from Japanese designers Kenzo Takada, Hiroshi Fujiwara, and Rei Kawakubo). This can be a nod to the kaiju. Loose garments are also summer friendly and are a practical choice with the warm weather on Litha's heels.
- **Pearls:** Like Godzilla, pearls come from the sea, and Japan is famous for producing the akoya saltwater cultured pearl. Japanese brands like Mikimoto and Tasaki dominate the luxury pearl market. Pearls symbolize wisdom gained through experience, a notion that mirrors their formation. What insight have we gained by Midsummer, having gone through Samhain, Yule, Imbolc, Ostara, and Beltane? How many layers of wisdom have we accrued? Genuine cultured pearl jewelry is indeed a luxury, but pearlescent jewelry such as that made from abalone or freshwater pearls is a more affordable alternative. Don't forget mother-of-pearl or pearlized buttons for shirts. This is a tiny detail that may go unnoticed, but one that you know has considerable symbolic value!
- **Tabi socks:** The tabi silhouette (sock and shoe) originated in the fifteenth century. Initially created to accommodate thong

footwear, shoes were made in this style for practical reasons: the design is rooted in reflexology; the split toe promotes better balance. However, it can't be denied that they give an animal-like appearance—you can literally put on the kaiju with a pair of tabi socks or shoes.

Books and Films to Read, View, and Inspire

Fukuda, Jun, dir. *Godzilla vs. Megalon*. 1973; Toho Co., Ltd.: Chiyoda-ku, Tokyo.

Honda, Ishirō, dir. *Mothra vs. Godzilla*. 1964; Toho Co., Ltd.: Chiyoda-ku, Tokyo.

Honda, Ishirō, dir. *Space Amoeba*. 1970; Toho Co., Ltd.: Chiyoda-ku, Tokyo.

Honda, Ishirō, and Terry O. Morse, dir. *Godzilla, King of the Monsters!* 1956; Toho Co., Ltd., Jewell Enterprises: Chiyoda-ku, Tokyo.

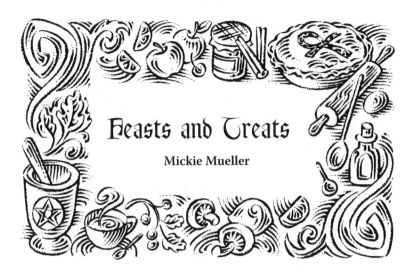

Feasts and Treats

Mickie Mueller

THE HEIGHT OF THE sun feels like a great reason to celebrate outdoors. The days are hot and long, and it's a perfect day to cook outdoors if you have the opportunity. Lots of people don't have grills though, so all these recipes can also be cooked indoors as well. This menu is full of the joy of the season and is fun to share with family and friends.

Grilled Watermelon Wedges

I know it's weird, but grilling or even pan searing watermelon transforms it into a richer flavor. The sugars caramelize and pick up smokiness if you're using a grill. It also changes the texture a bit, making it a nice sweet and savory umami bite. Try topping them with a squeeze of lime juice, thin sliced scallions and crumbled blue cheese.

Prep time: 10 minutes
Cooking time: 8–10 minutes
Servings: 6

1 small seedless watermelon
Optional: lime wedges, blue cheese crumbles, and thin-sliced scallions

A small seedless watermelon works best for this recipe. Cut the watermelon in half and then, flat-side down, cut each half in half. Slice each section into triangles that are about ½ inch thick. If they're large slices, you can slice them in half again. Leave the rind on each piece, as it helps the watermelon stay together and it's easier to grip the rind with tongs to turn them. Put the wedges on a hot grill and cook 2–3 minutes per side until grill marks show. Serve with lime wedges, sliced scallions, and blue cheese crumbles.

Chicken Sliders and Veggie Sliders

My daughter shared her chicken burger recipe with me, and I experimented with vegan burgers too. Making them into fun little sliders allows everyone to have as many or as few as they like. Plan on at least three sliders per person.

Prep time: 15 minutes
Cooking time: 20 minutes
Servings: 8

½ cup crushed rice cereal or breadcrumbs, divided into ¼ cups
1 pound ground chicken (Vegan option: textured vegetable protein for a veggie option; omit the egg and breadcrumbs, add 1 tablespoon flour.)
1 egg
½ small onion, minced
1 teaspoon garlic powder
½ teaspoon salt
1 teaspoon pepper
1 teaspoon poultry seasoning
Small-sized buns to serve the finished burgers on, like King's Hawaiian rolls

Put ¼ cup of the crushed cereal or breadcrumbs in a shallow dish and set aside. In a large bowl, mix the rest of the ingredients (except buns) with clean hands until well blended. Shape into ¼-cup patties that will fit on your rolls. Press each patty into the remaining crushed cereal or breadcrumbs to coat and cook either on the grill or in a skillet until both sides are golden brown and the chicken is cooked all the way through in the middle. Serve with your favorite burger toppings on the rolls.

Rainbow Pride Pasta Salad

I celebrate several LGBTQ+ family members, so when I accidentally created a beautiful pasta salad with vegetables in all the colors of the rainbow, they were all delighted! After the first time I presented it, I figured out how to include a blue vegetable too, which is the most difficult to find. If the blue is too weird for you, leave it out, but I'm pretty weird and not afraid to shock people with my pasta salad.

Prep time: 15 minutes
Cooking time: 8–10 minutes
Servings: 8

16 ounces (before cooking) tricolor or plain rotini (I use gluten-free penne.)
12 butterfly pea flowers (Find in health food stores or online.)
½ cup cauliflower, cut into ½-inch pieces
1 cup grape tomatoes, cut in quarters
½ cup frozen peas
½ orange bell pepper, diced
½ yellow bell pepper, diced
½ red or purple onion, diced
1 16-ounce bottle of Italian dressing of your choice

Cook the pasta according to the package, strain, and rinse with cool water. Brew a small cup of strong butterfly pea flower tea and soak the cauliflower pieces in it for one hour. Mix all the chopped vegetables in a large bowl with the pasta. Add the blue cauliflower and salad dressing, toss, and refrigerate 1 hour.

Edible Flower Gelatin Gems

These individual, jiggly, handheld desserts feature an edible flower encased in clear but delicious gelatin on a creamy base, and I'll include alcoholic and vegan options. If you're lucky, you can find edible fresh flowers at your local florist, farmer's market, or healthy food market, or you might be growing some organic flowers yourself. Be careful to properly identify flowers and make sure they're not grown with pesticides. You can also purchase freeze-dried edible flowers online. Make these a day ahead of time and keep refrigerated in the molds.

Prep time: 15 minutes
Inactive: 5 hours
Servings: 18–20

Clear Layer

Nonstick cooking spray

Disposable shot cups, ice cube trays, or mini muffin pans

4 cups white grape juice, white cranberry peach juice, or sweet sparkling wine, separated

2 envelopes unflavored gelatin or agar-agar (there's usually 4 in a box)

Edible flowers, petals, or herbs; try roses, pansies, calendula, nasturtiums, lavender, dandelion, mint, basil, or thyme (see notes about safety above)

White Layer

2 cups hot water

2 envelopes unflavored gelatin or agar-agar (there's usually 4 in a box)

1 14-ounce can sweetened condensed milk (there are coconut versions that work great if you're dairy free)

For the clear layer, spray the molds with nonstick cooking spray. Add 2 cups of juice to a bowl and sprinkle 2 envelopes of gelatin on top of the juice and set to the side. Bring 2 cups of juice to a boil and whisk it into the bowl with the gelatin and juice, mixing until the gelatin is dissolved. Fill your molds three-quarters of the way using a small pitcher with a pour spout or a small ladle. Use tweezers or chopsticks to put an edible flower or several upside down into each mold, pushing the flower to the bottom and then pulling the bottom of it back to the surface. Repeat with all molds. Place the molds in the refrigerator to chill; set a timer for 30 minutes.

After 30 minutes, leave them in the fridge and begin making the white layer. Pour 2 cups hot water into a bowl and sprinkle 2 envelopes of gelatin onto the surface of the water and allow to set two minutes. Whisk in the sweetened condensed milk and allow the mixture to cool on the counter 15 minutes. Next, top each mold off with the white layer, gently pouring or spooning it in with a ladle. Return to refrigerator for 4 hours. Mine slid out easily with only a little coaxing, but if you have trouble, fill a sink with warm water and briefly submerge each mold only to the rim for 30 seconds and turn out the gelatin gems onto a plate. Keep them in the fridge until ready to serve.

Your guests will be delighted and intrigued. If you wish, you can prepare some with a couple fresh berries in each as well. Get creative; reimagine this recipe as a parfait with several layers or make the whole thing clear, use interesting molds, and have fun with it.

Crafty Crafts

Lupa

Now that summer is here, local wildlife may have a tougher time finding clean water to drink, especially if your area is in a drought. If you don't already have a natural source of fresh water where you are, one of the best gifts you can give to your local wildlife is a birdbath.

The water birdbaths hold is, of course, perfect for smaller birds to clean themselves as part of their preening process. This helps them remove parasites and dirt and keeps their feathers in better condition. Healthy feathers not only help them with temperature regulation regardless of the weather but also maximize their efficiency when flying—something that can literally be a matter of life and death for a wild bird.

But birdbaths also provide local wildlife of all sorts with water, and you may be surprised at what sorts of animals show up at yours! Depending on where you are, your visitors may include insects like bees and butterflies, mammals like squirrels or deer, and even snakes that are able to wind their way up to the bowl. All of these creatures will appreciate a cool drink on a hot day.

Recycled Dishes Birdbath

There are lots of premanufactured birdbaths out there made of cement, plastic, and other materials. However, I want to show you how you can make a birdbath out of recycled materials available at any thrift store or yard sale. In fact, you might even have the makings of a birdbath right at home!

What is this amazing medium? Dishes! Old glass and ceramic dishes can be stacked in all sorts of fun combinations to create a birdbath designed to your specifications. Because they're already waterproof, they'll hold up to the weather year-round. And piles of old dishes can be bought for next to nothing, handpicked from shelves of secondhand selections. (Or just clean out your own cupboards for stuff you're not using any more!)

Materials
Dishes
Epoxy
Optional: Ruler

Cost: $7–$200, depending on how tall your birdbath is

Time spent: 2 hours, not including sourcing dishes or glue drying time

Before you start, though, you'll need to come up with a basic design. Most birdbaths feature a wide base, a narrow pedestal, and then a bowl on top. Choose a bowl that's easy to clean because you'll need to sanitize it on a regular basis to keep the birds from spreading diseases and prevent algae growth. Because glass and ceramic bowls can be heavy, you'll want to make sure whatever you choose for a base will be wide and heavy enough to keep the birdbath from tipping over and breaking.

You'll also want to consider how tall you want to make the birdbath and whether you'll need to be able to move it around easily for cleaning or yard work; glass and ceramic are heavier than plastic, and your birdbath may put on some weight pretty quickly! Avoid

any pieces with very thin walls, like many drinking glasses, that could shatter with too much weight or stress; remember that a gallon of water weighs over eight pounds, and that will add to the overall weight of the birdbath. Finally, think about whether you want to include particular colors or designs.

Next, it's time to start collecting materials! Whether you're going out thrift shopping or just pulling together stuff around the house, you may find your design changes according to what you actually have on hand. Maybe you find a bowl that you want to design the entire birdbath around, or perhaps you want to use dishes that you have a strong sentimental attachment to.

Once you've selected some possible components, try carefully stacking them to see how they fit together. You probably won't be able to stack them all at once, at least not without adhesive. Just try stacking two or three that will go together to see whether they fit well enough, both with regard to balance and appearance. Again, you're going to want something wide and heavy for the base, like a thick ceramic salad bowl or heavy glass serving tray. Make very sure it rests flat on the ground with no wobbling! The pedestal can be made of any combination of cups and mugs, teapots, even plates and saucers. Again, make sure that each set of pieces you're going to be stacking on top of each other will do so evenly and without big gaps between the dishes. Also, wider pieces are better closer to the bottom to improve balance and weight distribution, and avoid narrow, tall pieces like drinking glasses unless their walls are very thick and sturdy.

When you choose the top dish for the pedestal, pick something that is fairly wide so it has a lot of surface contact with the bottom of the bowl. Also, don't pick anything too thin or flimsy so that the weight of the bowl at the top doesn't cause stress cracks to form on the bottom over time; remember that each piece is only supported by an area the size of the piece below it, and anything that overhangs doesn't have any direct support at all.

Now it's time to put everything together! You'll need a very strong epoxy like E6000 or two-part Gorilla Glue. Pay close attention to how long it takes for the adhesive you choose to dry and then fully set. You may need to glue one dish on at a time, allowing the epoxy to set thoroughly before adding the next one. Also, keep the dishes centered on each other as much as possible; once one becomes off-center, it could cause the entire birdbath to be unbalanced and more likely to tip over. If you want, use a ruler to determine the center of each dish and lightly mark that spot with a marker, then center the next dish over that spot and use your ruler again to be sure that it is centered before gluing it into place.

Once you have put all the dishes together, take the birdbath into your bedroom. Hold it by the bowl over your mattress (extra blankets are a good idea), and then shake it hard a few times to see if it comes apart. If it does, the bed will cushion whatever dishes fall off and minimize the chance of breakage. You'll need to glue them back on, but at least you didn't have your work fall apart outside!

Now you can take your birdbath and place it outside! Choose a nice, level spot where it won't be easily knocked over. Add clean, fresh water, and you're done! You should change the water daily whenever possible and clean the birdbath with a 1:9 bleach to water solution at least weekly, more often in warmer weather. If you see a sick bird in the bath, you may want to bring it back inside for a few weeks, cleaning thoroughly before you put it back out for local wildlife to enjoy again.

The Natural Magic of Love

Dallas Jennifer Cobb

WITH THE SUN ARRIVING at its most northerly position, Litha is the longest day in the Northern Hemisphere and a celebration of fire. The great fire in the sky, the sun is the source of all life, bringing the radiant energies of photosynthesis, warmth, gravity, and sanity to us. Fire represents the sun, which is at its furthest north trajectory, and now will stop and turn to travel back to the south, bringing the shortening of the days.

This day of the most sun and the longest period of daylight was a sacred day celebrated throughout many Pagan and earth-based faiths. Stonehenge and other henges were built to celebrate the fullness of light, a longtime symbol of divine inspiration.

Love is the strongest of human emotions; it is a feeling deeply wired in our psyche and developmental stages.

On this day when we celebrate the wealth of light, let us also celebrate the wealth of love in our lives.

It is easy to feel unloved when we demand the attention from outside. Today we will cultivate a love that begins within and resonates out.

By lighting our own interior light, we shine and radiate, becoming a beacon of light that others will see and be attracted to. Like moths gathering around a porch light, be the brightness that attracts others by cultivating your own internal self-love.

Feeding Your Fire Ritual

If you can, plan to wake up before the sunrise and stay up until after the sunset. Witnessing the length of the longest day enables us to contemplate how much light, energy, sanity, and power is available to us to work our magic. Where I live, there are fifteen hours, twenty-nine minutes, and thirty seconds of light on the longest day. That is a lot of daylight to work magic with. A lot of light in which to "see."

Tell yourself that you will pause once each hour for every hour in which you are awake today and find something that you love. If you have a cell phone, you can set a timer; if you wear a Fitbit or Apple Watch, set that hourly reminder.

Make a ritual of pausing whatever you are doing. If you are driving, pull over for goodness' sake! Pause and take a moment and say:

I love… and fill in the rest of the statement. It doesn't have to be complicated or grand, just make a list of what you love:

I love my dog and how she snuffles. I love the yard and the shade of the big maple trees; they keep my grass green. I love hot, strong coffee in the morning, the smell of my favorite aromatherapy. I love my daughter and how when we text we often write the same thing to one another at the same time, then both type in "Synchronicity." I love how the lake looks different every day, and the beach is constantly shifting. I love all bodies of water: the lake, stream, river, pond, and oceans.

As you go through the day, you will be in different environments and with different people. When you let your love naturally arise in these locations, you will compile a list that is as wide as it is deep, as diverse as it is sweet.

Consciously naming what you love moves the love from a passive, background energy to a central fire burning bright within your heart, your spirit, and your life.

Anytime you need a little warmth, return to your list and feed your fire.

Sacred Self-Love Spell

I spent many years yearning for someone, anyone, to love me and save me. It took a long time and a lot of healing to finally realize that my most reliable relationship was with myself. I cultivated a sense of being my own strong mother, and that part of me learned how to love, protect, support, and nurture my broken, abandoned, and desperate child self.

It has taken a lot of time and therapy to learn to trust myself and slowly begin to soften to be able to receive love. And when I hear negative or dismissive messages, or have a tendency to abandon myself or my boundaries, I slow down and do this Sacred Self-Love Spell, and I'm able to return to the awareness of my need for tender care of the vulnerable and wounded parts of me.

Between 11 a.m. and 3 p.m. local time, devote ten minutes to this Sacred Self-Love Spell. Find a spot where you can sit in the sun, expose as much of your skin as you are comfortable with, and relax.

Ten to fifteen minutes of natural exposure (without sunscreen) to sunlight daily increases our natural production of vitamin D, and makes us happier and generally healthier (Mead 2008).

Close your eyes and focus on the radiance and feeling of warmth the sun provides. Imagine the rays of the sun are beaming nature's love down on you, and your skin receives that loving caress. Feel the pleasure and how your body relaxes. Know that in the sunlight, all parts of you are lovable. All parts are accepted. Feel the happiness soften and make you receptive.

Allow yourself to be enraptured momentarily by the comfort, joy, and absolute delight of sacred sunbathing, and know that anytime you need to feel loved and held, you can turn your face or body toward the sun for a few minutes of therapeutic sunbathing.

Receive the radiant energy shining upon your body and know you are loved.

Reference

Mead, M. Nathaniel. "Benefits of Sunlight: A Bright Spot for Human Health." *Environmental Health Perspectives* 116, no. 4 (April 2008): A160–A167. https://doi.org/10.1289/ehp .116-a160.

Litha Ritual

Suzanne Ress

WHETHER OR NOT THEY are invited to join you at your Litha ritual, there likely will be one or more fairy folk present. To stay on a fairy's good side while also letting him know, in a subtle manner, that you're aware of his presence, I've designed this ritual, which can be done as a group or by a solitary practitioner.

A Midsummer Ritual to Appease a Solitary Fairy

Several days, or at least a day, ahead of time, you will need to find an enchanted wood. Ideally, this will be an oak grove, but even a single oak tree in a quiet setting will suffice. Lacking access to oak trees, any inviting wooded area away from regular human activity is all right. The most important aspect of an enchanted wood is that its feel is welcoming. You should be able to sense this clearly. The trees, plants, and other wildlife in your selected locale must invite your presence there. This welcoming feeling comes, in large part, from the fairy, or fairies, who dwell there. Fairies are curious about humans, and if one beckons to you spiritually, it is so that he may observe you for his own entertainment. Allowing him this possibility will please him.

Materials Needed

A yellow or white cloth square (like a bandana or a cloth napkin)

A glow stick, preferably yellow or green, for each participant

A yellow floral wreath with real or fake flowers

Bells, flute, recorder, harmonica, drums—any or all

A thermos or two of Midsummer Punch (recipe below), enough for all participants

A silver cup

A bag of white, peeled almonds, seven per participant (Nut allergy sufferers may substitute any small white edible thing they can tolerate.)

A fresh white bread roll

A handful of calendula flower petals, dried or fresh

Five umbelliferous flowers, white or yellow (such as dill, fennel, Alexanders, Queen Anne's lace)

Midsummer Punch: chill lavender syrup and tonic water, and a good quality gin, if desired. Just before leaving for the woods, mix 1 tablespoon lavender syrup with ⅔ cup tonic water (add a jigger of gin if desired) for each serving. Add a sprig of rosemary to the thermos.

Go to your selected woods about an hour before sunset on the day of the summer solstice. Participants should be dressed all in white.

Spread your fabric square at a place where there is enough open space for all participants to move freely around it. If the glow sticks are wrapped, unwrap them, but don't crack them on. Place the floral wreath beside the fabric square, and place the rest of the items—aside from the musical instruments—on the fabric square. Distribute the musical instruments to the participants, who should be standing around the wreath and fabric.

Call the quarters and draw down the moon, but do not close your circle. Instead, wait silently, breathing deeply, for several minutes or more. Spontaneously, when she feels the spiritual environment has become very still, the leader says,

Folk of the woods,
Take heart and thrive!

Each participant who holds an instrument shall begin to play it, whilst the others dance, each staying in their own space, not circling. The instrument players, if there are more than one, should pay attention to each other and try to create pleasing music.

After a while, the leader or other designated person shall switch places with the person to her left, and this should go on, two people at a time switching places, so that every person will eventually have made a full circle around the center—the leader moving deosil and the others widdershins. For solitary practitioners, this movement should be imagined only.

When everyone has gone around once, the leader shall call out,

This longest day we celebrate,
Embracing openly true fate.

Standing still now, let the music gradually die down, and return the instruments to the center. Some moments of silence shall ensue.

In these moments, the inhabitant fairy may make himself known to you by rustling greenery, the call of a raptor, a low-flying bat, or other things.

At the right time, the leader shall get the thermos and the silver cup from the center and pour himself a drink, drink it down, then pass the thermos and cup to the person to his left, etc.

After the drink has completed its round, the leader will retrieve the bag of almonds from the center, eat seven of them, and pass them to his right.

Once the almonds have completed their round, the bag is returned to the center, and the leader says,

Let's leave these presents,
For abiding spirits.

The participant to the speaker's left shall fetch the fresh white bread roll from the fabric cloth in the middle and begin to break it into small pieces. She shall throw each piece over her left shoulder, saying with each toss a pretty or rhyming fairylike word. It might help to think of such words ahead of time, but it can also be completely spontaneous. The words can be any, and it's okay to repeat the same one more than once. Some words that come to my mind are:

Dandelion
Musky
Capriole
Petrichor
Diwetha
Bluestem
Porphyry

The uttered words, whatever they are, should be sung like a song by the bread-tosser. Don't get hung up on the meanings of the words—only their sounds are important.

The person to the right of the leader shall get the handful of calendula petals and the umbellifer flowers from the fabric square, return to his place, and toss them a little bit at a time over his right shoulder, singing or chanting a single syllable with each toss. The syllables can be such as these or any others:

La
Fa
Re
Nu
Ji
Yo

After all of the flowers and petals have been tossed to the fairies, a complete silence should be held. Everyone must stand very still and make no sound at all, and this should go on for several minutes.

The fairy will become more obviously present. Breathe deeply and enjoy this; he will do no harm.

Finally, as darkness will now have begun to set in, each participant shall take a glow stick from the center and crack it on to light it. Use these for several minutes to draw pretty things, more gifts for the fairy, in the air, but do not speak. Quiet humming or whistling is okay.

When the time feels right, gather up the wreath, thermos, silver cup, fabric square, and musical instruments, and leave without saying goodbye, trailing glow stick light paths through the dark.

Notes

Notes

Notes

Lammas

The Balance of Give and Take

Kate Freuler

LAMMAS, ALSO KNOWN AS Lughnasadh, is a joyful, hopeful occasion, as it's the first of the three harvest celebrations. Corn, wheat, and other grains are the tangible results of the past months' labor. It's a time to give thanks while considering how to ensure future fruitfulness and success.

In Celtic lore, the sun god, Lugh, is married to the land on this day, which symbolizes the bond between the sun and earth. For this reason, trial marriages lasting a year and one day were traditionally begun on Lughnasadh. For more permanent unions, handfasting marriage ceremonies were performed. Some typical activities for Lammas are baking sacred bread, expressing thanks, making crafts from corn and wheat, signing pacts, and taking oaths. Included in the celebratory aspects of Lammas is the offering of a sacrifice. For life to continue and earth to keep sustaining us, we must give something in exchange. This understanding of reciprocity is explained through various myths and carried out in many ways past and present.

Old Stories of Sacrifice

For some people, the word *sacrifice* might bring to mind blood and ceremonial killing. While modern sacrifice rarely involves violence, long ago animals and people were offered to various gods and goddesses on occasion. On Lughnasadh, a bull was sacrificed to ensure future harvests, and in other cases, the king, who represented the sun, was killed and given to the land. These practices were replaced with offerings of food and drink over time.

The story of sacrifice on Lughnasadh is about Lugh's foster mother, an earth goddess named Tailtiu. Tailtiu cleared the land for planting across Ireland and then died from exhaustion. She gave her life so that there could be agriculture. She represents the plants that die to provide life-sustaining food. In honor of Tailtiu's sacrifice, Lugh created the holiday, which was an unusual combination of funeral rites alongside games and sports. It's because of this myth that there is an underlying theme of death on Lammas, which acknowledges the waning strength of the sun as summer nears its end. Even while celebrating the harvest, there's an understanding that for things to thrive, something must die the same way that the sun's presence dwindles and Tailtiu's life ended.

Nowadays, most modern sacrifices involve peaceful acts of offering food and drink to deity in exchange for progress, protection, and abundance.

There are a few different customs that have been handed down over time, mostly involving the sacrifice of bread or grains. In the Scottish highlands, a special dough called Lammas bannock was baked. While eating this bread outdoors, participants threw small pieces over their shoulders as offerings to various animals, like the fox and the eagle. In doing so, they asked that these predators not threaten their livestock.

In the Middle Ages in the UK, a loaf of bread marked with a cross was used in a Lammas protection ritual. The bread was broken into four pieces and crumbled in each corner of a barn to protect it.

In all of these instances, the reason for sacrifice is for the greater good, to give thanks, and to receive blessings.

Lammas is a time to reflect on the concept of sacrifice and what it means to you in modern-day terms. We make sacrifices every day without even realizing it. Being mindful of when and how we do so can make our actions more intentional, adding meaning to our everyday lives.

The Giving Earth

The earth knows all about sacrifice. The earth naturally kills many things to make room for new growth all year round. The rabbit is sacrificed to the fox. An ancient tree falls to become fertile soil for saplings. Humans, unfortunately, do not sacrifice quite so willingly, and it shows. We're currently in a climate crisis of incomprehensible proportions, a problem so big that many of us feel helpless to stop it. While it's becoming harder and harder for an individual person to create environmental change without bigger corporate entities getting on board, there are small things we can do that create a bond between our spirit and the earth. This bond is more important now than ever and needs to be passed on to future generations in hopes of saving the planet. We benefit the earth with our small choices, and in return, the earth keeps on giving.

There is a great imbalance created by taking without giving back, in our private lives and all around us. We take and take from the earth, depleting its resources to the point of self-destruction. It seems to be lost on many people that without the earth, we simply cannot survive. Period. When our earth is threatened, so is our existence. Even the most processed of materials, when broken down, cannot be made without earth's raw resources of petroleum, oils, minerals, metals, and so on.

Many of us are completely removed from nature and where food originates. Excessive packaging, premade goods, and the pristine, consumer-friendly convenience of the produce section have us rarely, if ever, considering where our sustenance comes from. It's sometimes forgotten that plants and animals die so that we can eat and live.

The act of a willing sacrifice is not only honoring the balance of give and take, but is creating a deeper bond between the self and the earth along with its spirits, gods, and goddesses.

Everyday Sacrifice

There is give-and-take in almost everything we do. We must contribute to relationships, friendships, and community in order to gain any benefits. We feed our animal friends to keep them alive, give our time to loved ones to maintain a relationship, and exert effort in exchange for anything worth having. Lammas celebrations can reflect even these small things. The sacrifices made on Lammas acknowledged the necessity of understanding that when you take something (the harvest), you must leave something for the future (the sacrifice). Even while celebrating abundance, we have to be mindful of the future.

Many of us are already doing everything we can to be more environmentally friendly, so I'm not going to preach about reusable grocery bags, recycling, or the benefits of public transit. Instead, I want to draw attention to how these small things can be framed as sacrifices and acts of gratitude to the earth. You are making sacrifices in ways you may not have considered before. When you approach these often mundane tasks with this attitude, it gives bigger meaning to little actions.

- **Convenience:** One of the driving forces of earth's destruction is convenience. Take plastic, for example. It's much easier and quicker to just throw leftovers or lunch snacks into a ziplock bag than to worry about reusable containers. Plastic wrap is much more efficient than a glass container that must be washed, dried, and stored. While an individual cannot control how food suppliers package their items, the changes we do make at home are worth noting. When we choose something less convenient but better for the planet, the earth benefits from this sacrifice.

- **Time:** These days there's been an encouraging uptick in the production of reusable things. Everything from food wraps made of beeswax to cloth diapers are available. But these environmentally sound choices can take up a little more time than their disposable counterparts. It takes time to wash those reusable containers or to hang clothing outdoors to dry. Laundering reusable cloth items takes longer than throwing out the disposable single-use version. Eco-friendly products usually require a little cleaning and maintenance. But reframing these chores as a sacrifice to the earth and its spirits can make them a little less daunting.

- **Physical energy:** Some environmental choices take work. For example, walking instead of driving around the corner to the store or pulling weeds from your garden by hand instead of using pesticides. The physical acts involved in eco-friendly activities can be dedicated to gods, goddesses, or the earth itself. Simply think of the deity or the spirit of the earth in general while doing the task and direct your energy to it. This energy is a gift to the earth in exchange for all the good it does for us. Instead of thinking about these things as a pain, try framing them as an act of love: a sacrifice of your physical energy for the planet that gives so much.

- **Money:** The saying "vote with your dollar" means to use your money to support the businesses that are doing things right—in this case, environmentally ethical ones. Understandably, many people just can't afford to do this right now. But if you do have the extra money, think of buying the slightly more expensive brand that has genuinely ethical practices or supporting local makers. Usually, that slightly higher price tag is because of the extra work that goes into creating ethical products. Every penny you spend on a better product counts, and those extra dollars can be considered a sacrifice to the earth.

Those are just a few ways to reframe environmental acts as sacrificial, but I imagine you can think of more. While doing a menial task like sorting out recyclables or handwashing reusable food wrap, take the opportunity to strengthen your bond with the earth. Here are some simple ways to put some spiritual meaning behind your actions.

- Create an affirmation to say when commencing a menial task involved with your eco-friendly choice. This can be a simple statement, like, "I dedicate my thoughts and action to [the earth or name of goddess or god] with love and gratitude. May I be blessed with abundance in the future."
- Keep a meaningful, earth-related photo where you can see it to remind yourself why you're taking the time to do these things. It can be a picture of your deities, earth spirits, a forest, or even your favorite animal. This little reminder is often enough to inspire you to keep up the good work.
- Set aside a candle or type of incense that you light when you commence your task. This candle or incense affirms to the universe that you are directing your energy intentionally back to the earth in gratitude.
- Reward yourself once in a while. Keep track of the money you're saving by making certain environmental choices and then buy yourself a treat.

In the end, none of us are perfect when it comes to our environmental footprint, but we can at least keep trying to the best of our ability. Sacrifice isn't always flowers, candles, and wine. Sometimes it's our thoughts, efforts, and actions that matter most.

References

Marquis, Melanie. *Lughnasadh: Rituals, Recipes & Lore for Lammas*. Woodbury, MN: Llewellyn Publications, 2015.

McCoy, Edain. *Sabbats: A Witch's Approach to Living the Old Ways*. St. Paul, MN: Llewellyn, 2001.

Cosmic Sway

Bernadette Evans

THE MOON ENTERED THE sign of Cancer on July 31 at 11:19 p.m. There's an instinctual protective energy when the Moon is here. You're concerned for the welfare and state of your family, friends, and home. Intuition and sensitivity are more acute, and you feel the energy of those around you. Going within to hear your spirit feels like second nature to you.

The Moon is in its waning crescent cycle. It's time to release what you don't want anymore. Tap into your own magic to align with your dreams and wishes.

This holiday is celebrated at the height of summer, August 1, when temperatures can get quite hot. Lammas, which is sometimes called Lughnasadh, is when you begin to bring in some of your harvest. You get to enjoy the fruits of your labor if you have a garden. If you don't have your own garden, go to the local farmer's market and enjoy someone else's vegetables and fruits. You'll be rewarded with fresh juicy tomatoes, mouthwatering strawberries, and more. Nurturing your body and spirit with all the goodness from Mother Earth is in keeping with the energy of the Cancer Moon. When enjoying the day with friends, remember to stay hydrated and drink water.

Dark Moon

It's time to dust off your dancing shoes and bop, sway, or pirouette your way across the stage (literally or figuratively). There's a New Moon at 12 degrees of Leo on August 4 at 7:13 a.m. Since New Moons are about planting seeds and new beginnings, what do you want? Maybe you secretly want to shine but are afraid of what others will say or think. Be brave and bold, and put yourself out there! There is only one you, and you have gifts to share with the world. The Leo Moon also wants you to take time to celebrate life and play. Grab some friends and do something spontaneous. Be creative, but most of all have fun!

Mercury Retrograde

Mercury had just entered the sign of Virgo when it started to slow down. It will station retrograde on August 5 at 12:56 a.m. at 4 degrees of Virgo. It will retrograde back to 21 degrees of Leo.

While Mercury is retrograde, you may want to revisit some ideas that have been percolating. When it's in Virgo, a health-related sign, you may want to revamp that area of your life. Maybe it's time to get serious about eating nutritious food and sticking to a workout regimen. Virgo is also concerned about work and day-to-day life. Is it time to make some adjustments that would make your life run smoother?

When Mercury dips its toes into the Leo arena, it's time to rethink how you present yourself to the world. Are you hiding? Go within and re-examine what brings you joy. Remember what used to make you laugh. Bring some of that back into your day-to-day life. Mercury will be retrograde until August 28, when it stations direct at 5:14 p.m. It will take approximately ten days before it starts to gain momentum and begins moving full steam ahead.

Full Moon

On August 19, there will be a Full Moon that goes by the moniker of the Full Sturgeon Moon. It will be at 27 degrees of Aquarius at

2:26 p.m. Full Moons are about releasing what's not for our highest good. Ask yourself if you've been in your head too much or solely centered on doing what pleases you with no concern for others. Somewhere there is a happy medium where you can please yourself and others.

This Full Moon will be squaring Uranus. Whenever Uranus joins the party, you could be in for some surprises or upsets. You may feel restless or rebellious. You get to choose how you handle the energy. It's possible you're handling it okay, then someone in your circle does or says something that is shocking or hurtful. How will you respond? Breathe; don't make any sudden moves or react in a way that you'll regret. Go for a walk or do something that calms your nervous system down. Remember, this too shall pass. Maybe you just need a change of pace or scenery. Life has become too routine, and you want to shake things up! Go for it. Be adventurous and bold.

Virgo Season

The Sun entered the sign of Virgo at 10:55 a.m. on August 22. This is an earthy energy that embraces work, health, and day-to-day matters. With the Sun residing here over the next month, you could focus on being healthier. What's the first thing you do when you wake up? Can you start a new routine? Do you need some time to yourself before the whole house gets up? Whatever you decide to do during this time, just do it without critiquing yourself. Do your best and let go of your inner critic.

Uranus Retrograde

Uranus will station retrograde on September 1 at 11:18 a.m. at 27 degrees of Taurus. It will station direct at 23 degrees of Taurus on January 30, 2025 at 11:22 a.m.

Uranus is like a huge rollercoaster with lots of twists and turns, ridiculously high precipices, and then scream-inducing falls. Okay, maybe it's not that bad, but it can certainly take you on a wild ride.

Now, the planet that loves to rebel, be eccentric and innovative, calms down. You get the chance to finally catch your breath. Events that threw you for a loop are seen more clearly for what they are. You can see from an objective lens. Let go of any angst that you're feeling related to moments in your life. Every upset leads you on a different path and transforms you in the process. Embrace it.

Dark Moon

On September 2, it's Labor Day in the US and Canada, which is in keeping with the theme of Virgo: labor, work, effort, etc. At 9:56 p.m., there's a New Moon at 11 degrees of Virgo. It's a quiet day with no other major aspects happening. This New Moon asks you to take stock of what you want in your life. Maybe you'd like to live a healthier lifestyle. You can't go wrong eating healthy fruits and vegetables and starting a fitness routine. This energy is known for hard work and being organized. Decide which area of your life needs the attention and give it some TLC.

This New Moon could be the perfect time to lend a helping hand to a friend or volunteer for an agency. Whatever way you go, being of service is also part of the Virgo Moon energy. Try not to be too picky or hard on yourself or others. It's easy to fall into the perfectionist trap; don't get caught up in it. Do your best and the rest will fall into place.

Full Moon

Before the Sun winds up its tour in Virgo and moves on to Libra, we have the first eclipse in the last set of eclipses for 2024. On September 17 at 10:34 p.m., there's a Full Moon and lunar eclipse at 25 degrees of Pisces. This Full Moon often goes by the name of Full Harvest Moon. This energy is sensitive, intuitive, dreamy, and creative. Think of the eclipse as a magnifying glass. Everything is that much bigger and close-up. The Full Moon shines a light on areas where you're doing well or struggling. You could be connecting with your higher self or meditating, or you could be getting lost in your work.

The nature of this Moon is sensitive. Some may say too sensitive. I think sensitivity is something to be aware of, but not cautioned against. Don't take on other people's energy because that will drain yours. Try not to be offended when someone says something that could hurt your feelings. Sometimes people blurt things out without thinking; don't get sucked in. This Full Moon finds the balance between having to do it all and embracing your intuitive side. They both want attention.

Reference

"Full Moon Names for 2023." *The Old Farmer's Almanac.* Yankee Publishing, Inc. January 5, 2023. https://www.almanac.com /full-moon-names.

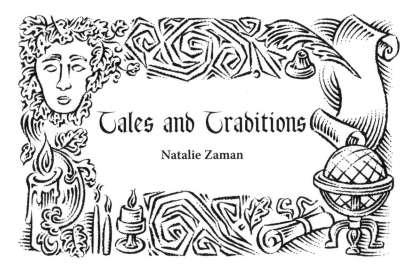

Tales and Traditions

Natalie Zaman

AT LAST, WE'VE COME to the first of the harvest festivals. The first fruits are gathered at Lammas, and they are usually the sweetest: stone fruits, berries, wheat, etc. As Gene Wilder's Willy Wonka says in the super trippy 1971 film (by way of Ogden Nash), "Candy is dandy!" (*Willy Wonka* 1971). Lammas is also a time of games and play, a tradition that can still be seen today: at this time of the year, country fairs and festivals dot the world with rides, games, and competitions, all against a backdrop of sultry warm weather and a (hopefully) bountiful first crop. A similar situation is afoot in *Charlie and the Chocolate Factory*. Mr. Wonka, ready to reenter the marketplace after a long hiatus, makes his return with a competition.

Willy Wonka: The Wise Fool

It would be foolish to think that Mr. Wonka is not a wise man. He is an astute judge of character and human nature, and he's acutely aware of the power of youth—not necessarily physical strength, but goodness, wide-eyed wonder, an innocence that is at its purest in childhood. While he might appear simple and foolish, even silly, he has a shrewd brain that is always working. Like the classic "Fool," there is more to his words and actions than what can be seen on the surface. Likewise, the festivities, fairs, and fun of Lammas are a happy mask behind which is much hard work and ingenuity.

- At Lammas, we pause in our work to gather in the first harvest, feast, and have some fun. If Willy Wonka does nothing else, he creates fun from his work. His chocolate factory is a feast for the eyes (and the stomach!). It's also a playground, but one that produces an interesting harvest in the lessons presented to the five "lucky winners."
- Lammas festivities included opportunities for revelers to show off their skills and test their strengths. Willy Wonka's competition to find a worthy successor to his empire certainly contains elements of luck. Ultimately, however, the strength of character for each golden ticket holder is put to the test. Each character is given opportunities to shine, and one by one they're eliminated—there can only be one winner.
- At Lammas, produce is brought to market, where quality and presentation go hand in hand. Willie Wonka's golden ticket scheme brings his chocolate to market—and is guaranteed to sell out for the anticipated payoff of a factory tour. The more bars you buy, the better your odds. A genius move!

Lammas *prêt-à-porter par* Wonkavision

What an extraordinary little man he was! He had a black top hat on his head. He wore a tailcoat made of a beautiful plum-colored velvet. His trousers were bottle green. His gloves were pearly grey. And in one hand he carried a fine gold-topped walking cane (Dahl 2004, 101).

Willy Wonka dresses for success and so can you by incorporating elements of his look into your daily rotation.

- **Gold:** Gold is the color of maturing wheat, the sun that ripens it, and the fruits on both vine and shrub. It is the first harvest, and part of the celebration of Lammas is a first assessment—what have we accomplished so far? Gold is also the color of the lion; Lammas heralds Leo season! Finally, gold is the color of the coveted "Golden Ticket"—those who possess one will learn the secrets of the Wonka chocolate factory. Whether as jewelry or simply the color itself, wearing gold is a statement of value, a concept heavily in play at Lammastide.

- **Color Blocking:** Color blocked looks are bold and powerful and impart the message of multiple colors in a pulled-together package. Wonka's hat is protective black—he has secrets to keep. It rests atop his brain, which could also hint at the germination of plans and ideas. (Black is the color of the earth, where seeds are planted, and the womb.) His plum velvet coat commands majesty, his green trousers, growth. His gray gloves hint at mystery, and the gold-topped cane, success. It's also notable that the colors of his jacket and trousers are those you'll find in fruits and vegetables ready to be enjoyed at Lammas. What shades do you need to put on to show and wield your power? (Note: the following are suggestions only; color associations are highly personal. What do these colors mean for you?)

  - Black: protection and germination
  - White: purity and transparency
  - Gray: fluidity and mystery
  - Yellow: happiness and positivity
  - Blue: peace and protection
  - Green: growth and healing
  - Red: passion and confidence
  - Orange: creativity and vitality
  - Purple: majesty and spiritualism
  - Pink: love and innocence

• **A great hairdo:** Willy would be nothing without the help of his staff, the Oompa-Loompas, who he employed to make the candy and ensure that his trade secrets stayed in his factory. (The Oompa-Loompas lived in the factory and had all their needs provided for; that and the fact that Willy saved them from starvation and predators solidified their loyalty.) While the films have taken liberties with the Oompa-Loompas' appearance, in the book they're described as tiny people with long, golden hair—the same color as the wheat cut at Lammas. (Please note that this is different from Dahl's original text, which was considered racially insensitive. It, like P. L. Travers's orginal text of *Mary Poppins*, was edited in the 1960s (*Charlie and the Chocolate Factory*) and 1970s and '80s (*Mary Poppins*) to remove offensive references.) This same wheat is plaited and woven into fantastical sculptures. If you have the tresses, try experimenting with new braiding methods. (Have a look at the *Glamour* article below for some ideas to get started.) If your hair is short, like mine, try a fresh cut for the sabbat (and the still-hot weather!).

Books and Films to Read, View, and Inspire

Dahl, Roald. *Charlie and the Chocolate Factory*. Illustated by Quentin Blake. London: Puffin, 2004.

Stuart, Mel, dir. *Willy Wonka & the Chocolate Factory*. 1971; Wolper Pictures.

References

Carell, Julianne. "How to Braid Hair: 10 Braided Hairstyles for Beginners to Learn." *Glamour*. April 22, 2020. https://www.glamour.com/story/cute-diy-braided-hairstyles.

Dahl, Roald. *Charlie and the Chocolate Factory*. Illustated by Quentin Blake. London: Puffin, 2004.

Stuart, Mel, dir. *Willy Wonka & the Chocolate Factory*. 1971; Wolper Pictures.

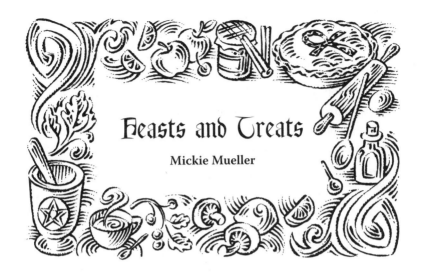

Feasts and Treats

Mickie Mueller

If you've read my recipes so far and made it to Lammas, you'll already know that I'm keeping dietary restrictions in mind. Here's a whole sabbat that's basically about wheat, grains, and yeah, bread. Wheat-eating and gluten-free friends, don't worry; I've got you all covered. Here are a few family favorites for a hot summer day from my kitchen to yours.

Easy Yogurt Bread Sun Rolls

I've seen this easy dough recipe going around for a while; it's versatile and a simple way to bake a delicious bread for Lammas—anyone can do it. You don't have to be an experienced baker for this one, you don't have to wait for yeast to rise, and you can make lots of different baked goods with it. You guessed it, I also have gluten-free and dairy-free versions. I've mixed in sunflower seeds and shaped the rolls like the sun. Depending on the ambient humidity and flour that you use, you might need to adjust the ratios of flour to yogurt a bit; it should be a soft, workable dough.

Prep time: 10 minutes
Cooking time: 20 minutes
Servings: 8 rolls

1½ cups self-rising flour or gluten-free self-rising flour; or 1½ cups
    all-purpose wheat or all-purpose gluten-free flour blend, plus 3
    teaspoons baking powder and ½ teaspoon salt
2 tablespoons shelled sunflower kernels (shelled sunflower seeds)
1 cup Greek yogurt, or dairy-free Greek yogurt
Egg wash made from 1 egg beaten with 1 tablespoon water, or if you
    don't eat eggs, 1 tablespoon melted butter or plant butter

Preheat oven to 350°F. Line a baking pan with baking parchment. Combine the self-rising flour, sunflower kernels, and Greek yogurt in a large bowl until it comes together into a soft ball of dough. Do not overwork this dough or it will become tough. Turn it out onto a floured board and divide into 8 pieces. Roll each into a round ball and flatten slightly. Use a sharp knife to clip about ½ inch into the disk of dough along the edges, making 8 clips total.

Place each one an inch apart on the baking sheet and pinch the clipped sections together with your fingers, then flatten, forming the triangular sun's rays. Brush with egg wash or melted butter and sprinkle with a few more sunflower seeds. Bake 20–25 minutes or until golden brown and it sounds hollow when tapped.

Your New Favorite Chicken Salad

This is a nice meal for a hot summer day; it's delicious on fancy bread, like the sun rolls in the previous recipe, croissants, or wraps. It's a beautiful balance of savory and sweet that'll leave everyone in awe of your chicken salad skills. It includes chopped apples, halved grapes, and a little honey mixed with shredded cooked chicken breast.

Prep time: 10 minutes
Servings: 8

⅓ cup mayonnaise or Greek yogurt, or 1 mashed avocado
1 tablespoon honey
½ teaspoon poultry seasoning, or 2 sprigs fresh rosemary chopped
    and 5 sprigs fresh thyme chopped

2 9-ounce cans of chunk chicken breast packed in water
½ cup red grapes, halved lengthwise
1 red apple, diced into ½-inch pieces
½ cup pecans, roughly chopped
¼ red onion, diced
Salt and pepper to taste

Add the mayonnaise, honey, and seasonings to a large bowl and mix well. Open and drain the chicken and put it in the bowl. Add the rest of the ingredients and mix until the chicken is flaking apart and everything is well combined and coated. Serve on bread of your choice; it's delicious topped with thinly sliced onions, lettuce, or alfalfa sprouts.

Absolutely Authentic Guacamole

I grew up in New Mexico, so I was excited when I learned how to make proper guacamole with a *molcajete*, which is basically a giant mortar and pestle. If you're not a guacamole snob like me, you can still use this recipe. The best guac starts with pico de gallo—a fresh blend of onions, tomatoes, chilies, and optional cilantro. I'll share my tips and tricks, and everyone will want your homemade guacamole!

> **Prep time:** 10 minutes
> **Servings:** 4–6

1 serrano chili or jalapeño (serranos are hotter), diced
¼ cup onion, chopped
Salt to taste
1 tomato, diced (a whole Roma or about ¼ cup of diced tomato)
3 ripe avocados, sliced in half, pit removed
2 tablespoons fresh cilantro leaves or parsley leaves, chopped
Juice of 1 lime
I use a molcajete for this recipe; if you don't have one, use a flat-bottom dish, like a 2-quart casserole dish, and a potato masher.

A quick word if you've never cooked with fresh peppers: You can adjust the spiciness by the variety of peppers you choose and how you prepare them. If you have sensitive skin, wear gloves. Slice the pepper in half lengthwise. Much of the heat comes from the seeds, so scraping the seeds into the trash with the tip of your knife will make it milder. Make sure you wash your hands well after chopping peppers and don't put your finger in your eye!

Don't be intimidated by avocados. Here's how to pick fresh ones: Ripe ones are usually darker in color and should also give a little bit when you push on them with your thumb but shouldn't be mushy. I was also taught that the stem will wiggle a bit if it's ripe or close to ripe. I often buy them the day before I know I'll need them and put them in a bag with a ripe apple; the apple will help them ripen up more quickly.

Add diced pepper, onion, and a dash of salt to the molcajete. Grind the ingredients until they're slightly mashed, and then add the tomatoes and continue grinding them until the tomato pieces become a bit juicy and the mix is aromatic. Use a spoon to scoop the insides of the avocado into the molcajete and proceed with the mashing until most of the avocado is creamy and well mixed in with the rest of the ingredients. Leave some small avocado chunks if you like. Add the cilantro and lime to finish it off and mix well. I like to taste it at this point and add more salt or lime juice if needed. If you want individual serving dishes, half an avocado shell works great. Serve with tortilla chips or fresh veggies.

Hibiscus Soda Pop

Perfect for a hot day, this is easily made with hibiscus tea, sparkling water, and sweetener of your choice. It's one of my husband's favorites. We use fizzy water from our Soda Stream, but you can also use a big bottle of club soda or store-bought sparkling water.

Prep time: 10 minutes
Cooking time: 10 minutes
Cooling time: 15 minutes
Servings: 4–6

1 cup sugar
1 cup water
3 hibiscus tea bags
Sparkling water

To a small saucepan add sugar, water, and tea bags. Dissolve the sugar over medium heat while stirring as the hibiscus tea infuses through the mixture. Once dissolved, you can remove it from the heat and let it cool. Once cool, squeeze the teabags into the liquid and throw them away.

Decant your hibiscus simple syrup into a bottle with a lid and store in the refrigerator for up to 3 weeks. Fill a glass with ice and fill one-quarter of the way with simple syrup and then to the top with sparkling water or club soda.

Frozen Banana Bonbons

These are so easy, and they are a perfect treat for a hot summer day. These frozen banana chunks are encased in a chocolate shell and dressed in toppings of your choice. I love these as much as ice cream!

Prep time: 10 minutes
Freezing time: 2 hours
Cooling time: 15 minutes
Servings: 4–6

4 bananas
1 cup chocolate chips
1 tablespoon coconut oil (the hard kind, not the liquid)
Toppings: shredded coconut, chopped nuts of your choice, freeze-dried strawberries, mini chocolate chips, candy sprinkles, crushed dried bananas

Prepare 2 small baking pans lined with parchment paper or aluminum foil. Slice the bananas into ½-inch slices. Melt the chocolate. I use the microwave; it takes less than two minutes. Stop it and stir every 15–30 seconds, and stir until completely melted.

Using a fork, dip each banana slice into the chocolate, covering it. Set it on the baking pan and immediately sprinkle with topping of your choice. Repeat until all the banana slices are covered. Place them in the freezer for 2 hours or until completely frozen throughout. Once solid, you can transfer them to a plastic bag.

I eat them right out of the freezer, but for a party you can serve them in a small bowl that's inside a bigger bowl full of ice to keep them cold a bit longer. Encourage guests to eat them quickly!

Crafty Crafts

Lupa

ONE OF THE FIRST harvests of the year is berries. All through the long days of summer, spring's flowers have been turning to fruit, which then ripens in the sun. Berries are among the smallest of fruits, and the colors denoting ripeness range from orange and red to deep blue and black, depending on the species.

Berry Ink and Paint

The colors of some berries are rich enough that they may be used to create natural dyes, paints, and inks. While the process of creating dyes and paints may be quite labor-intensive depending on the materials used, a simple berry ink is an easy and fun seasonal craft to start off with.

Materials
Berries
Metal strainer
White vinegar
Salt
Quill pen
Optional: Pestle or spoon, pot to simmer in, cornstarch or flour

Cost: $20–$75, if you need to buy supplies besides the berries

Time spent: 60–90 minutes not including foraging/buying berries

The first thing, of course, is to acquire some berries. You can certainly buy some at the grocery store, though the price for these may add up pretty quickly. If you have a local farmer's market or a u-pick berry farm in your area, that may help cut costs, especially at higher volumes. However, keep in mind that you're going to need to process and store all the berries you don't eat or otherwise use immediately, and they can go bad pretty quickly even in the fridge.

Another option that works for some people is foraging. This is the act of going out and gathering plants and other items from the wild, especially those that are edible, medicinal, or otherwise useful. (Some berries can be all three!) If you already have berries growing in your garden and yard, so much the better. However, if you're going to be foraging on public land, you'll need to contact whatever governmental agency is in charge of it to ask whether foraging is allowed, whether you need a permit, and if there's a limit on how much you can pick. For private property, always ask the owner for permission first before foraging. Also, be mindful of places where pesticides or herbicides may have been in use recently.

Safety is an additional concern when foraging in more rugged areas, especially off-trail. Take a friend, both to help you carry foraged berries and also in case of emergency. Dress for the weather and wear appropriate footwear. If you're going to be deeper in off-trail areas, make sure you have a map and a compass as well as GPS, along with other emergency hiking gear just in case; it may seem a bit like overkill just for some berries, but people have gotten lost for days or weeks starting with one little misstep. Finally, if you're foraging in an area that has bears, make some noise as you go along; bears also really love berries, and you don't want to accidentally startle one in a big thicket!

What sorts of berries should you look for? Blackberries and mulberries will both produce a lot of color; raspberries, red currants,

cherries, and blue or black elderberries are also an option. Other berries may work, but please be careful when picking anything you aren't absolutely certain isn't poisonous; if you're going to try sumac berries, for example, make sure you aren't accidentally picking poison sumac!

Once you have the berries at home, rinse them off and divide by species. Then put them one cup at a time into a metal strainer with a fine screen. Crush the berries with your fingers, a pestle, or the back of a spoon. You want to try to get as much of the juice out as you can. Some people prefer to simmer the berries in a pot of hot water for 15–20 minutes first to try to get more color out of them, especially with lighter-colored berries, but this probably isn't necessary for a basic ink made with darker berries like blackberries.

After straining the berries as much as possible, remove the pulp and seeds from the strainer (edible pulp can be used in a baking project later on!). Then pour the juice through the strainer a couple more times to remove any bits of berry skin or seed from it. For every cup of berries (not berry juice) that you started with, add a teaspoon of white vinegar and a teaspoon of salt. The salt keeps fungal growth at bay, and vinegar helps keep the color bright. Mix well, strain one more time, then let it sit for about a half an hour. Your ink should be ready to use! You can use an old-fashioned quill made from a turkey or domestic goose feather with the tip sharpened with a knife or a commercially manufactured quill pen. (Be aware that almost all wild bird feathers are illegal to possess in the United States due to the Migratory Bird Treaty Act; turkeys are a rare exception.)

If you've never written with a quill before, it takes some getting used to. Be careful not to put too much pressure on the pen or paper, especially if you're using a natural feather without a metal tip. You'll have to periodically dip the quill back into the ink to refresh it. Once you're done, swish the end of the quill in clean water to remove excess ink. If you need the inked paper to dry faster, you can spread a little dry sand on it, then carefully brush it off once the ink is dry.

Let's say you want to turn your ink into paint instead. Often berry ink will work as a watercolor paint right off the bat. However, it may be too thin even for watercolors, or you might want an effect closer to that of thicker paints. Try thickening it with cornstarch or flour, just a little at a time until you get the consistency you want. Or simmer the ink down slowly to remove water (this can affect the color of some inks, so test the color every so often).

Once you've got the hang of the basic process, you can experiment a bit! Try combining different types of berries in various proportions to see if you get unique colors. Berry ink and paint can be wonderful tools for magic or other creative uses. Do be aware that it is often photosensitive and can fade in sunlight, so it's best to keep both paint and anything you've created with it out of direct sun. It won't last as long as commercial paints, though keeping it in the fridge can preserve it a bit longer, and often the color may fade or turn to more of a brownish color. But for short-term spells and other temporary uses, or anything where you don't need the color to remain constant, berries can be a great natural source for ink and paint!

The Natural Magic of Belonging

Dallas Jennifer Cobb

LAMMAS IS DERIVED FROM the words *loaf mass*. It is a traditional celebration of the grain harvest, of the abundance of food that this time of year brings, and the baking of bread. Living in North America, I am blessed to enjoy an abundance of food throughout the year, though there are many in my community who do not have the same access.

I like to mindfully celebrate Lammas as a time to reach across social barriers and embrace all the people around me, creating ways to nourish and sustain everyone. We literally are "all one family" and need to continue to gently educate and cultivate equity in any way that we can. A time of plenty should be a time of plenty for all people.

Held in Community Ritual

In honor of Lammas, make time to gather in community, bringing your neighbors together. Your neighbors are the people who live on your floor, in your complex, on your street, or in your neighborhood. If you live rurally, it is the people whose homes, farms, and homesteads are closest to yours. Neighbors are the people who you will most commonly rely on throughout the coming days of dark and cold.

Send an invitation to your neighbors to "share in the bounty of the season" with a potluck. Invite each person or family to bring something to the table. I like potlucks because those with a lot to share can bring a lot, and those with a little to share can bring a little. I often set up a big cooking pot outdoors and contribute fresh, local corn on the cob with lots of butter. Bringing corn to the table invokes corn Goddesses from many cultures to join us, including the Indigenous Corn Mother, the Greek Demeter, the Celtic Cerridwen, and the Egyptian Isis. These Goddesses represent the nourishing power of the Goddess, which is present at this harvest time, and remind us of the adage "We will reap what we sow." It also provides the opportunity for kids to shuck the corn and harvest the outer sheaths to make corn dollies later.

Ask people to bring a small contribution for your local food bank to help extend the bounty of the season to those in need. It doesn't have to be much—a squash, a loaf of bread, or a jar of seasonally made preserves is easy to carry and goes a long way in the hands of someone who is hungry.

Set a specific time to "break bread" together so that everyone comes to the table together and can take part in the gathering of your neighborhood community and feel enriched by it.

My neighborhood is comprised of year-round residents who live in a village that gets swamped by tourism in the summer. When we gather around Lammas, we celebrate having survived the summer, and happily reconnect with one another.

While my neighbors know and like me, most of them are not Pagan. I like rituals like these that help us recognize the power and magic available to us all, whether or not we identify as Pagan. I am practicing my ways and honoring my faith while not pushing anything on anyone beyond an opportunity to gather, eat, chat, and laugh.

Place a basket for food bank items by the gate, door, or wherever people enter your home to gather the offerings your neighbors bring. Put the name of the food bank or organization on the box so people know where their offering will be going. It helps to connect their awareness to the ongoing need in the community. Don't tend to the box, so that those unable to bring a donation don't feel awkward.

When people are gathered, take a moment to say something. I know I hate to be lectured to, so I suspect others do too. Because of that, I try to work some spiritual and political meaning into what I say without hitting them over the head with it:

I am delighted that we can gather together in community and break bread. I am happy to have neighbors and supportive community. When I need help pushing the car out of a snowbank, I know you are here for me, and you know you can call on me. As we share our bounty of food, let us remember we all bring something good to the table, and we all need to be nourished and sustained. May the bounty of this table fill not just our bellies but our hearts and spirits that we may be nourished and sustained.

As people eat and talk, take a moment to "harvest" the joyful burble of conversation and laughter. Store that energy deep within your heart. As the long winter approaches, we will need all of these things to feed us.

After, drop the box of offerings off at the local food bank. As you give, also give thanks for the harvest, abundance, and community.

A Belonging Spell

So many of us long for a sense of belonging, and yet we experience alienation and feel like an outsider in so many realms. This simple somatic practice can invoke feelings of calm and help connect to a sense of belonging. I love that science is beginning to catch up with magic, and so much of the new neuroscience is researching and proving much of what we already knew anecdotally.

Havening Touch is a somatic practice involving the slow, gentle stroking or rubbing of hands, arms, and face. By stimulating skin receptors in a gentle and pleasant way, Havening Touch can reduce feelings of anxiety and stress and increase the flow of oxytocin (the bonding hormone).

Sit quietly and take stock of how you feel. Rate your level of stress on a scale from zero to ten, with zero being none and ten being extreme.

Breathe easily and let your hands come together, softly touching one another, almost like washing your hands, touching the palms, fingers, and backs of hands slowly and gently.

Continue breathing easily and let your hands gently rub up your arms, as if it were cool and you were warming yourself. Soft, slow strokes.

Gently touch your face, stroking your brow lightly as if wiping away sweat, softly cupping your cheek, and stroking your chin as though contemplating something.

Now take stock of your level of stress. Rank it on a scale of zero to ten again, noticing any shift.

Havening Touch can be done by one person to another, like how a parent soothes a child with touch. It can be done to yourself as self-comfort. The beauty of this technique is that it can be used in almost any situation. Feeling awkward in front of a crowd before making a presentation? Rub your hands together lightly as though in thought, and create a positive effect in your nervous system. Feeling like an outsider as you walk into a party? Gently rub your shoulders as if to warm up from a chill.

References

Daughter RavynStar. "Corn Mother." Journeying to the Goddess. July 2, 2012. https://journeyingtothegoddess.wordpress.com /2012/07/02/corn-mother/#:~:text=Matrifocus%2C.

"Havening Touch." Havening Techniques. Accessed December 13, 2022. https://www.havening.org/about-havening/havening -touch.

Lammas Ritual

Kate Freuler

IN CELTIC MYTHOLOGY, THE sun god, Lugh, was married to the land on this day, making Lughnasadh, or Lammas, a time for wedding ceremonies, pacts, and oath-taking. This included temporary trial unions, sometimes called Teltown marriages, that lasted a year and a day. In a sense, the following ritual is like a marriage in that you're making a commitment to the earth, just as the god Lugh did. Commitment often comes with various forms of sacrifice, which is another important element of the sabbat.

A Year and a Day

This ritual involves writing an oath to the earth vowing that you will carry out a specific environmental task for one year and a day. This mirrors the marriage contracts formed on Lammas and includes an element of sacrifice because you will be giving time and effort to the task. The oath will be a promise to make a small, ongoing change that benefits the earth for the specified time. It can be a minor daily act, such as committing to recycling, moving away from single-use items, or using only refillable water bottles. The important things are that it's sustainable for you and that it benefits the earth in some way. Some other reasonable examples are buying thrifted or ethical clothing, avoiding meat from factory farms, switching to natural cleaning and personal products, or using a composter if you have access. Before you begin, put some thought into what action you can realistically carry out for one year and a day.

You will be writing the oath on a piece of paper. You can use fancy stationery or decorate the paper to make it special. Imagery of the sun, grains, and corn are all appropriate, as are the colors yellow, orange, and gold. If you have an affinity for any earth deities, you might include them as well.

Below is a sample of an oath to the earth. You can copy it word for word or feel free to tweak it and make it your own.

The sun adores the earth,
The earth opens for the sun,
Together they create all life.
Like the sun, I offer the earth my love and gratitude.
I vow that for one year and a day I will [fill in the blank]
As an act of devotion to help heal and protect our planet
And future life.
I hereby make this promise of sacrifice in the name of [the earth or name your deities].
With this pact, it is done.

Sign your name at the bottom.

All you'll need for this ritual is your written pact, about half a cup of animal-safe grains (in case critters eat it after you're gone), and a yellow candle. If you're outdoors, you might want to put the candle in a holder that will protect the flame from the wind.

It's preferable to do this ritual outside, but if that's not possible, you can perform it indoors and then scatter the grains in a park or secluded area afterward.

Try to do this ritual as close to noon as possible. Ideally, the sun will shine brightly above you, but don't worry if the weather's not perfect. The ritual is meaningful regardless.

Light the yellow candle. Take a moment to breathe in the nature around you: the heat of the sun, the sound of breeze and birds, and the smell of the flourishing plant life. When you're ready, read your pact out loud to the trees and the land.

Lay the paper on the ground or a flat surface and pour the grains over top of it. Be sure to keep them confined to the paper. Hold your palms over the seeds and say: "I offer this sacrifice to the spirits of the harvest to signify my gratitude and ask that I continue to grow and flourish in the coming months. Please grant me protection, blessings, and health."

Carefully pick up the paper without spilling the seeds and face the east. Sprinkle one quarter of the seeds on the ground and say: "I offer this sacrifice to the east in gratitude for creativity and the power of my mind. May I always be able to find inspiration and wisdom."

Move to face the south and sprinkle the same amount of seeds onto the ground. Say: "I offer this sacrifice to the south in gratitude for passion and vitality. May I always find excitement and hope."

Move to face the west and sprinkle more seeds. Say: "I offer this sacrifice to the west in gratitude for intuition and emotion. May I always trust my inner self and seek the truth."

Facing the north, scatter the remaining seeds on the earth. Say: "I offer this sacrifice to the north in gratitude for health and prosperity. May I always be secure and stable."

Blow out the candle.

Keep your pact somewhere safe for a year and a day. Carry out the promise of your pact to the best of your ability. You can light the remaining candle during gratitude meditations or when you are just feeling appreciative of what you have in life.

To make this ritual a group event, place the grains in a bowl. Have each member of the group write their own pact. Form a circle around the grains and the lit candle. Moving in a clockwise direction, have each person read their pact aloud. Then, assign one person to each of the directions to give the grain sacrifice and speak the accompanying words.

Next Lammas, retrieve the paper to revisit your oath. Contemplate whether or not you were able to follow through and decide if the changes you made are things you can commit to permanently. If so, keep up the good work!

Notes

Mabon

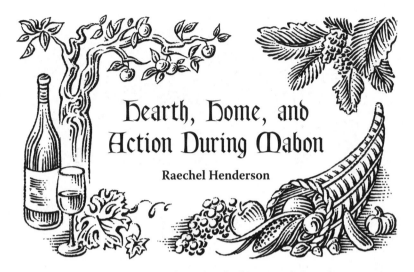

Hearth, Home, and Action During Mabon

Raechel Henderson

OF THE EIGHT SABBATS, it's Mabon's themes of abundance, gratitude, and feasting that resonate most deeply with me. After years of scarcity—relying on food banks, on food stamps, and on the kindness of others—the gratitude when I have had enough has helped me through those times when I was insecure. And those times when I have found myself with more than enough, I have made sure to pass on the extra to others who are lacking. These ideas—of thankfulness and sharing in my good fortune—have found their way not only into my practice as a witch, but as a follower of the goddess Hestia.

In my book *The Scent of Lemon & Rosemary: Working Domestic Magick with Hestia*, I wrote a bit about Hestia's relation to the world outside the home, how the household is the smallest building block of society, and related to our purposes here, how little she would care for corporate greed or political corruption. That the polis, or city, fall under her purview, that she straddles the two domains: the private and the public, gives us an idea on how she can be called on, especially in this season, to work magick in the public sphere, especially on those topics of social justice and politics.

Ever since I wrote about her, I have thought about how she connects the home to the state. This is a goddess who told the chief of the pantheon, Zeus, her brother, that she would not marry, that she would have bodily autonomy. She was honored by state officials who swore their civic oaths to her. The first of all sacrifices was given to her through her sacred flame.

This is a deity, or archetype, seemingly tailor-made for today's environment, when people are starting to rebel against the extreme compartmentalization that society has tried to enforce over the last couple of centuries. Our work affects our home life and vice versa. The decisions of lawmakers affect our quality of life, and so we take to the streets, to the ballot box, to online forums, even, to respond to those who would strip us of our autonomy.

Hestia is not only more than a kitchen goddess, she shows how the kitchen is connected to the halls of government. Homemade bread can fill our bellies, but if there is no flour because of shortages or if we cannot afford the flour or if we don't have time to bake because of exploitative hours, Hestia is involved as well.

"The personal is political," it is said, and this is especially true with regard to Hestia, as she oversees both. This makes her an especially good deity to work with when we want to make changes to the world. We can take our personal beliefs, talents, and goals and cast them on the larger societal stage through our work with organizations and politicians that align with our objectives.

Like Hestia, Mabon is both a private and public holiday. We bring in the harvest and put it up to secure our survival over winter. Apple picking, football games, walks through crunching leaves—all of these activities and more get us out of the house and into the public. Mabon is the time when we give our thanks, both privately and publicly, sharing our bounty with those less fortunate from donating to back-to-school supply drives to providing canned donations to food banks. Even if we do not grow our own food, we still benefit from the bounty that various farmers and ranchers have raised and sent down the production lines to the grocery stores and eventually to our tables. And while there is an emphasis on baking and feasting as ways to celebrate Mabon, there is so much more we could do.

This is the time of year when we can leverage our personal skills and talents to benefit our larger community. It's more than just handing out baskets of zucchini to unsuspecting friends and neighbors. It's getting together with friends to have a canning party where jellies, jams, and pickles can be made and then exchanged. Or giving coworkers cuttings of peppermint that has run rampant throughout the garden so that they might try it and have tea for the colder months. There's going through closets and boxes for coats and winter wear that are no longer needed and can be donated to shelters. And it is donating money to organizations because sometimes direct aid is the best way to share surplus.

Similar to how Mabon is more than just a kitchen sabbat, Hestia also rules over more than just baking. For a while now the emphasis and domain relegated to Hestia has been the hearth. In today's day and age that has meant the kitchen, as we equate our stoves, toaster ovens, and even microwaves to the hearth. Seeing as the hearth was also the central heating of the home for millenia, it's curious that we haven't assigned her to the furnace. All of this emphasis on the hearth, however, elides the other, second nature of Hestia: that of the polis.

Here in the United States, fall means politics and elections along with football, Thanksgiving, and pumpkin spice. Thanks to the extended campaign season, when political ads can start airing a year or more before the actual election, this tends to distort our experience of time and the seasons. This is where Mabon can come in handy, marking the beginning of autumn, a time when we pay attention to what we've harvested, what needs mending, and what needs thrown out. This applies as equally to the home sphere as the political one.

Mabon gives us a heads up. The sudden crispness in the air, the last full blooms of summer before autumn flowers take over, even the appearance of the now-perennial pumpkin spice lattes all signal that it is time to slow down. We are asked to take stock and see what state the world is in and how it might need fixing before winter comes in full force. Mabon asks us to pay attention after the whirlwind fun and sun of summer. What will we be reaping in the harvest and will it nourish us through the colder months? What, Mabon wants to know, is going on both inside and outside our homes? And what are we going to do about it?

Many of these symbols also correspond with Mabon: the candles, the spices, the kitchen connection. These provide a bridge between Hestia and the sabbat. This connection deepens the significance of calling on her for any Mabon rituals. Hestia can provide blessings for kitchen witchery or baking and preserving the harvest. She can be called upon to protect your home and all those who dwell within as the wheel turns and cooler weather is upon us (if you are in the Northern Hemisphere). Or she can be invoked to bless our social justice activities as we donate, march, and vote to make a more equitable world.

Hestia's symbols relate not only to her association with fire but to her status as a virgin goddess and to the few myths and hymns that involve her. As the first and last—a title that comes because she was the first of the Olympians to be swallowed by their father, Kronos, and thus the last to be expelled when Zeus defeated the Titan and freed his siblings—she is given the first portion of any sacrifice or offering. This title also indicates that she can be called upon firstly in tasks and be relied upon to stay until the job is finished.

The donkey is associated with her due to its braying that alerted her to an attempted sexual assault by another god. This places her on the side of all victims of sexual violence, making her an excellent ally for Take Back the Night rallies and other actions that target that particular form of violence.

The swine, or pig, has been associated with Hestia as well, most likely because of her dominion over the domestic sphere. This, then, puts issues of food production squarely under her influence as well.

She can be called upon to address food insecurity, food deserts, factory farming, and field-worker conditions, among a host of other concerns. Food has been affirmed as a human right by the Universal Declaration of Human Rights. Additionally, every society is only as strong as its weakest members, thus feeding them is a civic duty. Again, placing the issue of food and feeding both in the realm of the domestic and the public, where we see Hestia time and time again.

Not many herbs or plants are associated with Hestia. Chamomile was labeled as "Blood of Hestia" in alchemical grimoires of the past, while chaste trees have been mentioned. Herbs that correspond to the element of fire can be used in ritual and on altars to her, although avoid those ones that have an association with lust. Look at herbs, flowers, and trees that are concerned with protection. These can be used in incense, as decorations, or as offerings.

Other symbols that have come to be linked to Hestia are oil lamps, olive oil, and wine (as an offering). In most ancient artwork Hestia was depicted as a seated woman wearing a veil. That is, when she was depicted. Unlike other gods of the Greek pantheon, Hestia was rarely shown in human form. The flames in the hearth were often her only portrayal.

For myself, I keep a very simple altar to Hestia: a candle and a mortar and pestle, which I use in my work. Apples, crackers, portions of the baked goods I make this time of year all end up next to the candle. I lay them there to represent the abundance of my harvest. I lay down pennies or play money to represent the donations I can make to those charities I support. Some years the altar looks a little more bare than others. That is the nature of life, however. Some years it is more famine than feast. But I still lay down what I can, and I express my gratitude for what I have: When there isn't an abundance of food, then I am thankful for the roof over my head. If there isn't a roof over my head, as there wasn't for a while a few years ago, I mark my appreciation for friends who were willing to shelter me.

This year my gratitude will manifest in action. I am in a place where I don't have a great abundance of material things, but I do have time and energy and the will to make the world a better place. I can support my friends who find themselves hurt by current changes in societal and governmental attitudes toward them. I can hold space for them. I can aid in protests. I can vote. And I can call on Hestia to protect them both in their homes and out.

Hestia, and Mabon, remind us that change starts at home. The little acts of kindness ripple out. They affect people and situations that we may never know about, but that doesn't make our actions any less impactful. Start small: a gift of banana bread, offering to watch a friend's children for an hour, attending a rally, or even running for the school board. Local action embodies the spirit of Mabon and can benefit those beyond your immediate community.

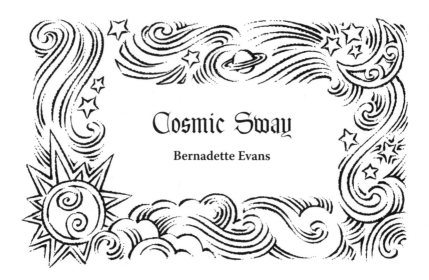

Cosmic Sway

Bernadette Evans

THE DAYS ARE GETTING cooler, and summer holidays are a thing of the past. Now the kids are fully immersed in learning at school and everyone is getting back into a routine. September 22 is the celebration of Mabon, the final holiday on the Wheel of the Year. It's the fall equinox, when there's an equal amount of daylight and darkness. Traditionally, this was a time when thanks were given to the gods, goddesses, and Mother Earth for the harvest. Being thankful and honoring Mother Earth never goes out of style. It's time to bring in the last of the fruits and vegetables from your garden. Maybe do some canning or pickling so you can enjoy your garden even in the winter months.

The sky is bustling with activity today, most of it in the wee hours of the morning. The aspects that may have the most impact are the Sun trine Pluto at 2:12 a.m. and the Venus square Pluto at 5:15 p.m. They are all in the last degrees of the signs, and Pluto is still retrograde. Is there a relationship that is over? Pluto likes to uncover what's been buried. The Sun-Pluto trine could be used constructively. There is power in this trine, but you'll want to use it wisely and for the good of all. Be direct and forceful when trying to make an impression on others. This energy that has been building needs to be expressed in healthy ways. Imagine what you'd like to create in your life and how it would transform the way you live. See it, feel it, and embody it.

The Venus square Pluto is a different type of energy. For one, it is a square, which means it could be challenging. Another way to look at a square, though, is that it gives us a kick in the butt to get moving. If everything was easy and flowing, you might not have the ambition to do anything. This energy between Venus and Pluto is about relationships and money. Easy topics, right! Maybe you're starting a new job or your work is transforming somehow. You could be switching up how you make money.

Your relationships are another matter. They may be going through a change, whether you like it or not. Take time to discuss these shifts with your partner. The not-so-pretty side of Pluto is the desire to control the other person or the situation. The reason most people want control is they're scared of what will happen with these new adjustments. Change can feel scary, but it can also transform your relationships by bringing depth and awareness to them on a whole new level.

Libra Season

On September 22, it's time to celebrate Libra season! The Sun enters the sign of Libra at 8:44 a.m. Just as the equinox is about equal amounts of light and darkness, Libra's primary focus is balance and fairness.

As Libra is an air sign, it really enjoys connecting with others. Why not invite neighbors and friends over to share some great food? Display all that yummy produce and listen to the satisfied ooohs and ahhhs emanating from friends as they bite into all that delicious goodness. Whatever you decide to do, being with others is at the forefront. You may enjoy lots of people and gatherings, or you may like a small group. It's about communicating, telling stories, listening to others, and being a good neighbor. It's a light, friendly energy.

Dark Moon

There's a New Moon and solar eclipse at 10 degrees of Libra on October 2 at 2:49 p.m. It's the last eclipse of 2024. Just as with the lunar eclipse on September 17, energies are amplified. An eclipse in Libra puts the focus on partnership, the other person. How are you as a business partner? Do you try to be fair at work? Maybe it's time to bring some of that famous Libra diplomacy into your workplace. How much time and effort do you put into your friendships? All relationships require love, time, and nurturing. Are you in a committed partnership? How much do you give of yourself? Give your partner more attention at this time and watch it bloom.

Jupiter Retrograde

Jupiter will station retrograde on October 9 at 3:05 a.m. at 21 degrees of Gemini. It will slowly make its way back to 11 degrees of Gemini. It will station direct on February 4, 2025 at 4:40 a.m. Jupiter loves to go big! It's the planet of expansion as well as the planet of overdoing. When this planet is retrograde, it may be time to go within. Normally, Jupiter is connected with generosity and spirituality, traveling, philosophies, and other cultures. So, often, you may look elsewhere for the answers. Take time to listen to what your spirit already knows. You'll be surprised by your inner wisdom.

Full Moon

Happy Thanksgiving to our Canadian friends! The Moon is in Pisces. You may be picking up all sorts of energies from others today.

The Sun square Mars activates a lot of energy. You could have energy to burn; use it constructively and do a physical activity. This aspect may also rouse aggression or irritability in yourself or others. Be careful of getting into unnecessary conflicts. Walk away.

Add the Venus-Uranus opposition to the mix and it could be a very interesting day. You may just feel restless and want to do something totally different. It's possible you'll attract a new, unusual, and surprising relationship into your life. It's just as possible that you want to experience some fun. Check something off your bucket list that you've always wanted to do. Take a break from your usual routine and live a little!

We've come full circle with the last Full Moon for this year's *Sabbats Almanac*, which is called the Full Hunter's Moon. It occurs on October 17 at 7:26 a.m. at 24 degrees of Aries. The Full Moon is about balance, the yin and yang of life. The sign of Aries means the focus is on what you want, but at the Full Moon in Aries, there's a need to look at what your friends and partners need too. It's a delicate dance that everyone needs to learn at some point. Once you master the moves, your relationships will flourish. Sure, you and your partner may have your toes stepped on and you'll yelp, then you'll move forward.

Reference

"Full Moon Names for 2023." *The Old Farmer's Almanac.* Yankee Publishing, Inc. January 5, 2023. https://www.almanac.com /full-moon-names.

Tales and Traditions

Natalie Zaman

MABON AND ITS ATTENDANT season is the final act, the last chapter of the year. It is a time of accounting and introspection: What have we accomplished? What could we have done better? It is a time of feasting, gratitude, and harmony; this is the last harvest of the wheel. It is also a season of knighthood. Michael, the warrior saint, is honored at this time. Michaelmas, his feast on September 29 (shortly after Mabon), honors not only him but all of the angels who fought in the battle for heaven. Knighthood is bestowed for deeds and character; knights are judged by their skills and behavior, how they carry themselves, and how they treat others. We all possess knightly qualities of bravery, chivalry, and loyalty—how else would we have made it to this point in the year?

Brienne of Tarth: Lady of the Knight

Many historical and fictional knights could represent the season of Mabon. In recent years, having followed the tales of *Game of Thrones* (via pages and screen), I feel that Brienne of Tarth brings a fresh perspective to the concept of knighthood. She embodies all of the traditional traits of a true knight—honor, valor, and an intense desire to only want to serve those she loves and to whom she has pledged loyalty. But being a woman, she is not allowed to be a knight; the title "Ser" is not for a lady. However, this does not stop Brienne.

Grateful for every opportunity to prove her mettle, Brienne stays true despite the betrayal and mockery she faces at every turn. Adapting to the changing times, Brienne does whatever it takes to live and speak her truth. She embodies the pragmatism that lies at the success of a Mabon harvest. As the days get darker and darker, it's comforting to know that the knight's spirit is here to protect us. Brienne of Tarth reminds us to set aside preconceived notions of what a hero should be and to be open to bravery, chivalry, and loyalty where it is least expected.

Mabon *prêt-à-porter par* House of Tarth

How can you arm yourself to prepare for the coming darkness? After Mabon, Samhain arrives quickly. Look to Brienne for some sartorial direction to put on valor, conviction, and protection for the season.

- **Armor:** For armor to work well, it has to fit correctly; it is highly personalized to a body's exact measurements. In the television series, Brienne does not have personalized, custom armor when she starts her quest for knighthood. Each house had its own particular "uniform," but the costume designer, Michele Clapton, took it into consideration that Brienne, being a woman (and a tall one at that), would probably have to pull bits and pieces together to make something that would work. You likely won't need to don armor and chain mail to survive your day—but particular articles of clothing serve that purpose. A vintage jewel found or inherited that brings the power of the past to your day, undergarments that hug and hold you in, or scarves and coats that literally protect you from the weather. What pieces in your closet make you feel empowered or even invincible? *This* is your armor; whatever the outcome of the year, however it unfolded, you have much of which to be proud. The end of the televised series has a few feel-good moments, one of which is the fate of Brienne, who gets many of the things she desires—karma in action!

- Knighthood: this is bestowed by Jaime Lannister, making her the first female knight of Westeros. In the televised series, he also gifts her with her first personalized set of armor.
- Leadership: she's made Commander of the Kingsguard for Bran the Broken.
- Identity: in the televised series, it is intimated that the last suit of armor Brienne is seen in is one that she's made for herself because "after all she has done and experienced, she knows what she needs, and what she wants as a knight and as a person" (Atkin, 2019).

- **Sun and moon:** The symbols of House Tarth are presented on a background of azure and rose. In many cultures, the sun is seen as a male symbol, and the moon is female. The character of Brienne shows that we embody all genders and their aspects, each in our own unique measure. We are both and all. The sun and moon imagery of this heraldry also reflects the season of Mabon. The autumnal equinox is a day when light and darkness are equal.
- **Blue:** Brienne hails from Tarth—a beautiful island off the coast of Westeros at the mouth of Shipbreaker Bay. It is known as the "Sapphire Isle" because of the deep and perfectly blue waters in which it is situated. In almost every scene in which Brienne makes an appearance (in the television series), she wears blue, a nod to Tarth but also to fluidity: Brienne's identity is like water—shaped by her and her alone. While the color is a reference to Brienne's home, it can also hint at the sky's deepening darkness as the days lengthen after the autumnal equinox.

There is always a new story waiting to be told, new connections to be made. I fully expect my royal court of the sabbats to shift and change as the years pass and I discover new casts of characters and new faces with familiar stories. Think of your experiences, your generation, and your culture. What cast of characters populates the screens, stages, and pages of the sabbats and seasons for you?

Books and Films to Read, View, and Inspire
Benioff, David, and D. B. Weiss, creators. *Game of Thrones*. 2011–2019; HBO.
Martin, George R. R. A Song of Ice and Fire series.

Reference
Atkin, Jessie. "Game of Thrones: 10 Hidden Details About Brienne of Tarth's Costume You Didn't Notice." Screen Rant. November 29, 2019. https://screenrant.com/game-of-thrones-brienne -costume-hidden-details/.

Feasts and Treats

Mickie Mueller

MABON IS A BEAUTIFUL way to celebrate a harvest fest that has no ties to complicated and problematic historical celebrations. It allows us to reclaim the things we love about thankfulness as we move forward into a more caring world. This is a menu that celebrates gratitude and abundance. If you can bring at least a few locally grown items into your feast, it's a meaningful way to connect with the spirits of the land in your area while supporting local growers.

Cornucopia Charcuterie

A cornucopia is a symbol of abundance. We purchased a bread cornucopia from a local bakery in 2017, and I decided right then that I wanted to make my own. This shaped bread can be made easily with store-bought bread dough, homemade wheat dough, or gluten-free dough. Fill it with tasty bites to create a delicious showstopper. Make it a couple days ahead of time so your Mabon is easier to enjoy.

Prep time: 30 minutes
Cooking time: 25–45 minutes
Servings: 4–6

1 disposable foil cookie sheet (mine was 15 × 10)

Metal, uncoated paper clip

Extra aluminum foil

Nonstick cooking spray

3 11-ounce cans of premade breadstick dough (for wheat version)

1 egg, beaten

1 tablespoon water

Charcuterie or other fillings of your choice

Egg wash made from 1 egg beaten with 1 tablespoon water, or 1 tablespoon melted butter or plant butter

Gluten-Free Version

1½ cup all-purpose gluten-free flour blend, plus 3 teaspoons baking powder and ½ teaspoon salt

1 cup Greek yogurt or dairy-free Greek yogurt made from coconut

Preheat oven to 350°F. Look up a couple photos of a cornucopia so you know what the shape is. Cut the edges off the cookie sheet with scissors (be careful; it's sharp), trace out a half circle onto the tin, and cut it out. Shape it into a cone shape, with the biggest opening about 5 inches across, and the tail end should also be open, about 1½ inches across. Secure at the largest end with a paper clip. Crumple some foil loosely to come through the tail end, with about 3–4 inches extending past the end of the pan, and shape it into the tail, which is hooked upward at the tip. Fill the form with loosely crumpled foil to help keep its shape, and wrap a flat piece of foil around the tail end. Spray a baking sheet with nonstick spray and *lightly mist* the foil form.

Wheat dough version: Open 1 can of dough at a time. Use the strips of dough exactly as they come out of the can. Starting at the tail, wrap the dough in a spiral from the tail toward the opening, keeping the dough slightly overlapping. When adding a new strip, pinch it together with the previous strip to join them. If you wish to make it extra fancy, you can braid the last three strips to make the rim of the opening, but this is just an option.

Gluten-free yogurt dough version: To make the dough, follow instructions for Lammas's Easy Yogurt Bread Sun Rolls, leaving out the sunflower seeds. Grab an egg-sized ball of dough and knead it 3–4 times. Roll it in a coil about ½ inch thick and 1 foot long. Starting at the tail, wrap it in a spiral from the tail toward the opening, pressing the dough against the form as you wrap it, but don't overlap the coils. When adding a new coil, pinch the ends together with the previous coil to join them. Watch for cracks, and pinch them back together.

For both the wheat and gluten-free versions, I found that holding the form and turning it as the dough is lifted from the counter onto the form makes this easier for one person to accomplish on their own. When it's finished, brush with egg wash or melted butter.

Wheat version, bake 350°F for 45 minutes. Gluten-free version, bake 350°F for 25–30 minutes. It's done when it's golden brown and sounds hollow when tapped. If the opening and tail get too brown, cover those with foil to even out the color. Allow it to cool about 10 minutes before removing the form gently, compacting it as needed. It can be stored for a few days on a platter covered in a linen tea towel. Serve on a platter or board filled with and surrounded by charcuterie of your choice.

Balsamic Glazed Chicken

As we call it at our house, "*That* chicken!" I literally dreamed this up one day when I was bored with all my chicken options, and then I looked it up and found out that it's actually a thing! I make the glaze right in the pan while the chicken is cooking. It's sticky, rich, and yummy and was so easy I told the household I can make it anytime.

Prep time: 10 minutes

Cooking time: 15 minutes

Servings: 6

¼ cup balsamic vinegar
2 teaspoons honey
Dash salt

Nonstick cooking spray
6 boneless, skinless chicken breasts or thighs
3 garlic cloves, minced
2 tablespoons fresh thyme leaves
Salt and pepper

Mix balsamic vinegar, honey, and salt. Prepare a skillet with cooking spray over medium heat. Sear the chicken on both sides until the chicken is cooked throughout. Remove from the skillet and set aside. Add the minced garlic to the pan and sauté 1–2 minutes until light brown, add thyme, and cook another minute. Pour in the sauce and cook on medium, allowing it to reduce for 5 minutes or so. Once the sauce has thickened just a bit, add the chicken back to the skillet and cook a few minutes more, turning the chicken in the sauce to coat.

Tomato and Cucumber Salad

If you haven't grown your own, you can pick up ingredients from your local farmer's market for the best flavor. This simple salad is a classic at my house and uses the harvest of the season. Lots of people make this with a sweet vinaigrette, but I love the richness of a balsamic vinaigrette in this version.

Prep time: 10 minutes
Servings: 4–6

1 cucumber
2 tomatoes (I hope you can find some homegrown ones.)
½ red onion
2 sprigs of fresh basil, chopped
2 tablespoons olive oil
2 tablespoons balsamic vinegar
Salt and pepper to taste, or Cavender's Greek seasoning

Peel the cucumber, quarter, and slice it. Chop the tomatoes into big chunks. (I quarter them and then slice the quarters.) Slice the onion and quarter the slices. Cut the basil into thin ribbons. Add the vegetables to a big serving bowl and top with the olive oil, balsamic vinegar, and seasoning, and toss to coat everything well.

Apple Galette

Even if you've never made a pie, this one is so easy, it's perfect for anyone—no pie pan needed, only a flat baking sheet. You can make homemade pie crust or use store bought. This rustic dessert is sure to please and is lovely served with ice cream or whipped cream. There are gluten-free pie crust mixes and recipes available. I loved making homemade pie crust back before my gluten-free days. Making one now is a bit more complex, so I just grab Bob's Red Mill gluten-free pie crust mix because the best thing about a galette is that it's meant to be fuss-free.

Prep time: 15 minutes
Cooking time: 40–45 minutes
Servings: 8

3 apples, cored and sliced in thin slices (You can peel them, but I don't.)
3 tablespoons brown sugar or coconut sugar
1 tablespoon lemon juice
1 teaspoon ground cinnamon
½ teaspoon ground nutmeg
½ teaspoon ground allspice
⅛ teaspoon ground cloves
Pinch of salt
Prepared and rolled-out pie crust dough, homemade or store bought
1 egg beaten

Preheat the oven to 400°F. Place the apple slices in a large bowl and add the sugar, lemon juice, and spices and mix well. Line a flat baking sheet (not a pie pan) with parchment paper and transfer your prepared pie crust dough onto the pan.

Arrange the apple slices in neat, concentric circles or freeform onto the pie crust, leaving about 1½ inches around the edge. Begin folding the crust up to cover the apple slices around the edges all the way around until your pie is open in the center and the outer edge is covered in crust. This will look rustic, and that's exactly how it's supposed to look.

Brush egg wash onto the crust and bake for 40–45 minutes until the crust is golden brown and the apples are tender.

Crafty Crafts

Lupa

As fall arrives and hints at winter's chill and long nights, it's a good time to be thinking about quieter, more reflective activities that lend themselves well to indoor settings. Some people take this as an opportunity to read and study; others plan rites for the future or consider how current traditions and practices may be updated. It's also an excellent time for creative pursuits like artwork and writing.

Wood Journal

A journal or other blank book is a great tool for times like these. You can, of course, buy all sorts of blank books at craft shops and bookstores. A three-ring binder is an especially versatile tool, as you can add in or remove pages as you see fit, even customizing what sort of paper you put in there. Unfortunately, many commercial binders are vinyl over heavy cardboard—not the most durable stuff in the world. This project will help you create something more long-lasting by making your book out of wood.

Materials

Pieces of wood
Way to cut the wood
Sandpaper
Binder rings
Paper
Ruler
Painter's tape
Pencil
Drill and drill bit
Optional: Hole punch, paints, leaves, or other decorations for the
   cover
   Cost: $50–$150, not including power tools for cutting wood
   Time spent: 2–4 hours; cutting your own wood will add to the
time

The first thing you'll need is the wood itself. If you're going to
work with standard 8 ½ × 11-inch paper, you want the wood covers to be a little larger than that, maybe 10 × 12 inches at the most
(most commercial binders are about 9 ½ × 11 ½ inches). You also
don't want it to be too heavy, so make sure the wood is no more
than about ¼ inch thick (⅛ inch may be a little easier to deal with).
If you already have a bandsaw, circular saw, or similar power tools
and know how to use them competently and safely, you can buy a
sheet of birch, basswood, walnut, or other nice-quality plywood and
cut it to size. Otherwise, there are smaller pieces available online or
in specialty craft stores that can be carefully trimmed down with a
manual coping saw. Or see if your local hardware store can cut you
something to size (they may have to special order it if all they carry
is plywood for construction projects).

Make sure the edges are sanded smooth to avoid cuts or splin-
ters; if the edges are rough, you can easily smooth them by hand.
Get a pack of sandpaper with a few different grits. Then sand the
edges all the way around both pieces, starting with the heaviest

grit sandpaper, then a medium grit, and finally the finest grit. You can even buff the edges with a soft cloth to remove any loose bits of sawdust and carefully check for any rough spots you may have missed.

Next, consider how you're going to put the binder together. There are a few options: one of the easiest is metal binder rings. These are usually nickel-plated steel rings that have a hinge on one side of the ring while the open ends clasp together with little notches. They come in a variety of sizes, commonly 1–3 inches in diameter. The more pages you want in your book, the larger the rings you'll need. Three should be sufficient to hold your book together, though you may want to make it four if you're going to have an especially large, heavy book.

Now, decide on what paper you're going to use. Most pre-punched paper, like loose-leaf notebook paper, will have three holes, so if you deviate from that number, you're probably going to have to punch holes in your own paper as well. As with notebook paper, you'll want the holes at the very top and bottom to be close to, but not right at, the paper's edge. Any other holes need to be evenly spaced between those two to distribute weight and stress in a balanced manner. You can find hole punches that punch three or four holes pretty easily on the market; anything beyond that and you're going to be stuck doing it by hand with a single hole punch, making sure that the holes all match up in every sheet of paper.

Once you have paper with the desired number of holes punched in it, take one piece and lay it over one of the sheets of wood, with the side of the wood you want inside the book facing up. Align the left edge of the paper (the edge with the holes) with the left edge of the wood and center the paper vertically so that the distance between the top edge of the paper and the top edge of the wood is the same as the distance between the bottom edge of the paper and the bottom edge of the wood. Then, while maintaining those distances, carefully move the paper right about ¼ inch so that there's now a ¼-inch gap between the left edge of the paper and the left edge of

the wood. This will create a little more protection for the left edges of your paper.

Carefully tape the edges of the paper down on the wood to keep it from moving, being careful not to cover up the paper's holes. Next, place the other side of the wood so that the side you want on the outside of your book is facing up. Place the first piece of wood, paper side up, on top of this other one so that they are perfectly aligned. Then use painter's tape all around the edges to keep them aligned, again not covering up the paper holes.

Now, use a pencil to mark a dot in the very center of each of the paper holes. Using a drill bit that is a little larger around than the metal of the binder rings, carefully drill through those dots until you have drilled holes through both pieces of wood. Keeping the wood taped together, put the binder rings through the holes and make sure they can move around a little bit; if they're too tight, drill the holes again with the next drill bit size up, then test the rings again.

You can decorate the wood covers however you like. A simple coat of stain can be nice, and you can carve or burn the wood before staining it. Or you can paint it using acrylic or oil paints; acrylic paint should be sealed once it is dry. For a fall theme, try pressing colorful leaves between heavy book pages until dry, then decoupage them on the covers with sealant (like Mod Podge); a few coats of clear varnish will help protect the delicate leaves, though you should still be careful with them and accept that the color will eventually fade. You can even create seasonal covers, one for each quarter or sabbat, and switch them out throughout the year!

The Natural Magic of Healing

Dallas Jennifer Cobb

IN THE WHEEL OF the Year, Mabon represents the west, the home of water. Often a ritual of thanksgiving for all the harvested grains, fruits, and vegetables we have stored for the year ahead, Mabon speaks to the cycle of composting and falling apart. The leaves of plants are tilled under the soil. Seeds are harvested and set aside for the following year. Stalks are chopped and thrown to compost, their nutrients breaking down to nourish future gardens and aerate the soil.

We ask: What is no longer needed? What can be released? How shall we give thanks? And where can we bring renewal?

Because it is Mabon, let us devote ourselves to water, the element of the west.

A Water Healing Ritual

Because Mabon is associated with the west and its element is water, I wanted to share a version of the water healing ceremony I do each year at this time. Aboriginal elders teach that water is the lifeblood of the earth and the life's blood of our bodies. And we can undertake healing of this element any time, all the time.

Walk to a body of water, thinking about how you want to heal the water. Use specific language, your language, and tell the water what you will do:

I am a water keeper. It is my sacred path to protect and heal the waters of earth. I join my Indigenous sisters and commit to protecting and safeguarding this source of vital lifeblood.

At the water, project your energy and intention to the water. Speak out loud:

I'm here by your side. I will not leave you. I will protect and heal you. I am thankful for you. You are the earth's lifeblood and my body's lifeblood. You are 60 percent of me and cover 71 percent of the earth. I will use my strong will, my free voice, and my wild spirit to pray for you, sing to you, and chant with you, for I know how necessary you are to all life.

Take a deep breath and chant a long *Aum* (see Imbolc's In Tune Spell for more information). Send intention out in vibration. Hold your hands in, over, or palm toward the water. Let your intention bless the water, raise its vibration, and engage the natural healing magic of water.

Repeat this daily, weekly, or monthly, healing and protecting our sacred life's blood: water.

Making Magical Water Spell

It is so easy to make magical water that it may become your go-to practice for transformation, reclamation, or empowerment spells.

Magical water is water changed by our interaction, charged with our energy, consciousness, and intention. Magical water can be made for any spell, ritual, sacred use, or rite.

You need a glass vessel with a lid. I love old-style canning jars with rubber rings and glass tops held by a metal screw-on lid, but feel free to use whatever you have at home. Glass is important because unlike plastic, glass doesn't leach BPAs (bisphenol A), contaminating the water.

You need the cleanest source of water you can find. You can use tap water, lake water, bottled water (remember, glass bottles are always better), or rainwater. If you live in a city and rely on treated drinking water, you can use a Brita or other charcoal-based water filter to remove the bigger particles of chlorine that water is often treated with.

Magic water can be made for drinking and working its magic within, and can be made to be used externally in spells and magical concoctions. Removing toxins from the water produces a higher natural vibration. And I think of it as an act of devotion, part of my sacred "water keeper" path. Always start with potable water and not from sources that haven't been verified.

It is useful to label your jars. I have used a Sharpee, adhesive labels I could write on, and even chalkboard-like stickers with chalk. (These are great because you can erase the label and wash the jar and use it for something else. But simultaneously they are unreliable because the chalk gets wiped off easily and then the label is gone.)

Instructions
Fill your jar with water. But don't put the lid on yet.

Cup the jar in two hands and hold it at about belly button level. You can leave it on a table or counter or hold it to your body.

Envision sparkling energy leaving your heart, pouring down your right arm, and into the hand. "See" the energy cross through the water into your left hand, back up the left arm, and to your heart.

Set up a continuous energy circuit—out to the right, through the water, and back through the left to recycle once more. Continue the cycling of energy. "See" the flow. Energy cycling helps heal and purify water.

To create a reserve of relatively neutral water to have for later use in varied magical spells and rituals, set some aside labeled "magic water," and use in subsequent magic. If you want water for a specific magical purpose, then:

Send a positive intention. While running your energy circuit, let your intention fill your imagination, vision, and energetic signature. See, feel, hear, and transmit your desired outcome in the positive: protection, transformation, self-love, peace.

Empower it with breath. Attune your own biological system to be part of the larger circuit. Your out-breath sends intention down through the right into the water, and your in-breath pulls energy up and through your heart. Feeling the cycle run through your energy, physical body, and specifically your heart, enables you to be "at one" with the water.

Label the jar for future use. I have created "Protection Water" and used it in a multitude of ways, including wiping down my daughter's sneakers, washing my cats' faces, dabbed behind my ears when I was going into a stressful situation, and for house cleaning and blessing.

The process of making magical water can be quick and fluid. When I fill a jar with my daily water, I often place a specific daily intention: Self-love. Acceptance. Ease. And each time that I drink from the jar throughout the day, I am magically affected by the intention I have set as the changed molecules enter my body and become part of my biology.

Mabon Ritual

Raechel Henderson

THIS RITUAL FOLLOWS THE structure of creating sacred space, gathering in the blessings and making offerings, expressing gratitude, blessing the tools, sending out magic for change, and then closing the ritual. Take time to prepare yourself before you perform the ritual so that you are in a Mabon mindset, one of acknowledging that the harvest is here, that you have reaped the benefits of the summer, and that you are thankful for what you have collected. Gather all the things you will be using in the ritual ahead of time so that you don't have to stop to get something in the middle of it.

Also, a note on working with Hestia: I am an agnostic witch in that I recognize the gods but I do not worship any of them. That's not to say I don't interact with them. I have worked with and learned from many, but it is more of a professional relationship rather than one of devotion. As such, while the included ritual calls on Hestia, it is not in a worshipful way, but as one would call on a friend to lend their support to one's endeavors. During the ritual, Hestia may ask that you do something in return. Give due consideration to her request, or offer to do something in return for her blessings like donating to a food bank or volunteering at a shelter. I have never found her requests to be onerous or outside of what I was already willing to do.

Working with Hestia

I suggest journaling to prepare for the ritual. Write about what Mabon means to you, how you see yourself working with Hestia, and what you can learn from her dominion over both private and public spheres. As part of the ritual you will need to write down a list of what you are grateful for and what actions you can take to make both your home and the wider world a better place.

Items Needed for the Ritual
Your gratitude list
Items to represent your blessings
Altar cloth and altar decorations
Candles and matches
Offerings
Journal

Select an item or two to represent your blessings this season. These can be anything from a few whole grain crackers to represent a food harvest; money, a paystub, or contract to represent your financial harvest; or even a clock or watch to symbolize the time you now have to dedicate to change.

Set up your altar, starting with your altar cloth in yellow, gold, and brown colors. The altar cloth can be as simple as a piece of burlap or a yard of yellow cotton. You can add a cornucopia or a bowl of apples, pears, and other seasonal fruit. A bouquet of flowers such as fleabane, goldenrod, snapdragon, or sweet peas is appropriate as well. Use yellow, gold, or brown candles. You can dress your candles with chamomile essential oil added to a carrier oil like olive. Alternatively, dress the candles by anointing them with olive oil and then rolling them in crushed and dried chamomile. Burn chamomile incense or make a mug of chamomile tea. Add images of donkeys and pigs if you wish to better welcome Hestia.

Work this ritual in the morning and during the waxing moon if you can to tap into the rising energies of the time. To deepen the themes of rising, baking, and harvesting, consider starting a batch of bread before the ritual. Once it is ready to rise, bring it along to place on your altar during the ritual. Collect what you will need—offerings, representations of your harvest, your gratitude list, and your journal—in a basket so that they are all together. Include any items you wish to bless, examples can be a representation of the funds you give to charitable organizations, signs you'll carry to protests, "I voted" stickers, or yard signs for your candidates.

When you are ready, open your ritual space however path or personal preference dictates. I start with lighting a candle and seeing a sphere of protective energy emanating from the flame to encompass the space. When I strike the match, I say, "Hail, Hestia!" to indicate to the universe what entity I will be working with.

Center and ground yourself. Allow the feeling of the space to seep into you. Focus on the scent of the incense, the warmth of the candles, the colors of the altar cloth, and the items you have placed on the altar. Let the sensations of fall, Mabon, warmth, and abundance fill you up. Once you feel you are ready, place your offering on your altar (either the rising bread, an apple, or some other offering to Hestia). Say, "To Hestia, first and last of the gods, I make my offering and call upon you to bless my endeavors here."

Place your representations of your abundance on the altar now. Say, "Hestia, I am thankful for all the blessings I have." Read off your list of what you are grateful for.

Place your tools for change onto the altar. Say, "Hestia, bless these, my tools for change." State your intentions with these tools—what you want to accomplish, how you will use them. Use what you have written in your journal as your guide. Stick with things you know that you can do. It is better to make a small promise you know you can keep than commit to grand designs you don't have the resources to accomplish. Remember, Hestia is a goddess of small, specific actions that yield results.

Say, "Hestia, I send out into the world my gratitude for the blessings I have gathered in. My abundance of resources, energy, determination, and attention I now direct out to effect change in society."

As you speak, see how the actions you will take with these tools will make a difference in the world. Clearly visualize yourself doing the things you have committed to. Go so far as to imagine how it would feel when you are successful. Hold that emotion for a moment and then send it out into the world. Know that you will accomplish what you have stated.

Once you have sent out your intentions, thank Hestia for joining you at the altar. Let the candles burn down if you can, otherwise snuff them out with thanks. Close your space in a way that your practice or personal preference dictates. If you had bread rising on your altar or in your ritual space, move it to the top of your oven or a counter space in the kitchen and let it finish rising. Once you have baked the bread, make sure to put aside the first taste for Hestia in gratitude. Eat the rest of the bread with friends, family, coworkers, or comrades—whoever you want to share Hestia's blessings with.

Take ten to fifteen minutes after the ritual to journal what you experienced and detail how you will go about doing the things you said you would do. Make a to-do list or add events to your schedule while you are feeling motivated so that you don't lose steam as the days progress. Remember, also, to give yourself grace in the following days. Change doesn't come overnight. Focus on the little things you can do and blessed be.